Museveni's Uganda

CHALLENGE AND CHANGE IN AFRICAN POLITICS

MUSEVENI'S
UGANDA

Paradoxes of Power in a Hybrid Regime

Aili Mari Tripp

LYNNE
RIENNER
PUBLISHERS

BOULDER
LONDON

Published in the United States of America in 2010 by
Lynne Rienner Publishers, Inc.
1800 30th Street, Boulder, Colorado 80301
www.rienner.com

and in the United Kingdom by
Lynne Rienner Publishers, Inc.
3 Henrietta Street, Covent Garden, London WC2E 8LU

Library of Congress Cataloging-in-Publication Data
Tripp, Aili Mari.
  Museveni's Uganda : paradoxes of power in a hybrid regime / Aili Mari
Tripp.
    p. cm. — (Challenge and change in African politics)
  Includes bibliographical references and index.
  ISBN 978-1-58826-731-3 (hardcover : alk. paper)
  ISBN 978-1-58826-707-8 (pbk. : alk. paper)
  1. Uganda—Politics and government—1979– 2. Museveni, Yoweri, 1944–
I. Title.
  JQ2951.A58T75 2010
  967.6104'4092—dc22
                                                            2010026514

British Cataloguing in Publication Data
A Cataloguing in Publication record for this book
is available from the British Library.

Printed and bound in the United States of America

 The paper used in this publication meets the requirements
of the American National Standard for Permanence of
Paper for Printed Library Materials Z39.48-1992.

5 4 3 2

Contents

Illustrations

Introduction

*It's me who hunted and after killing the animal, they want
me to go. Where should I go?*
—President Yoweri Museveni, 2008[1]

Hybrid regimes are fraught with contradictions. Their leaders adopt the trappings of democracy, yet they pervert democracy—sometimes through patronage and largess, other times through violence and repression—for the sole purpose of remaining in power. This creates a catch-22. Because leaders have
sought power through violence and patronage, they cannot leave power; the
personal consequences would be too great. Because there is no easy exit, they
must continue using violence and patronage to remain in power. Hybrid
regimes embody two divergent impulses: they promote civil rights and political liberties, and yet they unpredictably curtail those same rights and liberties.
They limit rights and liberties often enough that they cannot be regarded as
democratic—but not consistently enough to be regarded as fully authoritarian.
Uganda is such a hybrid regime, as have been most African countries after
1990. These countries are situated at a crossroads between democratization
and authoritarianism, rarely if ever reverting to full-blown authoritarianism of
the kind we saw during Idi Amin's rule in Uganda—but rarely transitioning
fully to democracy either.

When Yoweri Museveni's National Resistance Army (NRA) marched into
Kampala, residents were surprised to discover that there was no looting, as
there had been with previous armies. The NRA, governed by a strict code of
conduct, was strikingly disciplined. A former director of the Makerere Institute for Social Research, the late Dan Mudoola, referred to the NRA as almost
"puritanical and ascetic" (Mudoola 1991, 237). After two decades of turmoil
under the Amin and Obote governments, Museveni's takeover in January 1986
was seen by many Ugandans as a much-needed respite from chaos. Museveni
brought much of the country under his control, pacifying and drawing in various fighting factions under the rubric of a national army. The first cabinet
embraced most major political factions and parties. The government was led

by the National Resistance Movement (NRM) and its seemingly unique no-party Movement system. The NRM established a five-tiered hierarchical resistance council system of local government that had originated during the guerrilla war.

Uganda's president Yoweri Museveni was for a long time widely acclaimed by foreign correspondents, donors, diplomats, and some academics as a new style of African leader to be emulated for introducing key institutional reforms. He had inherited a legacy of institutional failure and collapse from previous administrations and had the opportunity to radically reform and recreate governance structures (Brett 1994a). He was commended for his almost single-minded pursuit of economic growth, fiscal discipline, and the free market. He restructured the civil service and improved civil service wages. He retrenched large sections of the armed forces, privatized parastatal companies, and returned confiscated properties to Asians who had been ousted by Idi Amin in 1972. Museveni also undertook currency reform and raised producer prices on export crops. Gradually the economy got back on its feet and growth rates took off as inflation dropped.

The country's real GDP growth rate in 2007–2008 stood at 8.7 percent, and according to the Treasury of Uganda, had grown at a rate of 6.5 percent since President Museveni took over, resulting in a seven-fold increase in the size of Uganda's economy. Poverty declined from 56 percent to 31 percent of the population from the early 1990s to 2005—even as Uganda's population doubled.[2]

Museveni was praised for tackling the HIV/AIDS epidemic and bringing the rates of infection down significantly. His ambitious decentralization policy and emphasis on grassroots participation have been widely regarded as models for other countries, and surveys like Afrobarometer showed that the local government system was regarded highly by the population. In the early years of Museveni's rule, Uganda's human rights record seemed pristine compared with that of previous regimes. He was seen as having brought peace and stability to a country that had been fraught by conflict for years. Even his efforts at the creation of a seemingly unique no-party state did not meet with much criticism initially, except from opposition parties.

Uganda was one of the first countries in Africa to significantly increase the presence of women within the legislature and government. Uganda adopted legislative quotas for women as early as 1989, thus increasing the number of women in parliament from claiming one seat in 1980 to 18 percent of the seats in 1989 and 31 percent of the seats by 2009. Museveni also brought women into key cabinet positions and had a woman vice president, the first in Africa, for ten years. The 1995 constitution had an extraordinary number of clauses addressing women's rights. Thus, at the outset, the NRM won the approval of large numbers of women who were convinced that this was a government that was committed to improving the status of women.

From many Ugandans' perspective, such glowing descriptions of the country's politics and economy were overly optimistic. As Ugandan analyst John Ssenkumba notes,

> To many Ugandans, the widespread conception, mainly held by outsiders, that their country is an oasis of stability, economic progress, and democracy is a frustrating mirage. For those without privileged protection from the unilateral exercise of governmental authority, however benign or enlightened this authority may appear to be, this image of Uganda as an arena of boundless political openings and relentless economic progress is grossly deceptive. (Ssenkumba 1998, 172)

These seemingly contradictory understandings of what had transpired in Uganda since Museveni took over reflect some of the paradoxes of hybrid regimes. They are neither the autocracies of the past, nor are they fully democratic. They range from semidemocratic to semiauthoritarian along the spectrum of hybridity, creating a duality of key elements of both democratic and authoritarian regimes that is explored in Chapter 1. In the case of Uganda, which falls on the semiauthoritarian end of the spectrum, many democratic institutions have been introduced, often to be subverted for nondemocratic ends simply to keep Museveni's government and party in power.

Political scientist William Muhumuza sums up the contradictions well:

> Museveni's government created an impression that it was on a steady path to strengthen democratic institutions. . . . Nonetheless, these institutions have ended up being used for propaganda purposes, they have not been enabled to perform their duties independently. Therefore, Museveni's motive to retain power in a pseudo democratic dispensation has significant implications for Uganda's political future. . . . Personalization of power leads to authoritarianism and corruption that may reverse Uganda's current gains. (Muhumuza 2009, 25, 40)

Howard and Roessler (2006) identify a key tension within hybrid regimes, arguing that they are inherently unstable because they provide opponents with a significant opportunity to challenge incumbents during elections. There are many other paradoxes in such systems. Museveni's exercise of power in Uganda has been replete with contradictions that are suggestive of some of the more general constraints on semiauthoritarian regimes:

- What had initially been a broad-based antisectarian government encompassing a wide spectrum of political interests and ethnic backgrounds became narrower and more exclusive in composition (see Chapter 2).
- Dissension within the NRM was both a product of the lack of leadership turnover and internal democracy, but, at the same time, it propelled the move toward multipartyism (see Chapter 3).

- Since 1986, when Museveni took over, the more the country seemed to open up political space, the more control the executive exerted. Ugandan politics under Museveni had initially been defined by an idiosyncratic no-party system (a de facto one-party system) until the introduction of multipartyism in 2005. The opening of political space at times became a pretext for control of civil and political society, and the more precarious the exercise of these rights became for those challenging the status quo. Advocacy was treated as antigovernmentalism and grounds for suspicion at best and repression at worst. The unpredictability of civil rights and other paradoxes of democratization are explored in Chapter 4.
- Decentralization and the creation of mechanisms for popular participation through a local council system were converted into a patronage-based political machine to maintain the ruling party in power. Center-local relations became concerned primarily with creating vertical lines of patronage and obligation and minimizing those horizontal societal linkages that became obstacles to staying in power (see Chapter 5).
- A key dilemma of power lies at the nexus of security and patronage. This is more characteristic of semiauthoritarian and authoritarian states than of electoral democracies or democracies that experience regular changes in leadership. Leaders pursue patronage in order to stay in power, not simply to enrich themselves or support their kin. They use patronage as a carrot to co-opt supporters and even, at times, their political opponents. They also rely on security forces as a stick to intimidate their opponents into submission. Rather than being sources of security, these forces became a source of insecurity for many, especially those in the political opposition. As governments feel more insecure, they rely increasingly on various extralegal armies and militias. Because rulers have used these tactics, they must stay in power. Leaving office will surely mean exile, repression, imprisonment, or death. It might even mean a trip to the Hague to be tried in the International Criminal Court. And so one often finds an impossible catch-22 situation in many semiauthoritarian (as well as authoritarian) states (see Chapter 6).
- Although much of Uganda experienced peace, the NRM government saw more internal conflict in almost all its border areas and in the northern and northeastern third of the country. It even engaged in incursions into the Democratic Republic of Congo in an apparent effort to expand its regional influence and to exploit resources. The conflict in the north of Uganda became one of the longest standing conflicts in postindependence Africa. These conflicts, which often took horrific dimensions, were frequently tied to long-standing grievances on the part of rebel groups but also to the army's need for new sources of patronage (see Chapter 7).

- The final chapter shows how economic growth, which has the potential in the long run to provide the basis for democratization, in the short run provides legitimacy to a system that relies on corruption, patronage, and violence to sustain itself. The chapter also explores some of the ways in which donors provide resources that unintentionally support nondemocratic practices and undermine the creation of productive and mutually beneficial synergies between state and citizens (see Chapter 8).

These, then, are some of the paradoxes of the Museveni government that this book explores. They emerge as persistent features of the semiauthoritarian regime type. The dilemmas are not primarily the result of the moral failings of an individual or even of a group of leaders; rather they are the product of the systemic and institutionalized features of semiauthoritarian rule in the context of a low-income country. In other words, there is no guarantee that another set of rulers in Uganda would behave all that differently under similar circumstances. When one looks at other countries facing similar constraints, comparable outcomes are evident, suggesting that the problems Uganda confronts are institutional and structural. Many of these dilemmas can be found in authoritarian regimes as well, but the difference lies in the extent to which semiauthoritarian regimes must also contend with the existence of democratic institutions and, at the very minimum, keep up the appearance that they too are indeed democratic. The undemocratic core of the regime makes this an almost impossible task, because there is a constant tension with the forces—in civil society, in political parties, in the media, within the elite, and in the legislature and the judiciary—that are trying to create a democratic reality out of those same institutions.

In authoritarian states, these challenges are much less pronounced. Sudan, for example, appoints its legislature, so it does not have to deal with the messy problems of how to ensure a desired electoral outcome yet give the appearance of a free and fair election. In authoritarian Eritrea, the government controls all broadcasting outlets and there have been no independent newspapers since they were banned in 2001. In Uganda, in contrast, the existence of a critical media poses a constant challenge to the regime, which promises freedom of speech in its constitution. Yet the government must engage in intermittent harassment and intimidation of the media in an attempt to control its content and influence. Under the authoritarian regimes of Milton Obote I (1962–1971), Idi Amin (1971–1979), and Milton Obote II (1980–1985), one could not envision the situation in Uganda today, where the Supreme Court constantly pushes back against executive encroachments and carves out its independence through key rulings.

By the same token, one cannot imagine within a democracy the kind of flagrant challenges of the kind experienced by the judiciary in 2005, when an extralegal armed militia, the Black Mamba, was sent to the High Court to rearrest opposition leaders at their bail hearing. These dual realities of partial democracy and partial authoritarianism exist in constant tension in a semi-authoritarian context.

The paradoxes of the Museveni regime are thus typical of the dilemmas confronting poor hybrid regimes, which are neither fully democratic nor fully authoritarian. This is not to say that their leaders should not be held accountable or that individual leadership qualities and values do not matter. Nor can one conclude in a deterministic manner that countries cannot depart from the predicted mold. Rather, it is simply necessary to recognize that the problems of governance in a country like Uganda generally transcend the behavior of individuals in power.

Thus, while this book focuses on Uganda's experience since 1986, it has broader implications for the study of those semiauthoritarian regime types that characterize the African landscape today, found in over half of all African countries. Its main contribution is to show the dual character of these regimes by studying one country in depth and to argue that they need to be examined in their own right, rather than as failed attempts at democratization or as mere authoritarian regimes in democratic guise.

The book is based on seven research trips to Uganda of several months each and one more extended stay. I first visited and became familiar with Uganda in 1968; my most recent trip was in September 2009. Although my initial work there involved the study of the women's movement and women and politics, it provided many insights that are reflected in the pages that follow.[3]

In developing the book, I conducted fieldwork in Kampala, Gulu, Jinja, Mpigi, Luwero, Mbale, and Kabale. This involved interviews and discussions with hundreds of leaders and members of national and local organizations, entrepreneurs, politicians, party leaders, policymakers, opinion leaders, academics, journalists, representatives of nongovernmental organizations (NGOs), businesspeople, representatives of development agencies, bilateral and multilateral donors, religious leaders, and many others in Uganda. I observed some of the proceedings of the Constituent Assembly in 1995 that culminated in the approval of a new constitution. I drew heavily on a systematic review of newspaper articles from *The Monitor, The New Vision, The Weekly Observer, The Independent, The East African,* and several other smaller papers. I also used online sources and unpublished reports by the Ugandan government, the US State Department, and various international and domestic NGOs as well as extensive secondary literature. I have made every effort to draw substantially on Ugandan sources and perspectives.

I owe a sincere debt of gratitude to all the Ugandans I have interviewed and learned from over the years. I am deeply appreciative to those who read and commented on the manuscript, including anonymous reviewers. Since I take my findings about the nature of the state in Uganda seriously, I will leave them nameless as a precaution, but my gratitude is no less heartfelt.

Notes

1. Cited in Onyango-Obbo 2008b.

2. *The Independent,* http://www.independent.co.ug/index.php/column/comment/70-comment/811-where-the-economist-went-wrong. Accessed July 6, 2009.

3. This research resulted in *Women & Politics in Uganda* (Madison, Oxford, and Kampala: University of Wisconsin Press, James Currey and Fountain Publishers, 2000); *The Women's Movement in Uganda: History, Challenges and Prospects,* coedited with Joy Kwesiga (Kampala: Fountain Publishers, 2002); and *African Women's Movements: Transforming Political Landscapes* (New York: Cambridge University Press, 2009), coauthored with Isabel Casimiro, Joy Kwesiga, and Alice Mungwa. I also published numerous articles and book chapters on related topics and on Ugandan politics more generally.

1

Museveni's Uganda in Comparative Context

The NRM fought to bring democracy, but it is now fighting democracy. . . .
The major political question today is democracy.
— Miria Matembe, former Member of Uganda's Parliament
and the Pan-African Parliament, 2004

Although much of the attention in the literature on African politics after 1990 has focused on the issue of democratization, the most important development of this period is at the other end of the spectrum: the slow but ongoing political liberalization of authoritarian regimes and their emergence as hybrids. Hybrid regimes (both their semidemocratic and semiauthoritarian variants) are neither liberal democracies nor autocratic regimes; rather, they are situated along a spectrum in between these two types.

Rather than focus only on the countries that are clearly democratizing, as much of the literature has done, this study suggests that it is also important to look at the softening that has taken place within authoritarian regimes, generating movements from authoritarianism to semiauthoritarianism and from semiauthoritarianism to semidemocratic regimes. These changes within authoritarian and semiauthoritarian regimes, I believe, are among the most profound changes that have occurred in Africa since 1990.

Hybrids are a challenge to the notion of the linear and teleological march of democratization from opening to breakthrough and finally consolidation. Carothers regards political party development, the strengthening of civil society, judicial reform, and media development as "chaotic processes of change that go backwards and sideways as much as forward, and do not do so in any regular manner" (Carothers 2002, 15). Given that most regimes in Africa today fall into this category of hybrids, it is my contention that we need to take a more serious look at them in their own right, rather than simply as countries that did not make it into the democratic fold. Moreover, it matters to people who live under these regimes: certainly one cares if one has an Idi Amin in power.

The limitations of social science as it has developed make embracing two contradictory realities at the same time nearly impossible, yet that is what hybrid regimes require of us. They embody two divergent impulses, both of which reflect a certain reality depending on what processes or actors one is analyzing. To say, as some do, that hybrids are only a façade for authoritarianism is not completely accurate, since there are times when rights are guaranteed and protected. On the other hand, to see such regimes as democratic belies the capriciousness with which those same rights can be withdrawn and the undemocratic ends to which democratic institutions have been used.

Hybrids also matter if one is concerned, as are Thomas Carothers (2002), Robert Bates (2008), Pierre Englebert (2000), and others, about state building. State building is often pitted against political liberalization according to the view that the former should take precedence over the latter. Democratization cannot occur without a state in the first instance. States can exist with or without democratization; moreover, states can be and have been built on authoritarian foundations. This study shows the necessity of both state building and political liberalization for moving these hybrid regimes out of the limbo they are in. Ultimately, state building cannot progress without a secure foundation of state legitimacy, especially when state building is combined with extreme poverty. Bratton and Chang (2006), for example, argue that state legitimacy is crucial for state building and that the most important feature of democratization that creates state legitimacy is the rule of law. They argue that state building and democratization therefore need to go hand in hand: there cannot be democratization without a state, but, by the same token, state building cannot easily take place in today's world without legitimacy, and the best way to secure legitimacy is through an emphasis on the rule of law, which is a central feature of democratization.

Political liberalization helps keep in check some of the worst abuses of power and corruption and thus has itself become a necessary ingredient for state building. The Ugandan case shows how the excesses of authoritarianism, patronage, and violence of the regimes of Amin and Obote ultimately led to state collapse and institutional decay. It was political liberalization, even in its limited form under Museveni, that initially offered a respite from a downward spiral at least until 1985. The experiences under the Amin and Obote regimes provide cautionary tales of what happens to state building when political liberalization is reversed in a poor country and when there are no checks on executive power.

Having said that, I must add that there are real structural impediments that make democratization much less likely in Africa than other parts of the world today. They have to do with lack of economic growth. Even a country like Uganda, which has fared better than most in terms of economic development, remains a long way from reaching the levels of growth that would qualitatively improve its chances of democratizing and remaining democratic without reverting to authoritarianism or semiauthoritarianism.

This chapter provides an overview of the changes that have occurred in Africa since the early 1990s, now that we have had more than two decades to observe the impact of political liberalization on the continent. It starts with a discussion of the ways in which various regime types are delineated, particularly the hybrid regimes, including the semiauthoritarian and semidemocratic ones. (See Table 1.1.) It discusses overall political liberalization trends in Africa since 1990 and contrasts the trajectories of authoritarian, democratic, and hybrid African political systems. It concludes by examining the key themes and characteristics of semiauthoritarian regime types in Africa as well as the ways in which these features have played out in Uganda since 1986. In particular, it focuses on the paradoxes of power as they relate to patronage and violence; power sharing with respect to ethnicity, clan, and religion; the challenges of political liberalization; societal efforts to protect civil and political rights; security; economic influences on democratization; and the ambiguous role played by donors in Uganda.

Delineating Hybrid Regimes

Larry Diamond (1996) argues that it was the prevalence of a wide range of electoral and pseudodemocracies that characterized much of the third wave of democratization, not just in Africa but globally. Building on the work of Terry Karl and Philippe Schmitter, Diamond shows that competitive elections were only a first and minimal step in the direction of democratization and that what was lacking was a deepening of the process that would not only encompass regular, free, and fair elections but also freedom of expression and association, equality under the law, rule of law, the separation of powers, and the protection of political and civil liberties.

If one looks at the descriptions of the general family of hybrid regimes, one sees that they are characterized by different scholars in a variety of ways that are not entirely compatible. They are variously referred to as pseudodemocracies (Diamond 1996), illiberal democracies (Huntington 1997; Zakaria 1997), electoral democracies (Diamond 2002), electoral authoritarian regimes (Schedler 2006), competitive authoritarian regimes (Levitsky and Way 2001, 2002), electoral hegemonic authoritarian regimes (Diamond 2002), contested autocracies (van de Walle 2002), virtual democracies (Joseph 1998), and so on. Further complicating matters is the fact that not everyone means the same thing by these categories, and insufficient research has been carried out to fully elaborate the political systems.

Semidemocratic Regimes

For the purposes of this book, semidemocracies (sometimes referred to as electoral democracies) hold regularly contested, closed-ballot, multiparty elections in which political parties have free access to the electorate through the

Table 1.1   Contrasting Characteristics of Regime Types

Liberal Democracies	Hybrid Regimes	Authoritarian Regimes
Civil and political liberties are generally guaranteed and protected	Repression of civil and political liberties is arbitrary, with recourse to the legal system	Civil and political liberties are repressed
Elections allow for regular turnover in leadership	Regular elections are held; however, they are subject to manipulation by incumbents. In semidemocracies, there is the possibility of a change in leadership. In semiauthoritarian regimes, incumbents use elections simply to legitimate their rule and stay in power at all costs	Elections may be held regularly; however, the outcome is generally predetermined
Legal system aims to promote civil and political liberties and uphold the rule of law	Laws contain contradictions with respect to civil and political liberties. These contradictions can be used to the advantage of those seeking redress	Laws do not ensure protection of civil and political liberties
There is separation of powers between the executive branch, the legislature, and the judiciary. Executives can be elected out of office	The executive impulse is to expand control. It is resisted by the legislature, the judiciary, the media, and civil society. The executive remains in power for as long as possible in semiauthoritarian regimes	The executive dominates without challenge
The multiparty system allows for changes in the dominant party over time	Multiple parties generally can operate, but the dominant party remains the same, with the largest number of parliamentary seats, for as long as possible	There is a single party or a de facto single party system
The army is civilian led and used primarily for protection against external threats; the military and police are controlled by elected officials	In semiauthoritarian regimes, organs of security may become sources of insecurity; paramilitary and extralegal security forces exist. The civilian-led army can be used for self-defense of the nation. The military may exert undue influence behind the scenes	Political power is subject to military dictates
There are institutionalized checks in the political system against abuse, nepotism, and favoritism not based on merit	Institutions are multipurpose, serving unofficially as vehicles for patronage and maintaining those in power. Patronage can be challenged	Power is distributed through patronage, repression, and co-optation
Mechanisms are in place to enforce transparency and accountability	Mechanisms to ensure transparency are unevenly employed and often distorted for other ends. They are introduced for the purposes of ensuring transparency and accountability	No pretense of transparency is made
Political institutions embody democratic values and practices	Democracy within political institutions is uneven, despite the introduction of mechanisms to ensure internal democracy	No pretense of internal democracy is made
Civil society is independent of the state	Civil society is not fully autonomous, though it has political space	Civil society is co-opted by the ruling party and/or state
Productive state-society synergies allow for give and take and a balance between vertical and horizontal ties	Relations with the executive branch are vertical. Horizontal relations within society are weak, but they may challenge vertical linkages	Ties with society are vertical

media and campaigning and in which there is not massive voter fraud. Semi-democratic countries allow for changes in party dominance and the alternation of the presidency. There is a lot of shifting between these regimes and semi-authoritarian regime types, because they have a tendency to lapse in their observance of political rights.

Andreas Schedler (2006) and Larry Diamond (2002) call semidemocracies *electoral democracies*. According to Schedler, they get elections right but do not institutionalize other aspects of democratization, including the rule of law, political accountability, good governance, and public deliberation. He suggests that the boundaries between complying with and violating democratic norms are imprecise, and bending the rules is at times part of the political game. The term *electoral democracies*, however, implies that these regimes are democracies when in fact there are limits in the extent to which they respect civil liberties and political rights or adhere to good governance and administrative transparency. At the risk of adding to an already overtaxonomized list of descriptors of regime types, I find that the term *semidemocracy* is more suggestive of the limitations on democracy and leads to less confusion, since it is easy for some to confuse the term *electoral democracy* with liberal democracy.

Semiauthoritarian Regimes

Semiauthoritarian regimes like Uganda today hold regular competitive elections; however, it is not clear that the rulers in these countries are interested in fully opening up the political process and relinquishing power. They do the absolute minimum to democratize in response to pressure from donors in civil society as well as from intraelite pressures. In Africa, they are characterized by presidents who win more than 60 or 70 percent of the vote, who return to power repeatedly, and who seek to lift term limits. Ruling parties dominate the legislature and dominate over the course of repeated elections.

Semiauthoritarian regimes are unlike semidemocratic regimes in that they do not allow for genuinely competitive elections. Frequently, massive voter fraud occurs, and opposition parties do not always have either free access to the electorate through the media or the same advantages as incumbents when campaigning—for instance, state resources and presidential backing. Incumbents invariably return to power and the dominant party remains dominant over long periods of time. However, as Diamond has pointed out, even liberal democracies do not have a truly level playing field, as incumbent parties or candidates are able to take advantage of easier access to the media, have a greater ability to raise funds, and may be able to (legally or illegally) use government transport and staff while campaigning (2002, 28). The difference between democratic and hybrid regimes in maintaining an unlevel playing field is ultimately a question of degree.

In most semiauthoritarian countries, there remain continuing violations of civil and political rights, although the overall picture of these regimes is improving in Africa. What distinguishes semiauthoritarian regimes from democratic ones is their lack of consistency in guaranteeing civil liberties and political rights. For example, they may allow for considerable freedom of the press and yet, at key moments during an electoral contest, they may suddenly limit such liberties, and media workers may find themselves charged with sedition for reports that only a few months earlier elicited no reaction from the government. Opposition parties, nongovernmental organizations (NGOs), members of parliament, and the judiciary may find themselves in similar predicaments, wherein the rules change unpredictably and extralegal or legal action is used to curtail freedoms of speech, assembly, association, and expression.

At the same time, it is the governments' regard for some of these liberties that distinguishes them from authoritarian regimes. Ordinary citizens may not find these regimes especially repressive because, as long as they do not belong to the opposition or engage in advocacy, they can often go about their daily activities with little consequence.

Semiauthoritarian regimes thus combine characteristics of both democracies and authoritarian states: they adopt elements of democratic institutions and rhetorically define themselves as democracies, but in reality they fall far short of meeting the basic criterion of liberal democracies, namely respect for civil and political rights. Unlike semidemocracies, they do not permit the meaningful electoral competition that allows for significant changes in leadership.

Semiauthoritarian regimes deliberately combine the rhetoric of liberal democracy with illiberal rule, as Marina Ottaway puts it (2003). For this reason, some, like Richard Joseph, have referred to these regimes as *virtual democracies* in which the ritual and symbolism associated with elections have provided an aura of adherence to democratization. Is it all a façade? Yes and no. Certainly, elections may serve as window dressing and are carried out as rituals of democratization. However, Murray Edelman (1964) has shown how all governments need political rituals like elections to provide collective meaning to the exercise of power, and people may need political rituals as venues to express common aspirations. The same political ritual may have different meanings for different people: leaders, opposition parties, the electorate, the international community, and foreign donors.

Edelman argues that authoritarian and totalitarian states may have the greatest need for such reassuring symbols, which is why they are the most keen to involve the population in political discussions, mass meetings, and events. It keeps peoples' energies diverted toward public displays of loyalty for the leadership; they remain focused on symbols and ideas rather than getting involved in private creative work that might be resistant to external manipulation (Edelman 1964, 8–9). Reasserting legitimacy and engaging the population in a predetermined ritual of affirmation of the legitimacy of those in power is certainly one function of elections in semiauthoritarian states. In particular, elections are often intended to mollify foreign donors who expect to see signs of democratization. But as Edelman explains, the element of political performance can be found in democracies and nondemocracies alike. For this reason, the idea of a virtual democracy is not entirely satisfactory in delineating hybrid regimes.

Andreas Schedler (2002) prefers the term *electoral authoritarianism* to describe semiauthoritarian regimes where elections are held, but opposition forces often cannot meaningfully challenge those in power. There are, nevertheless, some problems with the term and the emphasis it places on elections and authoritarianism. Howard and Roessler go so far as to say that "the defining characteristic of these regimes is a competitive process for the selection of national leaders that is often manipulated by the ruling party or incumbent to ensure its hold on power" (2006, 380). Between 1986 and 2005, Uganda had a no-party system, yet it shared most features of an electoral authoritarian regime, as Schedler and others define it. It certainly was not a politically closed authoritarian regime and it held elections in which people ran as individuals, not as party members. However, the elections are not the key distinctions between dominant party regimes and authoritarian regimes. Most autocracies hold elections even though the outcome may be predetermined. Some even have competing parties. Moreover, the term *authoritarian* does not sufficiently evoke the constraints on authoritarianism that can be found in such regimes; hence my preference for the term *semiauthoritarian regimes.*

Even though the boundaries between semiauthoritarian and authoritarian regimes may be fuzzy, authoritarian regimes make little pretense of incorporating democratic institutions beyond holding elections. Virtually all the same authoritarian tendencies can be found in semiauthoritarian regimes, but the difference between the two regime types is the degree to which one also finds democratic elements in semiauthoritarian regimes and the degree of repression of dissent. In semiauthoritarian regimes one finds, for example, challenges from the courts and the legislature to executive expansion. Civil society has political space for expression and assembly and can assert itself, whereas challenges to executive dominance are suppressed and have almost no impact in autocratic settings. Authoritarian regimes may also hold regular elections, but they are often ruled by a monarch, oligarch, military junta, or other type of autocrat.

Political Liberalization and Political Systems in Africa

Fareed Zakaria observes that democratization in Africa has been "a crushing disappointment. . . . Although democracy has in many ways opened up African politics and brought people liberty, it has also produced a degree of chaos and instability that has actually made corruption and lawlessness worse in many countries" (2007, 97–98). Others have argued that political liberalization has stalled in Africa since the democratization surge of the early 1990s (Carothers 2002; Herbst 2001). These judgments may be too hasty.

Since the 1990s, there has been a general shift toward political liberalization and democratization in Africa, with an increase in civilian-led regimes and a shift away from military regimes. There have been constitutional changes in thirty-eight countries and significant constitutional reforms in another eight countries. Multipartyism has been introduced in virtually all African countries, along with the holding of contested elections. Almost all African countries have experienced greater freedom of expression and association and an increase in political and civil liberties. Nevertheless, the overwhelming majority fall between the extremes of fully democratic regimes and fully authoritarian regimes.

The outcomes have been more dramatic in Africa than elsewhere around the globe, particularly with respect to authoritarian regimes. The proportion of democracies in the world increased by 19 percent in the "third wave of democratization," between 1975 and 2005, based on Freedom House figures.[1] The proportion of hybrid countries did not change at all, while authoritarian regimes decreased by 19 percent. In Africa, by contrast, although one saw the same 19 percent increase in new democracies in this period (1975–2005), much of the liberalization that occurred, especially after 1990, involved the softening of authoritarian regimes themselves and a movement away from politically closed autocratic systems. Thus, hybrid states in Africa increased by 17 percent, while authoritarian countries decreased by 36 percent (see Table 1.2, Figure 1.1, and Figure 1.2).

Table 1.2   Change in Regime Type: Contrasting Countries in Africa with the World (by percentage of total countries)

| | African Countries | | | Countries in World | | |
	Free	Partly Free	Not Free	Free	Partly Free	Not Free
1975	4	31	65	27	31	42
1980	6	35	59	32	33	35
1985	8	23	70	34	33	33
1990	9	29	62	40	30	30
1995	19	52	29	40	32	28
2000	19	39	42	45	31	24
2005	23	48	29	46	31	23
2008	23	44	33	46	32	22

Source: Freedom House, http://www.freedomhouse.org. Accessed December 12, 2009. "Free" roughly corresponds to "democratic," "not free" to "authoritarian," and "partly free" to "hybrid."

Figure 1.1   Global Democratization, 1975–2008

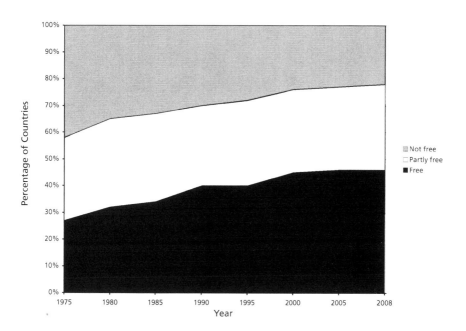

Source: Freedom House, http://www.freedomhouse.org. Accessed December 29, 2009. See note 1 at the end of Chapter 1 for further discussion of these categories.

Thus, the main shift that took place since the 1990s was away from authoritarianism toward semiauthoritarianism and involved some political opening within authoritarian regimes themselves. However, since the early 1990s in Africa, most semiauthoritarian countries have continued to improve their civil liberties and political rights ratings. Clearly, there have been a fair number of reversals in democracies and hybrids and the pace of political liberalization has slowed down after the initial surge, but, interestingly, authoritarian regimes have continued to gradually improve, with only three authoritarian countries experiencing reversals in civil liberties and none in political rights since 1990 (see Table 1.3).

The patterns that emerge in contrasting the four regime types found in Africa today are distinct and striking. By 2008, 21 percent (ten countries) of sub-Saharan African countries could be considered "free" (to use the Freedom House categorization), which is double the number two decades ago.[2] Fifteen countries (32 percent) were "not free," down by half in twenty years, while the

Figure 1.2   Democratization in Africa, 1975–2008

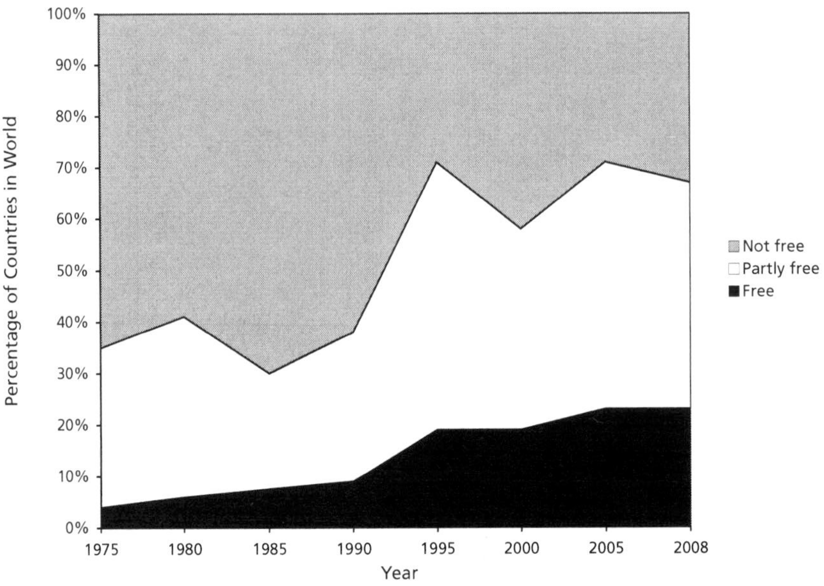

number of "partly free" countries totaled 47 percent (twenty-two countries) or twice the number than existed in 1989 (see Tables 1.4 and 1.5).[3]

Staffan Lindberg's (2009) examination of elections from 1989 to 2006 further confirms these trends. Lindberg finds that free and fair elections have become increasingly frequent in Africa. Overall, more countries are holding elections, with an increasing number achieving minimum standards of fairness. After the initial spurt in competitive multiparty elections, the percentage of presidential elections leading to alternations in power declined with the second and third elections. However, the fourth and later elections have seen a significant rise in alternations of power, even compared to the first elections. This leads Lindberg to conclude that the power of leaders to undermine democratic behavior is being constrained to a greater degree than in the past, which corresponds to the overall patterns I am finding with respect to civil liberties and political rights.

Emerging Democracies

Existing democracies had less room for improvement and therefore did not experience significant changes. However, nine countries have transitioned to democracy and remained democratic since 1990. Lesotho, Senegal, and Ghana

Table 1.3   Change in Political Rights and Civil Liberties in African Countries, 1990–2008

	Political Rights	Civil Liberties	Overall Ranking
Free countries			
Improvement	0 (0)[a]	17 (1)	0 (0)
Reversal	60 (3)	50 (3)	33 (2)
No change	40 (2)	33 (2)	66 (4)
Subtotal	100 (5)	100 (6)	100 (6)
Partly free countries			
Improvement	64 (16)	66 (6)	31 (5)
Reversal	12 (3)	22 (2)	25 (4)
No change	24 (6)	11 (1)	44 (7)
Subtotal	100 (25)	100 (9)	100 (16)
Not free countries			
Improvement	77 (14)	61 (20)	58 (15)
Reversal	0 (0)	9 (3)	0 (0)
No change	22 (4)	30 (10)	42 (11)
Subtotal	100 (18)	100 (33)	100 (26)
Africa overall			
Improvement	62 (30)	56 (27)	41 (20)
Reversal	13 (6)	17 (8)	13 (6)
No change	25 (12)	27 (13)	46 (22)
Total	100 (48)	100 (48)	100 (48)

Source: Freedom House, http://www.freedomhouse.org.
Notes: N = 48 countries.
a. The first number is the percentage of countries that have changed; the second number (in parentheses) is the number of countries.

were the most recent countries to democratize in 2000 and 2001. Another three countries, Malawi, Zambia, and Gambia, crossed the threshold and then reverted to being semidemocracies.

Democratic regimes in Africa have generally emerged from countries that had already instituted multipartyism and introduced a good measure of civil liberties and political rights. This suggests that hybrid regimes can provide important stepping stones to further democratization in Africa, as has been the case in other parts of the world, where countries with improved civil liberties created favorable conditions for transitions to democracy (Linz and Stepan 1996; O'Donnell and Schmitter 1986). Indeed, countries that have had earlier experiences with democracy are more likely to succeed in subsequent attempts, more so than countries that have no democratic traditions (Plattner 1998), so it makes sense that political liberalization takes place in stages, even though the potential for reversal is high. Increasing evidence for democratization by elections is emerging globally, suggesting that each round of competitive elections spurs

Table 1.4   Sub-Saharan African Regime Types, 2009

Democratic	Semidemocratic	Semiauthoritarian	Authoritarian
Benin (2,2)	Comoros (3,4)	Angola (6,5)	Chad (7,6)
Botswana (2,2)	Liberia (3,4)	Burkina Faso (5,3)	Equatorial Guinea (7,7)
Cape Verde (1,1)	Malawi (4,4)	Burundi (4,5)	Eritrea (7,6)
Ghana (1,2)	Mozambique (3,3)	Central African Republic	Guinea (7,5)
Lesotho (2,3)	Senegal (3,3)	(5,5)	Sudan (7,7)
Mali (2,3)	Seychelles (3,3)	Cameroon (6,6)	Swaziland (7,5)
Mauritius (1,2)	Sierra Leone (3,3)	Congo-Brazzaville (6,5)	Zimbabwe (7,6)
Namibia (2,2)	Tanzania (4,3)	Côte d'Ivoire (6,5)	
São Tomé e	Zambia (3,3)	Djibouti (5,5)	
Príncipe (2,2)		Democratic Republic of	
South Africa (2,2)		Congo (6,6)	
		Ethiopia (5,5)	
		Gabon (6,4)	
		Gambia (5,4)	
		Guinea-Bissau (4,4)	
		Kenya (4,3)	
		Nigeria (5,4)	
		Rwanda (6,5)	
		Togo (5,5)	
		Uganda (5,4)	

Notes: Freedom House ratings for political rights and civil liberties, respectively, appear in parentheses. Somalia is divided, in conflict, and without an internationally recognized state. Madagascar was in the semidemocratic category before experiencing a coup d'etat in 2009; its status is undetermined. Niger was a semidemocratic country until 2008, but has experienced a series of setbacks since and is still in flux.

Table 1.5   Trajectory of Regime Change in Sub-Saharan Africa, 1989–2008

Countries	1989	1999	2008
Not free	33	15	15
Partly free	11	24	22
Free	3	8	10

Source: Freedom House, http://www.freedomhouse.org. Accessed July 11, 2008.
Note: N = 47. Eritrea is excluded from that number because it was not independent in 1989, and Somalia is excluded because it became stateless in this time period.

greater political liberalization (Bunce and Wolchik 2006; Hadenius and Teorell 2007; Howard and Roessler 2006; Schedler 2002).

Staffan Lindberg (2009) has found that the number of successive, repetitive elections are the best predictor of civil liberties in Africa, although one might argue that it also works the other way around—that civil liberties create the necessary conditions for repetitive elections. Jason Brownlee (2009) has also found, in a crossnational study of fifty-eight regimes from 1975 to 2004, that hybrid regimes have better prospects for democratization than authoritarian regimes.

In 1989, on the eve of democratizing trends across the continent, only Botswana and Mauritius could be considered democratic. In the years that followed, Benin, Cape Verde, Ghana, Lesotho, Mali, Namibia, São Tomé e Príncipe, Senegal, and South Africa democratized. Unlike semiauthoritarian regimes, the countries that transitioned to democracy in the 1990s and after 2000 remained democratic, with only two (Zambia and Malawi) reverting to semidemocracy and one, Gambia, reverting in 1994 to "not free" status, as Freedom House characterizes it. Interestingly, of these democracies, Botswana, Mauritius, Lesotho, and South Africa are parliamentary democracies. These systems are considered more conducive to democracy than presidential systems, where power is more likely to be concentrated in the executive branch (van de Walle 2003).

Hybrid Regimes in Africa

Unlike semiauthoritarian regimes, semidemocratic regimes either experience regular changes in leadership through presidential and parliamentary elections or have the potential to do so. Where a single party is dominant, it does not go unchallenged. These regimes may have problems with civil liberties and political rights, but for the most part they allow for opposition parties to operate openly, and civil society operates freely. There is considerable fuzziness in the demarcation between semidemocratic and semiauthoritarian regimes and a lot of movement back and forth between them. Nevertheless, semidemocratic regimes emerged as a distinct type, albeit one from which a third of the countries that moved into this category in Africa reverted back to semiauthoritarianism between 1989 and 2009.

The majority of semiauthoritarian regimes (twenty-three countries in all) moved to this regime type from authoritarianism between 1990 and 1992. A few countries, including Burundi, Sierra Leone, and Liberia, liberalized later than the rest, delayed by conflict. Côte d'Ivoire, Eritrea, and Zimbabwe experienced a complete reversal to authoritarianism; however, the extent to which most semiauthoritarian countries move back and forth from the authoritarian category to the semiauthoritarian category is quite extensive. Countries like Mauritania, Central African Republic, Kenya, and Togo, for example, have vacillated considerably. They often manifest patterns of personal, clientelist-based rule that are reminiscent of African authoritarian regimes, with the executive holding a preponderance of power and rarely experiencing election losses. This distinguishes them from semidemocratic regimes like those of Malawi, Tanzania, and Zambia, where executive leadership regularly changes through the ballot box.

As this book shows, the contradictions that are built into semiauthoritarian political systems create tensions that simultaneously pull the state toward both democracy and authoritarianism. Pressures from the media, opposition parties, and civil society to further democratize are countered by tendencies to centralize authority within the executive branch, enhance the powers of the military and security forces, and eliminate any real or perceived threats to the dominance of the party in power. The lack of significant economic development contributes to this uncertainty, making democratization a less certain outcome. These countries may adopt seemingly democratic institutions, as Uganda did when it became a multiparty state in 2005, only to serve profoundly undemocratic objectives. In semiauthoritarian regimes like Uganda and Angola, unlike those that are more democratic, elections are not intended to allow for a change of the ruling party or executive in power. Only a handful of countries in the 1990s, including Ghana, Lesotho, Namibia, South Africa, and Senegal, actually moved from the "partly free" to "free" Freedom House category, suggesting that the transition from semiauthoritarianism to democracy is an extraordinarily difficult transition to make.

The softening of authoritarianism in Africa and the emergence of semi-authoritarian regimes can be explained by many of the same factors that account for democratization on a global scale in the 1990s, including the end of the Cold War, an end to key conflicts, donor pressures, diffusion influences, splits within the elite, and new demands by citizens. Societal actors began to exert greater pressure for political reform through lobbies, the media, networks of NGOs, legislative representatives, and the courts (which challenged the constitutionality of various laws). Demands for greater associational autonomy from the state also grew.

The Changing Nature of Authoritarian Regimes in Africa

Although much attention is paid to the countries that have become democracies, the most significant changes in Africa have happened within authoritarian regimes, with two-thirds moving out of this category between 1990 and 2008 and the remaining eleven countries experiencing political reforms, however limited. Military regimes have mostly disappeared and exist primarily as a transitional form of rule. Officers either run for office or create a space for the autonomous influence of the military behind the veil of civilian rule (Diamond 2002, 27). The old-style personal dictators who ruled Africa with impunity are virtually nonexistent today. No longer can one find rulers like Uganda's Idi Amin, Central African Republic's Jean-Bedel Bokassa, and Equatorial Guinea's Macías Nguema—men who eliminated potential dissent with such brutality and ruthlessness that they earned international notoriety. Power in dictatorships was virtually equated with these strongmen, who personally directed the administration and political institutions, arbitrarily passed laws to suit their own purposes, banned independent political organizations, maintained power through various forms of patronage, and used the military as a personal army. They used the state to perpetrate violence against citizens, with little regard for the law. In Uganda, the orgy of murder—which included the killing of the chief justice, Benedicto Kiwanuka, in 1972; Makerere University's vice chancellor, Frank Kalimuzo, that same year; and the Anglican archbishop Janani Luwum in 1977, in addition to two cabinet ministers—came to characterize the Amin regime (1971–1979). Milton Obote's second government (1980–1985) was little better and state terror was equally random, as the Youth Wing of the ruling party, the Uganda People's Congress (UPC), searched villages for rebels. It is estimated that politically inspired violence caused the deaths of 800,000 or more Ugandans between 1971 and 1985. Dan Mudoola points out that under Obote, Amin, and others who ruled Uganda for brief periods after independence, the army, which dominated politics, was widely regarded as an instrument of repression in service of various political factions (1991, 236). It was undisciplined and predatory.

Gone also are the Afro-Marxist regimes once found in Angola, Ethiopia, Guinea Bissau, and Mozambique—regimes that on ideological grounds suppressed challenges to the ruling vanguard party. Backed by Eastern-bloc countries and heavily reliant on the military, leaders of these regimes nationalized key private corporations and financial institutions, abolished private landownership, banned the hiring of labor, nationalized urban rental housing, and introduced other far-reaching social reforms.

Today we also do not find populist military oligarchies, such as that of Ghana under Jerry Rawlings in the early 1980s and of Burkina Faso under Thomas Sankara. Young military leaders who came to power in the late 1970s and 1980s led such regimes. They used state-orchestrated mass mobilization organizations (for example, people's committees, public tribunals, and local councils) to establish what they claimed was a new egalitarian moral and social order. Despite the rhetoric of participation, elections were often suspended, and decisionmaking was carried out by an inner circle close to the president (Bratton and van de Walle 1997, 80).

Compared to the past, most authoritarian regimes today conduct multiparty elections, however irregularly. They do so under circumstances that cannot be considered free and fair: electoral victories are accomplished through repression of the opposition, suppression of the media, and questionable electoral practices. While some of the previously mentioned older features of authoritarianism have disappeared, these authoritarian regimes still do not permit a changing of the guard through the ballot box. Most important, there is little pretense made of protecting civil and political rights, and there are few checks on human rights abuses. The present authoritarian states, including the multiparty ones, vacillate considerably between semiauthoritarianism and authoritarianism; however, the overall pattern is one of continued improvement of civil and political rights within authoritarian regimes (see also Tables 1.2 and 1.3).

The Challenges of Semiauthoritarianism in Uganda

Catch-22: The Power Imperative

The need for the incumbents to stay in power is what drives much of policy-making and politics within semiauthoritarian regimes. Violence and patronage often intersect in ways that make power difficult if not impossible to relinquish, because the personal costs are simply too high. Semiauthoritarian regimes are similar to authoritarian regimes in this regard. State-based patronage is an obstacle to democratization because of the way it is used to perpetuate the political order. Some scholars have focused on the ways in which leaders pursue power in semiauthoritarian regimes in order to access state wealth to support their kinship networks (Ekeh 1975; Hyden 1980), to sustain ethnically based networks (Joseph 1987), or simply to aggrandize themselves. Given the large and growing number of entrepreneurs in the Ugandan business sector and the ample opportunities for enriching oneself through a wide variety of economic activities given sufficient capital and connections, it is clear that there are easier ways to make money to sustain one's clientelistic networks than acquiring state power. In fact, few government officials can be counted among the wealthiest people in Uganda, and most of the wealthy who are in government made their fortunes prior to entering into office.

State wealth in Uganda is thus pursued primarily in order to maintain power and perpetuate the status quo. The Museveni government took power by force and, in the process, made its share of enemies. It has ruled at times by coercion and suppression of its opponents. Given the zero-sum nature of power in Uganda, the alternative to being in power has been exile, death, torture, or imprisonment. Idi Amin and Milton Obote fled into exile. Opposition leaders like Olara Otunnu, Kizza Besigye, Samson Mande, Anne Mugisha, and others of the Forum for Democratic Change (FDC) have chosen exile at different times rather than face an unpredictable fate within the country. Some opposition leaders and activists were tortured or intimidated into choosing self-exile. The fact that so many of Museveni's leading opponents are one-time military personnel only contributes to the National Resistance Movement (NRM) leadership's sense of insecurity. This need to pursue power at all costs is at the crux of the paradoxes of power in semiauthoritarian states.

Democracies do not have these dilemmas, because their leaders did not generally come to power through the barrel of a gun, nor do they need to sustain their power through repression or the threat of repression. They can step aside when they are voted out of office without fear of retribution. Authoritarian rulers, like semiauthoritarian leaders, may worry about being ousted, but they have less to worry about compared with their semiauthoritarian counterparts in contending with a critical press, vocal political opposition, scrutinizing legislatures, activist judiciaries, and civil society watchdogs. For semiauthoritarian and authoritarian rulers, remaining in power is the objective to which all other objectives are subordinated. Thus, corruption and patronage are not merely means of personal aggrandizement, nor are they simply about maintaining clients and being a "big man" or patron. Rather, they are means to sustain political control. The use of patronage to buy off people and the use of repression and violence or the threat of violence to suppress one's opponents are among the only ways that rulers can ensure that they remain in power when elections no longer suffice. Hence semiauthoritarian rulers like those in Uganda find themselves in a bind: they cannot leave office because the personal cost is too high, given their past record of suppressing the opposition and diverting state resources. On the other hand, they need to engage in further violence and diversions of resources in order to remain in office. Thus corruption and violence become the reasons they must continue to perpetuate their rule as well as the means by which they continue to do so.

The Challenges of Power Sharing: Politicized Ethnicity, Clan, and Religion

One of the main constraints on democratization is the divisive politicization of ethnicity, religion, caste, and other identities. Semiauthoritarian regimes have a difficult time overcoming such polarization because, in spite of the rhetoric of nationhood, meritocracy, democratic elections, and power sharing, the need to hold onto power trumps other considerations. Thus, shortcuts to power are often based on narrower ethnic, clan, or religious appeals. One of the main ways these ties are forged is through state-based patronage. In Uganda, the Museveni regime was to have overcome these divisions by building a broad-based government of consensus. One of the central paradoxes of the regime is that despite continuing claims of having a broad-based antisectarian government, which had a basis in reality at the outset of Museveni's rule, as time went on, the leadership of the military and cabinet began to draw heavily from Museveni's home region in western Uganda. There are many avenues through which patronage is distributed, including jobs, resources, contracts, licenses, permissions, scholarships, and other perks. In some countries, especially those with a dominant party, the party apparatus and related mass organizations may still provide an important avenue for the distribution of clientelistic resources. In other countries, however, these party-based networks crumbled with the onset of multipartyism and the delinking of the ruling party from the state. In Uganda, the ruling National Resistance Movement has established patronage networks throughout the country through the use of local government. The civil service is another such network of patronage, and perhaps the most important network is the military. These clientelistic networks, while consolidating key sources of support, at the same time undermine governance and erode the viability of institutions and leadership based on merit.

Museveni's NRM, also known as the Movement, initially distinguished itself by claiming to encompass and represent all interests, factions, parties, and citizens in Uganda in order to combat sectarianism, which had plagued Ugandan politics for decades. The notion of sectarianism in Uganda involves more than the simple politicization of religious differences; it encompasses all forms of potential exclusion. The early, broad-based NRM government, which had sought to incorporate a wide spectrum of political, ethnic, religious, and other interests through political appointments and consensus building, was replaced by a smaller clique of loyalists whose activities were cloaked in secrecy. Political appointments increasingly took on a more pronounced regional and ethnic character. The military and security forces were most obviously configured along ethnic lines. By the mid-1990s it was already clear that the NRM had tightened its grip in a way that left little room for meaningful power sharing. By the late 1990s, however, the all-too-familiar pattern of personalized rule and ethnically based, clientelistic politics became increasingly evident as corruption scandals involving Museveni's close associates and family surfaced. Many felt that patronage was being distributed too tightly along ethnic and regional lines.

There was growing dissatisfaction with Museveni's leadership in the north and other parts of the country, as well as a frustration on the part of those who felt they had not been given their slices of the national cake.[4] But if they posed a challenge to Museveni at the ballot box, they did not pose a military threat. The north, which had dominated Ugandan politics during Amin and Obote's time, was too war weary, and Buganda—which included the seat of power, Kampala, and had played an important economic and political role under colonialism—had no aspirations to unseat the NRM by force.

Challenges of Institutionalizing Democracy

Semiauthoritarian regimes have a difficult time institutionalizing democracy because of the power imperative. In semiauthoritarian states, power is generally concentrated and personalized in the executive branch (van de Walle 2003), and usually bolstered by a military and security apparatus. This is not to say that there is no role for the legislature and judiciary. Indeed, in Uganda we see that those institutions have some capacity for autonomous action, but their autonomy is constantly being challenged and compromised in the effort to keep the executive in power.

One finds that electoral outcomes in these regimes generally involve victory for the dominant party and incumbent president, who enjoys many years in office. Museveni, who intends to run again in 2011, will have by then been in office twenty-five years. President José Eduardo dos Santos of Angola has been in power since 1979; Cameroon's Paul Biya has been president since

1982. When constitutional constraints like term limits get in the way, they are likely to try to remove such obstacles.

At times, the leaders of semiauthoritarian regimes are propelled by popular support, emboldened by elections and referenda that keep them in power. However, elections are not the source of their power (Ottaway 2003), although they may be a source of legitimacy. Schedler describes situations in such regimes, where "electoral contests are subject to state manipulation so severe, widespread, and systematic that they do not qualify as democratic." Those in power manipulate the electoral rules, exclude opposition parties and candidates from participating in the elections, restrict political and civil liberties, limit the access of political opponents to the media and campaign finance, impose suffrage restrictions on voters, use coercion or money to lure the opposition to their side, and/or simply carry out blatant electoral fraud at election time (Schedler 2006, 3). They may intimidate candidates or voters, use resources diverted from the state to fund opposition candidates, and employ various legal and illegal advantages of incumbency that are not conducive to a level playing field, thereby ensuring victory for the party in power.

As is the case within authoritarian regimes, the dominant party generally remains in power from one election to another, sometimes over the course of decades. Nicolas van de Walle (2003) has noted the preponderance of party systems that emerged in Africa after the 1990s, wherein one dominant party (with over 60 percent of parliamentary seats) was surrounded by small, unstable parties. Opposition political parties are generally personality driven, not programmatically driven, and remain weak. Uganda, for example, is dominated by the NRM, which claims 65 percent of parliamentary seats, while the Forum for Democratic Change (FDC) claims 11 percent of the seats, the Uganda People's Congress (UPC) 3 percent, the Democratic Party (DP) 2 percent, the Justice Forum of Uganda (JEEMA) one seat, the Conservative Party (CP) one seat, and the independents 11 percent of the seats (Electoral Commission of the Republic of Uganda 2006).

Other tensions can be found in Uganda as well. For example, initiatives to democratize have often resulted in undemocratic outcomes. Uganda is neither the dictatorship of Idi Amin nor of Milton Obote II, nor a democracy, even though it holds regular and competitive elections. It is therefore not surprising that the very moment Uganda introduced multiparty elections in 2005, it also expanded the powers of the executive branch. This was a quid pro quo arrangement, one that epitomizes the paradox of semiauthoritarian rule in Uganda: steps toward political liberalization are often controlled and framed in ways that further centralize authority.

Rather than signifying a shift toward democracy, Uganda's adoption of multipartyism in 2005, in fact, represented the culmination of a series of developments that sought to entrench the Movement and Museveni in power without seriously opening up the system to a variety of contenders. Museveni introduced several political reforms when he came to power in 1986. He instituted a no-party system in which elections were to be conducted on the basis of personal merit rather than affiliation with a political party, because of the historic association of parties with sectarianism. The system was to be in place for an indeterminate period, until Uganda reached a state of modernization suitable for multipartyism, although its principles were poorly articulated beyond the prohibition against party-nominated candidates (Kasfir 1998, 50–51). Museveni also allowed for the existence of an independent press and autonomous organizations. Uganda's human rights record had improved considerably over previous regimes, as had army discipline.

However, the Movement sought to control and manage all steps toward political liberalization in Uganda. Around 1995, the regime began to actively limit political space and centralize power, both within the Movement and within the country. Museveni's no-party political system was enshrined in the 1995 constitution, paving the way for Movement dominance in a de facto one-party state and the elimination of any organized opposition outside of the Movement. By then, most opposition leaders in the DP and the Uganda People's Congress (UPC) had been purged from top positions. The internal divisions and fallout within the Movement after 1995 were among the most striking developments.

The move toward multipartyism in 2005 needs to be understood in light of Museveni's bid for a third term and his expansion of executive powers. Popular discontent with the Movement made its system politically untenable, but the way in which multipartyism was introduced—in particular, the fact that it became a quid pro quo for lifting presidential term limits—strongly suggests that it was part of an effort to further concentrate power. The pressures to consolidate executive power became stronger with each election in response to Museveni's waning support. In 1996, he beat the leading contender, DP leader Paul Ssemogerere, by 54 percent, winning 76 percent of the vote; in 2001, he beat leading contender Kizza Besigye by 41 percent, winning 69 percent of the vote; and in 2006, he beat Besigye by 22 percent, winning 59 percent of the vote. In all elections, irregularities and intimidation of the opposition were observed; thus these electoral figures represent only the official outcome and need to be regarded with a measure of skepticism. In 2008, Museveni announced his intention to run again in 2011, even as new plans were in the offing to change the constitutional requirements for electoral victory. The 2011 election promises to be much tighter, with 2009 polls by the Steadman Research Group showing that Museveni has less than half of the country's support.[5]

Thus, even as the country opened up to multipartyism, the Movement became more entrenched. Up until that time, the government had continued to restrict the freedom of association for those who had ties to parties, particularly the FDC; it had harassed and intimidated the opposition and media workers critical of the government; and it had attempted to force through undemocratic legislation in parliament without a quorum. The country's rulers increasingly relied on extralegal militias to intimidate political detainees even after the shift to multipartyism.[6]

Many of the NRM's allies fell out of favor or became highly disillusioned with the Movement. Mounting repression of opposition parties and coalitions, including the Reform Agenda coalition and later the Forum for Democratic Change, only strengthened their resolve as their followings grew. The Museveni government charged some of its more vocal critics with treason and sedition. Often such charges were used as a pretext for indefinitely detaining people, only to be dropped later. Political prisoners have numbered in the thousands; there have been alleged extralegal killings of opposition party members; and torture has been carried out and widely acknowledged even by the parliamentary- and government-appointed commissions. Preelection harassment of the opposition was widespread in the 2001 elections but less so in 2006.

Some of the sharpest criticisms of the lack of democracy came from within the Movement. One of the biggest fissures occurred in November 1999, when, in a public statement, Dr. Colonel Kizza Besigye, a former member of parliament who had served in the National Resistance Army as Museveni's personal physician, accused the Movement leadership of being "dishonest," "opportunistic," and "undemocratic" (Mwesige 1999). In the 2001 and 2006 presidential elections, Besigye ran against Museveni, and he and his supporters faced serious government-led intimidation.

In many ways, Museveni's flirtation with democracy is reminiscent of the first postindependence regime of Milton Obote (1963–1966), which was characterized by multipartyism, some civil society mobilization, and limited debate in the legislature. Like Museveni, Obote claimed he was creating a national identity by minimizing the salience of ethnicity, but ethnic politics remained at the core of his strategy of maintaining power. Power became increasingly centralized in the executive and the military, and Uganda became a one-party state. As with Museveni's early vision of the NRM, the UPC was to encompass all Ugandans in its membership. As Joe Oloka-Onyango argues, both leaders believed in the superiority of their political organizations and their capacity to manipulate the political elites. Both feared opposition politics, which, Oloka-Onyango suggests, has been the Achilles heel of both men. Obote suppressed the right- and left-wingers in the UPC, just as Museveni moved against reformists in the Movement and the Baganda who supported the restoration of a political monarchy through a federal system (Oloka-Onyango 2004). Ironically, Museveni may most resemble the man he considers his antithesis. However, a major divergence occurred in 2005: Museveni introduced multipartyism in order to ensure his continued rule, while Obote had moved in the opposite direction to create a one-party state toward the same end.

The Challenges of Participation: Civil and Political Rights

In most semiauthoritarian countries, there remain continuing violations of civil and political rights, although, as we have seen, the overall record for these regimes is improving in Africa. This is yet another contradiction of Museveni's Uganda. Semiauthoritarian states are generally locked in a tug of war with an autonomous civil society, which exerts pressure for political reform through lobbies, the media, networks of NGOs, legislative representatives, and the courts. Demands for greater associational autonomy from the state persist. Although civil society, political parties, and the media have greater room to maneuver, their position is always precarious, and uncertainty about the limits of activism prevails. The state is especially suspicious of activities that might be considered antigovernmental. This suspicion poses challenges to any kind of advocacy, which by definition is about influencing policy change. Civil society remains constantly under the threat of being co-opted by the state and remains weak.

The imperative of keeping Museveni and the Movement in power came to overshadow other objectives of participatory democracy as they had been articulated via the establishment of a hierarchy of local councils, from the village level up to the district level. Local councils had been intended as vehicles for grassroots participation in governance. Gradually they were transformed into a patronage machine that linked the localities to the center and proved especially useful at election time.

Most institutions that could challenge some of the more undemocratic aspects of the government are weak and have been manipulated, co-opted, or undermined. Parliamentarians have been able to resist some elements of the expansion of executive power, but the general weakness of the legislature and the power of patronage have made parliament fairly defenseless against assaults on its integrity. Ironically, the judiciary, which historically has also had relatively little independence from the executive branch, has played a greater role in defending its autonomy and the rule of law. Together with sections of the media, opposition political parties (at times), and parts of civil society, the judiciary has resisted the expansion of executive power and its extralegal activities. Yet all four groups have operated primarily on the defensive, trying to hold on to rights rather than pressing for greater freedom.

The Role of the Military

Whereas Africa was characterized by dictatorships in the 1970s and 1980s, civilian rule became the norm in Africa after the 1990s, particularly in the form of hybrid regimes and democracies. International norms had changed in ways that shifted decisively against army rule and the coups that, prior to the 1990s, had been a familiar part of the political landscape. However, this shift toward civilian rule did not completely diminish the role of security forces in Africa. Clientelism is the underlying basis upon which political support is built, and the most important source of that support is the security forces. In democracies, the military and the police are controlled by elected officials (Dahl 1998, 147). In semiauthoritarian states, that control is contested at best; in the more authoritarian of these regimes, military dominance is only thinly disguised as civilian rule.

Although Uganda is no longer a military regime insofar as the military does not exert overt control of the state, power nevertheless rests with the security forces, whose main goal is not only to protect the country's citizens from external threats but also to protect those in power from internal threats to their rule by citizens. Given the lack of democracy, the centrality of the security forces has, in practice, ironically led to increased insecurity, as the state frequently defines its enemies broadly as people who do not agree with its policies or with those in power. This becomes yet another paradox of many semiauthoritarian regimes.

John Clark found that those African countries that went furthest with political liberalization and had positive economic performance were the least likely to experience coup attempts, whereas all countries experiencing coup attempts and military-related instability since the early 1990s had shown limited improvement in political and civil liberties (2007, 147). Similarly, Michael Bratton demonstrated how central the military was in both facilitating and preventing the transition to multiparty elections in Africa, especially in the early 1990s. The role of the military was the key predictor of the trajectory of a country's political liberalization, as the military leaders were less inclined to give up their institutional privilege if the president was their ethnic patron and was about to lose power in the process. If the military split and sided with the opposition, prodemocracy forces had better chances of succeeding, but if the military sided with those in power, they faced repression (Bratton 1997, 89).

In Uganda, the scenario has been mixed, contributing to the semiauthoritarian limbo the country finds itself in. A group of ex-military officers, mainly from the western part of Uganda, broke with Museveni and aligned themselves with the opposition FDC party. These elite splits and pressures from within the military created a situation that ultimately forced Museveni to allow for some political opening and multipartyism. At the same time, Museveni reconfigured recruitment practices within the army to increasingly draw its leadership and elite forces from the west in order to prevent further dissension within the military and ensure a loyal security system.

The Challenges of Security

The shift toward hybridity and democratization has in general resulted in an improved security situation on the continent. Significantly fewer civil wars have been initiated, especially since 2000, and more wars have been coming to an end. This is one of the most important developments on the continent. Conflict ended in Namibia and South Africa with the end of white minority rule in the early 1990s. Civil conflicts also came to an end in countries like Mozambique (1992), Rwanda (1994), Chad (2002), Angola (2002), Sierra Leone (2002), Liberia (2003), Burundi (2004), southern Sudan (2005), and northern Uganda (2007). Three major conflicts ended between 1990 and 1999, and twelve ended between 2000 and 2005. This is not to diminish the significance of conflict in eastern Democratic Republic of Congo, Somalia, or Darfur or to suggest that continued peace is assured in southern Sudan, northern Uganda, and elsewhere, but rather to acknowledge the major change that has taken place with the decline of long-standing and/or high-intensity conflict.

The decline in conflict can be attributed to a variety of factors, including the end of the Cold War; the use of UN sanctions against countries and individuals; the increased use of international and regional peacekeeping forces; more attention to preventative diplomacy and behind-the-scenes diplomacy; the greater importance of peace negotiations and settlements in Africa, as well as the rising influence of peace movements and women's movements; and interventions by donors, donor states, and regional and multilateral organizations. The increase in political liberalization has also played a role. International awareness has heightened around issues relating to child soldiers, blood diamonds, and violence against civilians, resulting in changing norms and practices.

In more recent years, Uganda has come to follow this overall trend toward peace in Africa; but for most of the Museveni era, much of the country was plagued by insecurity. The insecurity had multiple sources, ranging from attacks in the west and northwest by the Allied Democratic Forces (ADF) in the late 1990s to attacks by Karimojong pastoralists in northeastern Uganda. The most troubled region has been the north, where, after Museveni's takeover, the spirit-medium Alice Lakwena mounted her Holy Spirit Movement until it was suppressed in 1987. Another Acholi rebel, Joseph Kony, launched his own army, the Lord's Resistance Army (LRA), to fight Museveni's Uganda People's Defence Forces (UPDF). The conflict, in which the LRA targeted northerners as well as government troops, resulted in the further marginalization of an already disaffected population in the war-torn districts. By 1996, 2 million northerners were internally displaced, and 1.5 million of them were residing in camps in eighteen districts. The government had moved them into the camps in the late 1980s, often by force, claiming that it wanted to protect them from LRA attacks and abductions. About 25,000 children and adults had been abducted, and thousands of children were forced to walk to urban areas at night for safety.

Museveni's contradictory strategy of simultaneously fighting the LRA, attempting to negotiate with them, and offering their fighters amnesty was a recipe for protracted war. The conflict continued until a tentative ceasefire was negotiated in August 2006 between the LRA and government negotiators in Juba, only to be followed by a series of failed peace talks. The LRA moved its operations out of Uganda and became a menace in the broader central African region, expanding the scope of its attacks in 2008 to Central African Republic, Democratic Republic of Congo, and southern Sudan.

In spite of the Ugandan government's attempt to portray itself as a source of peace in the region, its actions in the northern part of Uganda and in Democratic Republic of Congo suggest otherwise. Its overriding imperative in these conflicts has been one of maintaining the loyalty of the military to the government at any cost.

Economic Influences on Semiauthoritarian Rule

From 2000 until the global financial crisis starting in 2008, much of Africa experienced nearly unparalleled economic growth. Uganda was one of the big "success" stories. Although economic decline or collapse may have initially provided the impetus for political reform in many countries, later economic growth may have become a factor in sustaining the regimes of semiauthoritarian countries and providing legitimacy to incumbents, at least in the short run. In other words, economic growth, which generally is seen as creating conditions for democratization in the long term, may have acted as a suppressant to further democratization in semiauthoritarian countries, where it helped legitimize the status quo. Uganda's experience bears out this paradox.

Overall, the relationship between political liberalization and economic growth appears to have strengthened over time in Africa. One finds that civil liberties and GDP per capita are correlated between 1970 and 2008, as are political rights and GDP per capita in this same time period. The relationship also holds with a five-year lag that would allow for the economic changes to have an impact.[7] There was no statistically significant correlation between civil liberties/political rights and GDP per capita in 1985 compared with strong correlations by 2008.[8] Although these findings need to be corroborated with other dependent variable measures and analyzed in conjunction with other explanatory independent variables, they do point to some important longitudinal trends that warrant further investigation. Moreover, earlier studies in Africa did not uncover such correlations between economic growth and democratization (Lindberg 2009; van de Walle 1999). My suspicion is that the difference between these earlier studies and my own can be attributed to the fact that neither was tracking the relationship between economic growth and civil liberties longitudinally and through the economic upswing in Africa.

The Ugandan case suggests that the relationship between economic growth and political reform is more varied and complex than most existing explanations allow. Existing explanations are not entirely applicable to the Ugandan case. Economic factors are said to influence democratization in a number of ways. Economic crisis may cause splits within the elite, creating opportunities for the opposition to mobilize and claim new legitimacy for itself while weakening the bargaining power of the incumbents (Haggard and Kaufman 1995). Some political scientists have argued that in Latin America and Europe soft-line elites would need to forge pacts with hard-liners to prevent a reversal to authoritarianism (Malloy and Seligson 1987; Remmer 1991). All transitions, according to O'Donnell and Schmitter (1986), are the product of such elite divisions.

However, Bratton and van de Walle (1997) have argued that elite divisions have not played such a role in Africa, where transitions in neopatrimonial regimes were driven by mass popular unrest in response to economic and fiscal crisis. This may have led in turn to elite divisions, but the pressure came from below. The reform coalition generally came from outside the group in power, and, rather than representing hard-liners or soft-liners or forming elite pacts, they represented different factions of insiders and outsiders competing for the spoils of patronage. Part of the struggle in neopatrimonial regimes was over the rule of law itself: constitutions and electoral laws were at the center of controversy. The law became the main means through which resources could be accessed. Control of the media and electoral campaign assets were a means to that end. Businesspeople and the middle classes aligned themselves with the opposition because they were frustrated by state ownership, the state's lack of support for the private sector, corruption, and overregulation.

This explanation for political liberalization in Africa only partially clarifies what happened in Uganda and other countries in Africa, where pressures for reform came primarily from within the ruling elite and military and from elite factions, some of which left the government. To some extent there were pressures from the judiciary and legislature, although many of their actions were defensive rather than proactive. And although there have been societal pressures, particularly from lawyers and from the media, civil society in general has been quite weak. Mass pressures may have been a factor in initiating political liberalization in some countries in the early 1990s, but civil society could not be relied upon to sustain such pressure over time. Labor also has been too weak and unorganized to be a force for change in most countries, with a few important exceptions, and business has been too tied to the incumbent governments and has benefited too much from various cozy arrangements to be a source of pressure.

In Uganda, the pressures for reform came from within the elite and military at a time when the country's economy was on an uptick rather than in a downturn. Economic growth served to further legitimize the status quo, thus galvanizing the political opposition, which wanted a more equitable division of the country's political power and economic resources. The opposition drew on the rhetoric of changing international norms regarding democratization and were influenced by democratic developments in other African countries. The Ugandan case suggests that while economic crisis may have resulted in popular pressures for political reform in the early 1990s, by 2010 economic prosperity created its own impetus for change in a country like Uganda, where economic growth had become a source of legitimacy for the NRM's monopoly of power.

Donors' Ambiguous Role

Most semiauthoritarian rulers have gone only as far with political reforms as they have felt necessary to satisfy domestic and donor pressures. Their ultimate agenda is to stay in power at all costs, and as a result they may resort to profoundly antidemocratic measures. Africa's semiauthoritarian regimes may liberalize politically in response to donor pressure but simultaneously carry out as much repression as they can get away with in order to cling to power.

In Africa, elections are often funded by donors and monitored by international and local organizations, which have set new standards for electoral fairness within countries (Young 1999, 34–35). Some see democratization in Africa as having been almost entirely donor driven (Decalo 1992). Africa's heavy reliance on international donor funds meant that the political process had to be opened up to at least some degree, and some feel that donor influence helped mitigate against the emergence of the kinds of dictatorships that had been seen in the past, pushing countries away from authoritarianism into semiauthoritarian rule or democracies. Levitsky and Way (2001, 2002) argue that, in general, authoritarianism is more difficult to entrench in countries that have extensive ties with the West. The donor-recipient relationship, however, needs to be examined over time, especially in the case of semiauthoritarian countries. In Uganda, aid has facilitated democratization by supporting civil society and encouraging political opening. Yet at the same time, many Ugandans saw foreign aid as an endorsement of some of the most authoritarian tendencies of the government. Donors continued to support the country even when antidemocratic and interventionist foreign policies were adopted.

In Africa, the correlation between foreign aid and democratization has declined over time. In 1990, there was a correlation between civil liberties and foreign aid per capita[9] as well as between civil liberties and aid as percentage of GDP.[10] The correlation also held for democratization in general and foreign aid per capita[11] as well as democratization and aid as a percentage of GDP.[12] But these correlations disappeared by 2005, suggesting that aid may have served as an impetus for political liberalization in the early phases of democratization or as a reward for countries that liberalized, but that it became a prop for semiauthoritarianism as time wore on.[13] More detailed analysis and consideration of interactions with other variables would be useful.

Conclusion

As we have seen in this chapter, Uganda today embodies many of the contradictions of semiauthoritarian rule in Africa. Political spaces opened up in Uganda and elsewhere in Africa after the 1990s, as emerging civil societies and the media began to assert themselves. Judiciaries began to press for more autonomy, as did legislatures (Barkan 2008). Pressured by foreign donors, domestic opposition groups, and sections of the military and elite, countries like Uganda began to liberalize—although Uganda held out longer than most of its African neighbors in instituting multiparty politics. Moreover, when Uganda did introduce multipartyism, Museveni simultaneously expanded the powers of the executive. Uganda was no longer being led by tyrants like Idi Amin and Milton Obote, yet some uncomfortable parallels remained evident: familiar forms of "safe houses" (detention centers) and extralegal militia emerged, the military's adventures in Democratic Republic of Congo went unchecked, and constitutional constraints on the executive branch were gradually eliminated. The democratic future of Uganda hangs very much in the balance given the weakness in, co-optation of, and divisions among those forces that generally are sources of democratic change: civil society, political parties, the business class, sections of the military, and elite groupings. Moreover, the donors send mixed messages regarding political reform and thus must be considered an unreliable source of pressure.

Finally, a central paradox of the semiauthoritarian state is situated at the nexus of power, patronage, and the state's monopoly of violence: these states rely excessively on the use of violence to repress their opponents. They similarly rely on state-based patronage to maintain support. They cannot relinquish either without relinquishing power and to do so would put them at risk of being subject to the same repression they have inflicted on their opponents.

These contradictions within Uganda are typical of the challenges facing other semiauthoritarian regimes and help explain why the latter have such difficulty moving beyond the initial phase of political opening. Overall, Uganda today is better off along most measures compared to 1986, especially in terms of its record on economic growth, human rights, civil liberties, political rights, peace and stability, and the independence of the judiciary and legislature. At the same time, the post-1986 period has seen enormous instability in one-third of the country that has only recently subsided; political freedoms have been suspended for most political parties for most of this time period; executive power has expanded; the military dominates; and the independence of the judiciary and legislature is constantly being challenged. Such ambiguity is at the heart of semiauthoritarianism.

Notes

1. Freedom House rates countries as "free" (rated from 1 to 2.5) if they allow for competitive elections and come reasonably close to ensuring freedom of "expression, assembly, association, education and religion." Countries are regarded as "partly free" (rated from 3 to 5) when political corruption, political discrimination against minorities, foreign or military influences, civil war and violence, unfair elections, and one-party dominance weaken the quality of freedom. In terms of civil liberties, these countries may experience censorship, state and nonstate sources of political terror, and lack of free association. Yet they may nevertheless enjoy some political rights, including the right to organize political groups and access to other societal means of influencing the government. "Not free" countries (rated from 5.5 to 7) may be ruled by military juntas, one-party dictatorships, religious hierarchies, or autocrats. Political rights are minimal or absent. Countries may be faced with civil war marked by extreme violence or warlord rule in the absence of an authoritative functioning government. Not free countries have virtually no freedom or civil liberties, and political rights are severely restricted. Most African regimes today span the range of Freedom House ratings from 3 to 6.

I take these numbers only as rough indicators of the trends I identify. It is unclear to me, for example, what change Freedom House noted between 2002 and 2003 that would have merited a one point (out of seven) change in Uganda's score for improved political and civil liberties, especially given the precarious environment within which the opposition was operating. Countries like Uganda rate as electoral democracies on the Freedom House charts because of their openness to multipartyism, but, as this book will show, they exhibit clear semiauthoritarian tendencies when confronted with challenges in electoral competition. Similarly, Liberia was ranked as an electoral democracy during one of its most trying times from a human rights and civil liberties standpoint, when the country plunged into civil war (1997–2000). One could quibble with many other rankings. Nevertheless, they point to some relative differences within and between countries over time.

2. Freedom House, http://www.freedomhouse.org/template.cfm?page=439. Accessed April 25, 2010.

3. Extrapolated from Freedom House data.

4. Cake serves as a popular African metaphor that harkens back to King Leopold of Belgium's description of Congo as a "slice of this magnificent African cake" (Hochschild 1999, 58).

5. Uganda National Farmers Federation, http://www.unffe.org/index.php?option=com_content&view=article&catid=15:articles-a-opinions&id=47:the-challenges-of-modernising-land-legislation-in-uganda&Itemid=21. Accessed July 2009.

6. These include the Kalangala Action Plan, the Civic Defence Team, the Violent Crime Crack Unit, the Joint Anti-Terrorism Taskforce, and the Black Mamba. They are linked to the regular police and military but seem to operate outside normal channels of authority.

7. Civil liberties and GDP per capita: Pearson's $r = .143$, $p < .01$, $N = 414$; political rights and GDP per capita: $r = .139$, $p < .01$. Introducing a five-year lag yields approximately the same results: civil liberties and GDP per capita $r = .141$, $p < .01$;

political rights and GDP per capita $r = .138$, $p < .01$. Freedom House, http://www.freedomhouse.org/template.cfm?page=439; United Nations Statistics Division, http://unstats.un.org/unsd/databases.htm. Accessed July 11, 2008.

8. GDP per capita: $r = .397$, $p < .05$, $N = 48$; political rights: $r = .299$, $p < .05$. Freedom House, http://www.freedomhouse.org/template.cfm?page=439; National Accounts Estimates of Main Aggregates, United Nations Statistics Division, http://unstats.un.org/unsd/databases.htm. Accessed July 11, 2008.

9. $r = .27$, significant at the $p < .10$ level, $N = 48$.

10. $r = .247$, significant at the $p < .10$ level.

11. $r = .257$, significant at the $p < .10$ level.

12. $r = .266$, significant at the $p < .10$ level.

13. *Human Development Reports 2007/2008,* http://hdr.undp.org/en/statistics/. Retrieved March 2008. Freedom House, http://www.freedomhouse.org/ratings. Retrieved March 2008.

2

The Rise and Demise of a
Broad-Based Government

*I would like to make some brief remarks about this subject which delegates
have been referring to as the national cake. Most of us born to work in
kitchens know that, where a cake is, there must be a baker. So, I find the
discussion around sharing and eating the cake childish at the very least
and irresponsible, selfish, and parasitic at worst. Sections of the press and
some politicians have made "eating" acceptable and have placed it right at
the centre of political debate. Struggling for the trappings of power is now
at the centre stage; it has become acceptable and even fashionable. Values
[that] we women care about such as caring, serving, building, reconciling,
healing, and sheer decency are becoming absent from our political culture.
This eating is crude, self-centred, egoistic, shallow, narrow and ignorant.
We should ban eating from our political language. Madam Chairman, . . . it
is a culture [that] we must denounce and do away with if we are to start a
new nation.*
> —Winnie Byanyima, head of Uganda's Constituent Assembly
> Women's Caucus, in an address to the Assembly, August 3, 1994

One of the biggest challenges confronting semiauthoritarian regimes involves
the difficulty of breaking with autocratic tendencies to politicize ethnicity, religion, and other such identities as a basis for building clientelistic power bases.
Because of the imperative to stay in power and the elusiveness of legitimacy,
they must rely increasingly on shortcuts such as ethnic and kin affinities to
maintain their ever-shrinking base. Thus, they remain locked in what appear
to be zero-sum political equations that are hard to break, except by force. As
much as Museveni attempted to distinguish himself from the dictators that had
ruled Uganda before him, he espoused the same kind of antisectarianism that
Amin and Obote had adopted and was ultimately challenged by the same
dilemmas they faced in trying to create a workable ethnic matrix. The problem
of building viable political coalitions was especially challenging for Museveni, because he remained in power so long that new challengers from within
the National Resistance Movement (NRM) also began to get impatient with
his monopoly on power. At the same time, he had to contend with a relatively

free press, increasingly politically active kingdoms, and a growing civil society, all of which introduced their own demands and pressures.

Up until 2005, the NRM advocated a no-party system known as the Movement system. The rationale for the Movement system was tied to Uganda's past. The NRM blamed parties for fostering sectarianism and perpetuating the ills of the preceding regimes; it wanted to create a political system that would undermine the power base of the older parties (Muhumuza 2009). The term *sectarianism* was used by the NRM to refer to any form of exclusion based on religion, ethnicity, caste, or other societal division. The NRM argued that preindustrial countries like Uganda were not ready for parties because of the persistence of sectarian tendencies. Moreover, it saw parties as elite institutions that believed they could represent popular interests, whereas the Movement and its original hierarchical structure of local councils were vehicles for direct grassroots political participation by the masses.

Opponents of Museveni said his antisectarian stance was nothing more than populist rhetoric and that he was playing the ethnic card just like his predecessors, only with greater finesse. There was a growing popular perception that many of the plum government jobs were going to western Ugandans from subregions like Bunyoro, Ankole, Kigezi, and Toro as well as the Kasese and Bundibugyo districts—and especially to members of Museveni's Ankole ethnic group.[1]

This chapter provides background to the idea of broad-based government as introduced by the NRM when it took over in 1986. It discusses the ethnic political matrix that Museveni inherited when he came to power and some of the factors that had led to such ethnic polarization (see Figure 2.1). The chapter describes the origins of the notion of a politics of consensus; the early years of the NRM, when the broad-based government idea was first introduced; and the way in which the broad-based coalition began to unravel, especially after the 1994 Constituent Assembly (CA) elections. It also shows how, even under this new, regionally based political system, northerners—who benefited least from the Museveni regime—voted primarily along political rather than ethnic lines in the 2006 elections.

The Impetus for Broad-Based Government

Museveni's antisectarian discourse was originally intended to relieve several historic tensions. One such tension has been between Roman Catholics and Protestants. The former have frequently been associated with the Democratic Party (DP), whereas Protestant non-Ganda have been affiliated with the Uganda People's Congress (UPC), although the party affiliations have never fallen strictly along these lines. Uganda is evenly divided between Roman Catholics and Protestants, who, according to the 2002 Census, each make up

Figure 2.1   Map of Uganda's Ethnic Groups

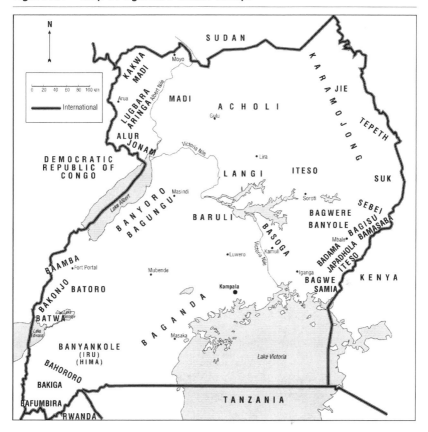

Credit: Eva Swantz

42 percent of the population, while Muslims constitute another 12 percent. In spite of their large presence in Uganda, political power has eluded Catholics. In contrast, the Church of Uganda (Anglicans), with which 36 percent of the population is affiliated, was tied to the colonial establishment before independence and later to Obote's regime and the UPC.

Another historic conflict has been between the northerners and the Baganda.[2] Baganda demands for federalism (*federo*) are seen by Museveni as one manifestation of the sectarianism that he needs to undercut. In January 2003, more than 100,000 Baganda held a peaceful demonstration demanding the restoration of *federo* for Buganda and the return of Kampala to the kingdom. These pro-kingdom sentiments eventually led to unrest, with thirty killed in rioting in Kampala in September 2009. Tensions between Museveni and the

Baganda were further inflamed in March 2010 during clashes between security forces and citizens who came to witness the remains of the Kasubi tombs that had been burned in what was believed to be arson. The tombs were burial grounds of four Baganda kings.

The demands for *federo* are rooted in the historic institutions, wealth, and political cohesiveness that had allowed Buganda to dominate the rest of the country under British rule (1894–1962). The Baganda are the largest ethnic group in Uganda, constituting 17 percent of the population, and Buganda has always been regarded as the largest, wealthiest, and best educated of the country's kingdoms (the others are Bunyoro, Toro, Ankole, and Busoga). This historic legacy has continued to influence its relationship with the rest of the country and has made Buganda, where the seat of national power is situated, a thorn in the side of every postindependence Ugandan government.

Since colonialism, the Baganda have been perceived as a major political force to contend with, despite the fact that they have not collectively had direct political power since independence. Because of Buganda's political and economic strength, the British decided to keep the south demilitarized and enlisted in the army the Acholi and Langi peoples of the north and the Itesot from the east. These patterns of economic, political, and military polarization were the basis for many conflicts in the postindependence period; however, some of the fiercest conflicts were among northerners themselves, especially during the Amin and Obote regimes.

Given the destructive consequences of the politicization of ethnic, regional, and religious hostilities and the countless lives lost in such conflicts, it is not surprising that Museveni's antisectarian rhetoric continued to have wide appeal. His Movement politics were premised on the view that Ugandans belonged to a single class of peasants and therefore did not need parties to reflect differing class interests. The NRM was exempted from the restrictions on parties because it did not claim to be a political party. Instead, it purported to be a no-party movement, even though, for all intents and purposes, it acted like a party. In many respects it resembled the old one-party systems of Africa, in which the party was often fused with the state to the extent that the two were almost indistinguishable. Had it officially declared itself a party, the NRM would have faced the same restrictions it had placed on other parties; therefore, to survive as a legal entity, it needed to maintain its no-party fiction.

The NRM portrayed itself as breaking with previous governments that had been characterized by religious sectarianism, especially by tension between the mainly Protestant UPC and the predominantly Catholic DP and between Buganda and the rest of the country. In part, they were facing the dilemma inherited from colonial rule, one that every postindependence government in Uganda has faced: how to build a coalition large enough to maintain power (Kasfir 1998). A central part of this challenge has involved figuring out how to deal with Buganda.

Obote, Amin, and the Dominance of the North

In fact, Museveni's travails in attempting to create a nonsectarian nation devoid of ethnic and religious divisions had its antecedents in the Obote I and Amin governments (see Table 2.1 for a list of Uganda's governments). Milton Obote, the first prime minister and second president of Uganda, had initially tried to minimize the salience of ethnicity and create a national identity. Rather than dampening ethnic sentiments, however, his efforts to destroy Baganda symbols served instead to fuel Baganda ethnonationalism.

Obote initially recognized the kingdoms, including Buganda, but eventually the coalition crumbled as he withdrew support for Buganda, leading to the constitutional crisis of 1966. This resulted in the exile of King Edward Mutesa, who had been president of Buganda since independence, and was seen as an attack on the Baganda as an ethnic group, who became politically marginalized after this crisis.

Given the British legacy of elevating Buganda to a special status within the colonial administration, Buganda's position within Uganda became an even greater source of tension after independence. Uganda's first constitution—the 1962 independence constitution—was established in the context of a newly formed alliance between Milton Obote's Protestant-led UPC and the Baganda Kabaka Yekka party (KY, or King Alone). The two parties had come together in an unlikely and ultimately untenable coalition to challenge the Catholic-led

Table 2.1   Executive Leaders of Uganda, 1962–2010

Years	Ruler	Title	Leader's Political Party or Movement
1962–1966	Milton Obote	Prime Minister	Uganda People's Congress
1963–1966	Mutesa II of Buganda	President	Kabaka Yekka
1966–1971	Milton Obote	President	Uganda People's Congress
1971–1979	Idi Dada Amin	President	none
1979 (April–June)	Yusufu Lule	President	Uganda National Liberation Front
1979–1980	Godfrey Binaisa	President	Uganda National Liberation Front
1980 (May–December)	Paulo Muwanga	President	Uganda National Liberation Front
1980–1985	Milton Obote	President	Uganda People's Congress
1985–1986	Tito Okello	President	Uganda National Liberation Army
1986–present	Yoweri Museveni	President	National Resistance Movement

DP. The DP's leader, Benedicto Kiwanuka, had become chief minister of Uganda in 1961. KY was focused on the fate of Buganda and the kingship (rather than that of the entire nation), and its members believed that the DP, although led by a Muganda, was not interested in the kingship. The KY-UPC members outnumbered the DP in the new 1962 parliament, ensuring that Obote could form a government that would oversee the transition to independence that same year.

The first constitution, which was negotiated in London among various parties and interests, provided for a Westminsterian form of government wherein executive powers would be vested in the prime minister, who, with his cabinet, was head of government. Queen Elizabeth II of Britain remained head of state and appointed a governor until 1963, when the constitution was to be amended to install a president. Under this constitution, Uganda instituted a unitary system, with Buganda enjoying autonomous status with greater rights and privileges than other districts in Uganda. The country's other kingdoms—Ankole, Busoga, Bunyoro, and Toro—enjoyed only quasiautonomous status. Buganda's parliament, Lukiiko, served as an electoral college for its representatives to the Ugandan National Assembly.

The special status of Buganda was perceived by many Ugandans as problematic, especially after Mutesa became the president of Uganda in 1963, while the UPC head, Milton Obote, served as prime minister. The *kabaka's* (king's) dual loyalties to Buganda and Uganda led to a constitutional crisis in 1966 (Mutibwa 1992, 58). The matter had come to a head during a 1965 referendum, whereby Uganda was to decide on the so-called Lost Counties, which would have allowed the residents of these counties to choose between remaining part of Buganda or returning to Bunyoro. The Banyoro and Baganda had been enemies through much of the nineteenth century. The enmity had been fueled by the efforts to take over Bunyoro in 1894. Its king, Chwa II Kabalega, resisted, but Bunyoro was captured by a British-Buganda alliance. Kabalega was exiled to the Seychelles. The British rewarded Buganda by giving it six counties of Bunyoro territory, which came to be known as the Lost Counties. These counties had particular cultural and historical significance to Bunyoro, and their appropriation by Buganda contributed to the perception that the Baganda were receiving preferential treatment from the British (Doornbos and Mwesigye 1995; Mukholi 1995; Mutibwa 1992).

In the 1965 referendum, the counties voted to join Bunyoro, leading to a split between the Baganda leadership and Obote. The ill-fated anti-DP alliance between Buganda's KY party and Milton Obote's UPC was already fraying, but after the referendum vote it crumbled. KY fell apart and many of its members joined the UPC in support of the Buganda faction that had opposed Obote, who was a Langi from northern Uganda. In fact, one of the reasons Obote was able to consolidate power at this time was because of defections by

DP and KY parliamentarians who switched to UPC in the hope of benefiting themselves and their constituencies (Kasozi 1994, 71–73). King Mutesa sought military assistance from the British, but before he and the Buganda faction of UPC could make a move, Obote arrested five ministers and charged their faction with plans to have Buganda secede from the rest of Uganda.

These developments led to the constitutional crisis of 1966, in which Obote assumed full executive powers and suspended the 1962 constitution in direct violation of the original constitution. The king sought Buganda's secession, demanding that the central government remove itself from Bugandan soil. The government appealed to the United Nations for support. Obote's forces marched on the Buganda stronghold in Mengo and brutally suppressed the royalists, killing at least 2,000 civilians. Mutesa fled into exile to Britain.

On April 15, 1966, parliamentarians found a new draft constitution in their pigeonholes and Obote, who came surrounded by troops to parliament, forced the members of parliament (MPs) to adopt what came to be known as the "pigeonhole constitution." The National Assembly was ordered by Obote to become the Constituent Assembly, which debated the constitution for three months prior to its adoption in September 1967 in a controlled process. Obote then imposed the adoption of the new constitution and declared himself president without elections. By the time Amin took over in a 1971 coup d'etat, over half of the cabinet members who had been in place at the time of independence were now imprisoned under the emergency powers that Obote used to consolidate power and eliminate any potential opposition. He sought to stay in power at all costs, regardless of whether institutions retained their integrity or human rights were respected (Oloka-Onyango 1993, 25).

This new constitution established a unitary and highly centralized state. It abolished the position of the prime minister, placing all executive powers into the hands of the president. Moreover, the executive powers were expanded at the expense of the judiciary and the legislature. The constitution abolished all kingdoms in Uganda, and Buganda's special status was eliminated. Buganda was divided into four districts, its name was wiped from the political map, and its parliamentary building, Bulange, was transformed into the headquarters of Uganda's Ministry of Defence. The kabaka's palace at Bamunanika outside of Kampala became an army barracks. This enraged the Baganda. Even though many were not enamored with the king himself, they were loyal to the idea of the kingship and the traditions it represented. The new constitution paved the way for further consolidation of the UPC as the single ruling party, now that the Buganda monarchy and the DP were out of the way.

After 1966, there was a sense that northerners dominated politics, given that the positions of president and commander in chief of the Uganda Army (Milton Obote), the minister of defence (Felix Onama), commander of the Uganda Army (Idi Amin), inspector general of the police (Erinayo Oryema), and head of intelligence (Akena Adoko) were all in northern hands (Amaza

1998, 152). The northern dominance persisted with the takeover of Idi Amin in 1971; however, new divisions emerged within the north itself, including a rift between the West Nilers and the Acholi, Langi, and Itesot and also between the Kakwa and Nubians and the Madi and Lugbara. Amin's takeover resulted in the widespread killing of Langi and Acholi soldiers as well as those West Nile officers who did not switch sides fast enough, sowing the seeds for later animosity and violence (Low 1988, 45).

Amin sought initially to take advantage of Obote's mistakes and posed as a supporter of ecumenicalism, religious tolerance, and noninterference in religious affairs. One of his stated reasons for staging a coup against Obote was to give Uganda a renewed sense of common purpose. He criticized Obote's attempts "to form a second, unlawful, and unconstitutional army drawn from one small area within Uganda; . . . nepotism and favouritism intended only to advance one small area of the country; . . . attempts to divide Uganda on tribal lines"; and "use of senior officers to divide the country by dividing the security forces" (Gwyn 1977, 69). As this book will show, these critiques recurred with each successive administration.

Amin established the Department of Religious Affairs and organized religious conferences in 1971 and 1972. He sought to heal divisions within Ugandan society, including those between the Muslim community and among Protestants (Kasozi 1994, 107; Mazrui 1977, 35; Ward 1995, 81). It was not long before he suspended politics in order to restore national unity, blaming political parties for promoting sectarianism. What emerged instead was a unity of oppression between the Baganda and the rest of Uganda, between the Protestants and Catholics, and within the Church of Uganda against Amin's rule.

Thus, like Museveni, Obote and Amin had initially found the rhetoric of antisectarianism to be popular and appealing but were forced to abandon it because they were unable or unwilling to address the grievances that lay beneath the ethnic and religious discourses. Ultimately they all contributed to exacerbating the ethnic and religious tensions and creating new lines of discord.

Obote's second regime (1980–1985) was based on Luo commonalities between the Acholi and Langi, although he relied increasingly on the Acholi to do most of the fighting with Museveni's National Resistance Army (NRA). Army Chief of Staff David Oyite-Ojok was killed in a helicopter crash when he was reportedly shot down by the NRA in 1983. In his place, Obote appointed another Langi, Smith Opon-Acak, who was not regarded by many military officers as qualified for the position. In doing so, Obote thus challenged the Acholi-Langi alliance in the army. Promotions in the army were based not necessarily on experience but on the extent to which the individuals posed a threat to those in power (Kabwegyere 1995, 225). The promotion of Smith Opon-Acak appeared to have been made on grounds of loyalty. This led frustrated officers like Tito Lutwa Okello and Bazilio Okello and others to overthrow Obote in 1985 in a coup d'etat.

Tito Okello turned against Obote's Langi soldiers, forcing Obote to flee (Low 1988, 50–51). After Okello's takeover, the Acholi and Langi became embroiled in conflict. However, the Acholi themselves were divided between the Gulu and Kitgum factions. Their Uganda People's Democratic Army (UPDA) itself eventually disintegrated because of a lack of agreement between two of its leaders, Brigadier Odongo Latek from Gulu and Bazilio Olara Okello from Kitgum.

Museveni went to the bush to fight Obote not only because of the alleged rigging of the 1980 elections but also to dismantle a system of government that was run by the military and had institutionalized state violence based on sectarianism. The Acholi, however, felt that the NRA was also removing a government dominated by northerners; from their point of view, the NRA takeover was part of a struggle between southerners and northerners (Gingyera-Pinycwa cited in Mutibwa 1992, 154; Omara-Otunnu 1987). According to the Human Rights Commission, most people in central Uganda, where the war against Obote was fought, felt that it was primarily against northerners and not a war for democracy (Finnström 2008, 74). The conflict itself took on ethnic dimensions as it was fought primarily in Luwero among the Baganda, who backed the NRA in ousting northerners from their area. It is estimated that about 300,000 mainly Baganda civilians were killed and over 500,000 were displaced from their homes.

The Origins of Broad-Based Governance

When Yoweri Museveni first took over in 1986, he followed his predecessors in introducing a government that was nonsectarian and broad based. The notion of broad-based government had its antecedents in the Ugandan National Liberation Front (UNLF), which, together with its military wing, the Uganda National Liberation Army (UNLA), and with the help of the Tanzanian army, overthrew Idi Amin in 1979 and governed until the 1980 elections. The UNLF was led by Yusuf Lule and was comprised of an amalgam of ethnically antagonistic forces, including Milton Obote's Kikosi Maalum; the Uganda Freedom Union, led by Godfrey Binaisa, Andrew Kayiira, and Olara Otunnu; Museveni's Front for National Salvation; and the Save Uganda Movement under UPC loyalists Akena p'Ojok, William Omaria, and Ateker Ejalu.[3] The UNLF idea of a politics of consensus was later incorporated into the Uganda People's Movement (UPM) platform in the 1980 elections and was eventually adopted by the NRA during its war against Obote's government.

The Tanzanians created a transitional government in Uganda in 1979 that had the task of returning Uganda to civilian democratic rule. However, a coup d'etat by forces backing Obote allowed him to control the 1980 elections in such a way as to win in the face of what many believed should have been a DP victory. The NRA was formed in 1981 out of frustration with the perceived manipulation of elections and was an amalgam of Museveni's Popular Resistance Army and Lule's Uganda Freedom Fighters. The idea of a politics of consensus was enshrined as the third point in Museveni's ten-point program for the political arm of the NRA, the NRM, and was an affirmation of the latter's opposition to regionalism, tribalism, and religious sectarianism. The NRM claimed to seek a broad national coalition of democratic, political, and social forces to unite the country and obtain a national consensus. The NRM was to reflect the broadest interests of the country.

The NRM-Led Government: The Early Years

When the NRM came into power in 1986, it sought to pacify the opposition by incorporating leaders representing a variety of political interests, including guerrilla factions that Museveni had been fighting only a few months earlier. A law extended amnesty to all combatants, police, and personnel in prison and state security agencies who might otherwise have been subject to prosecution. Former rebel groups were incorporated into the NRA, including the Uganda National Rescue Front (UNRF), whose leaders had been associated with the government of Idi Amin.

The NRM sought to build a government of national unity, heal the divisions created by party differences, and appease a wide range of groups by giving them representation within the Movement and government. Museveni courted and brought into his alliance the promonarchy Ganda, Protestant clergy, large sections of the Catholic establishment that were frustrated with the Democratic Party, members of the UPM, his own supporters who had backed him along ethnic lines, former Amin supporters from West Nile, and some leftists from the eastern part of the country (Oloka-Onyango 1997). Excluded from this initial coalition were members of the Okello government, the UNLA, and the UPC, although soon after the UPC came to be represented in the government. The DP stronghold had been in the south and in Buganda, whereas the UPC was mainly based in north and east Uganda.

One of the first pieces of legislation passed by the NRM was an antisectarianism statute in 1988. Eriya Kategaya, chairman of the Political and Diplomatic Committee, was assigned to make overtures to different political forces to create this consensus (Besigye 1999). Elections to the legislative body, the National Resistance Council (NRC), were based on individual merit rather than on party affiliation, in keeping with the rationale that this would minimize sectarian conflict embedded within party difference.

The first post-1986 cabinet reflected this effort to balance political and ethnic representation. It included a broad cast of characters, primarily from the

DP, which held at least ten key ministries, including Internal Affairs, Finance, Agriculture, Commerce, Constitutional Affairs, Energy, Justice, Regional Affairs, and Economic Development, as well as the position of attorney general.[4] The cabinet also included the leader of the Conservative Party, Buganda monarchist Jehoash Mayanga-Nkangi, who had served in 1966 as the last prime minister of Buganda. He served as minister of education under the NRM. Rebel leaders Dr. Andrew Lutaakome Kayiira and Dr. David Lwanga became ministers of energy and environmental protection. Even more surprisingly, UNRF leader Moses Ali became minister of tourism and wildlife. Ali had been minister of finance in Idi Amin's government. The UPC had a small presence in the cabinet with only two full ministries: Transport and Communication and Youth, Culture, and Sport. The cabinet later included UPC leaders Adonia Tiberondwa, Yona Kanyomozi, and Francis Butagira.

The Narrowing Alliance

Although the rhetoric of antisectarianism has persisted to this day, appointments in government and the military increasingly went to a narrower group of loyalists, undermining the claim to broad-based government. At the same time, the patronage networks expanded. Since 1986, the number of ministers and ministers of state has expanded from thirty-three to sixty-nine. By comparison, the People's Republic of China—a country with a population of 1.3 billion—has only twenty-two ministers (Namutebi 2009a). By 2007 there were over seventy-one presidential advisers and assistants (compared with four advisers in 1994). By 2007, more than a hundred diplomats represented the nation abroad (Mwenda and Tangi 2007). The original legislative body, the NRC, had thirty-eight members; by 1988 it had eighty members, and by 2008 there were 332 members of parliament representing eighty-three districts. The expansion of parliament to ninety-seven districts in 2009 would further increase the number of parliamentarians.

As the conflict continued in the north after the NRM takeover and the tensions between north and south Uganda persisted, the NRM was not inclined to incorporate many northerners into its government. While the south and west were well represented in the cabinet, the north was not, with northerners claiming only four cabinet positions between 1986 and 1988 and another eleven serving as deputy ministers or ministers of state (Mwenda 2007b, 24). By 1996, only a few multipartyists could be found in the cabinet. The 2003 cabinet reshuffle, in particular, drew criticism for being exclusionary as eleven cabinet seats were held by westerners, while northerners retained three positions and easterners held two positions. By 2008, the core cabinet continued to reflect this imbalance with twelve appointments from the west, eight from the central region, two from the north, and five from the east.

Constitutional Deliberations

With the Constituent Assembly (CA) elections in 1994, many felt that the broad-based nature of the NRM had all but evaporated. This happened, according to Kizza Besigye (1999) with the arrests and treason charges against multipartyists, who were accused of using their positions in the government to undermine the NRM. Tensions emerged between the NRM leaders and those who were considered broad based and hence less deserving of their positions. There was a growing sense by NRM leaders that they could dispense with broad-based politics without political cost because the NRM was so popular.

The CA elections represented a turning point, marking the end of broad-based politics. The NRM began operating as a de facto party, covertly setting up special committees in the districts to back NRM candidates, while decampaigning multipartyists running for the CA and even some NRM candidates who supported the idea of broad-based government. Initially a Movement Group in the CA was formed from the ten presidential appointees and special interest representatives, who, together with six elected representatives, lobbied for the NRM position. Pressure from within the NRM resulted in the formation of an official Movement Caucus, which no longer represented a broad range of views, but rather served as a mouthpiece of what had become in essence a political party (Besigye 1999). The problem, as many supporters of multipartyism saw it, was that no other grouping was allowed to caucus openly as a political party.

By 1995 it was clear that the NRM had tightened its grip in a way that left little room for meaningful power sharing. The crucial debate over the future of multipartyism in the CA was resolved in July 1995 after four days of deliberations and a walkout by multiparty forces. The NRM prevailed, casting 199 votes in favor of continued no-party rule, with sixty-eight opposed and two abstentions.

As power became more concentrated within the NRM, many of the Movement's old allies fell out of favor or became highly disillusioned with it. The Catholics' allegiances were divided during the 1996 presidential race between Museveni and his DP opponent, Paul Ssemogerere. By the mid-1990s, the Buganda-NRM relationship had fallen into disarray, as the government sought to play sections of the royalty against one another while keeping King Ronald Mutebi in an apolitical position. Were he to venture too far beyond his role as a cultural symbol of Buganda, he would risk losing various privileges and sources of government funds. The debate over the Land Bill in 1998 revealed the depth of Buganda disillusionment with the regime, although in the end a compromise was worked out that Baganda members of parliament were pleased with: a District Land Board would administer former public land in Buganda in the name of the kabaka (Katunzi 1998).

By the late 1990s, however, the perception was growing among nonwesterners that Museveni favored his "own people" when it came to government appointments and that the Ankole Bahima, in particular, were unduly benefiting from "State House scholarships, State House welfare programs, presidential donations, and appointments to key and strategic military and security offices" (Mwenda 2008a).

The differences between the hardcore NRM supporters and those who endorsed a more broad-based vision of the Movement based on individual merit led to tensions particularly in Kabale, Ntungamo, Kasese, and Iganga. Those who advocated for multipartyism were harassed and suppressed on the assumption that freedom of mobilization for any other organization or party besides the NRM would lead to unrest and confusion. Although not legally banned, opposition leaders could not hold meetings, sponsor candidates for office, or raise funds, and therefore in reality they were banned. It was very difficult to run for office unless one was approved by the NRM leadership. At the local level, the resistance council (later local council) structure operated as part of the NRM machine. The electoral commission was made up entirely of presidential appointees. These constraints on the development of democratic institutions and the ensuing insecurity felt by opposition leaders set the stage for the growing perception that power was now serving the interests of a few in the western part of the country through clientelistic arrangements.

After the 1996 election, in which northerners overwhelmingly voted against Museveni, he announced openly that he would not share the political cake with areas that voted against him but only "some bits of the development cake" by constructing roads in their areas. The metaphor clearly referenced ministerial appointments: "When it comes to the political cake, it is another matter," Museveni claimed. "Where do we get a minister from? Now people are waiting for Kony to come from Sudan and take over government. Let them wait; that is when they will share the political cake" (Williams 1996). (Joseph Kony is the rebel warlord who destabilized the north from 1988 to 2006, viciously brutalizing his own Acholi people and other northerners.)

The Changing Ethnic Makeup of Army and Political Leadership

Nowhere was the shift in power more evident than in the army and, in particular, in its leadership. Because the British colonialists had recruited heavily from the north and the east in the 1930s and 1940s to build their army in Uganda, by the time of independence, 80 percent of the officer corps came from these regions, while the remainder came from the central and western regions. At the time of independence, the top military men included Tito

Lutwa Okello (an Acholi), Suleiman Hussein (a Nubian), and two Itesot: Okuni Opolot and David Livingstone Ogwang. These patterns of military recruitment continued throughout the Obote and Amin governments up until Museveni's takeover in 1986. At that time, the Acholi formed the largest group of officers, followed by the Itesot (Omara-Otunnu 1987).

To understand the balance of power in Uganda past and present, it is necessary to look at the configuration of all the security forces. From the outset of Museveni's government, the army was seen as the core of the state; the NRM was merely its political wing. The NRA High Command was at the center of the power structure. Key positions initially went to the *historicals,* or the twenty-six men who started the bush war with Museveni against Obote in February 1981. The army rank and file themselves were an amalgam of several rebel armies from different parts of the country.

Right from the start, the leadership of the NRM security forces drew heavily from the western part of the country. The External Security Organisation was dominated by Amama Mbabazi and others from Rukungiri, while the Internal Security Organisation was controlled by Bahima members of Museveni's own Banyankole subgroup. Banyarwanda officers like Paul Kagame appeared to be in charge of military intelligence initially ("NRM Friction Spills to Spy Agencies" 2008). Andrew Mwenda (2008a) argues that since the Banyarwanda were not citizens, they were seen as "safe"; they would never be accepted as legitimate leaders and therefore could not pose a threat to Museveni's rule. Relations with them soured later, however, when the Rwandan Patriotic Front, led by Kagame, took over Rwanda in 1994 because, according to Mwenda, they refused to cooperate with Museveni. Jeje Odongo, an easterner from Katakwi, had been commander of the armed forces, but by 2001 he had been replaced first by James Kazini and then by another westerner, General Aronda Nyakairima. By 2010 there no longer were any nonwesterners in the core group of commanders. In fact, since its formation during the guerrilla war against Obote, all but two of the NRA-UPDF (Uganda People's Defence Forces) armed forces commanders under Museveni have been from the west.[5]

Museveni appears to have moved most possible presidential aspirants out of his orbit and off a trajectory that would allow them to make a bid for the presidency. The current chief of the UPDF, General Nyakairima, is a career officer from Rukungiri, reportedly with no political aspirations; his deputy lieutenant, General Ivan Koreta, who hails from Mbarara, and Joint Chief of Staff Brigadier Robert Rusoke from Kabarole are also career officers (Museveni 1997, 168). All the top military officers are from the west, with the exception of the commander of the Land Forces, who is a Muganda, and the chief of staff of Land Forces, who is an Atesot from the east.[6]

Most of Museveni's closest associates since 2005 have been top military leaders, all from the west—including his son, Major Muhoozi Kainerugaba, who was promoted in 2008 to the rank of lieutenant colonel and commander in charge of Special Forces; his half brother, General Salim Saleh (from Nyabushozi); General David Tinyefuza (who is a Muhima from Sembabule, which is technically in the central region but shares a border with Mbarara in the west); and General Elly Tumwine (from Kiruhura) in the west. He also reportedly lends his ear to Lieutenant Colonel Moses Rwakitarate and was said to be close to Brigadier Noble Mayombo (from Fort Portal) until the latter's death in 2008. One of Museveni's closest associates in 1986 was First Deputy Prime Minister Eriya Kategaya from Rwampara in Ankole, who was one of the historicals but who temporarily left the NRM over his objections to Museveni's bid to lift presidential term limits in 2005. The western imprint is also seen in the fact that all five generals who make up the High Command of the army are from Ankole.[7] The four lieutenant generals are from Ankole (west), Teso (east), West Nile (northwest), and Buganda (central).

After the military promotions of five westerners to the position of general (Museveni, Tumwine, Saleh, Tinyefuza, and Nyakairima), an official of the UPC and a group of lawyers, Advocates Pro Bono Group, petitioned the Constitutional Court to declare the appointments a violation of the constitution, which stipulates that the UPDF must have a national character. The army responded with a sworn affidavit by General Nyakairima, claiming that the aforementioned personnel were promoted to general because they were the best trained and most exemplary officers in the country (Nganda 2009).

Parliament had already formed its own subcommittee on defense to investigate ethnic imbalances in army promotions. It was also concerned about military representation within the parliament. Apac Woman representative Betty Amongi had questioned the preponderance of army representatives (seven out of ten) from the west (Lumu 2009).

These appointments suggested an effort by the NRM to build coalitions of support throughout the western part of the country. Some of these ties were also solidified through regional Bahima ties, Basiita clan connections, the general Ankole commonality, and western identification in general.

Cynthia Enloe's work on state security maps is instructive here. She argues that military commanders and state elites make ethnicity instrumental by constructing their armed forces in a way that reinforces and revitalizes ethnic identification, because the civilian population is forced to respond to a particular military configuration. The extent to which the ethnic configuration of the military has an impact depends on how coercive the military is toward the population and how prominent security considerations are in the state elite's policymaking. The interethnic mappings are based on what makes the state elites feel most secure and how politically dependable they believe the various ethnic groups are. The mental ethnic maps might consider which ethnic groups live along sensitive frontiers, whether they fulfill sensitive economic roles, whether they have political resources to challenge the state, and whether they have access to state structures. Each group is treated according to its political reliability based on predictions of how it will behave given their culture, emotional bonds, and common sentiments about particular neighboring countries (Enloe 1980).

The reliance on western leadership may seem efficient and safe in the short run. But in the long run it may backfire. Based on recent trends, such as the large number of defections among western leaders to the opposition, those who seem most trusted may not be up to the task or may prove to be less than reliable. By the same token, loyalties to the Movement throughout the country can be discerned by looking at voting patterns of citizens, making ethnic calculations dangerously unnecessary.

In Uganda, all the factors described by Enloe have come into play because the perceived ethnic makeup of the military and its leadership is seen as a prime example of favoritism toward the west in ways that are polarizing for such a multiethnic nation as Uganda. Because Uganda's present security mapping comes out of a history of ethnically configured armed forces, Ugandans have clear preconceptions of what the map looks like.

A Political Map

Although power has become increasingly concentrated along ethnic lines, it does not map directly onto popular political sentiments (although it certainly influences them). The results of the 2006 presidential elections tell us something about the ethnic political matrix that has evolved in the country. The two top contenders (Museveni and the FDC's Besigye) were both from the west. The other presidential contenders were from Buganda and from Lango in the north, although the contender from the north, Miria Obote, wife of Milton Obote, herself was a Muganda. Based on Electoral Commission (2006) data for this election—which, however, has been contested due to rigging— Museveni won all but one of the eighteen western districts and all but one of the sixteen central districts, while Besigye won all but five of seventeen northern districts, where opposition to Museveni was strongest. Museveni won ten out of fifteen eastern districts, while Besigye won only five. In other words, westerners won the bulk of the votes, regardless of the actual breakdown between the two contenders.

There was greater variability in the parliamentary elections in terms of party identification, but some of the overall patterns were the same. Prior to the election, a 2005 Afrobarometer survey asked respondents whether they approved or disapproved of the way President Museveni had performed his job in the preceding twelve months. The survey found that 94 percent of westerners, 84 percent of easterners, 83 percent from the central region, and 56 percent of northerners said they approved or strongly approved of Museveni's performance. Only in the north was there a striking deviation from the general pattern, with 42 percent disapproving or strongly disapproving of the president's performance.

What this suggests is that ethnicity matters, but it matters differently to different groups. The northerners, including both the Langi and Acholi, overwhelmingly voted for a westerner even though they had other choices, including someone representing their region. They voted largely for Besigye, who had the same basic political and military profile as Museveni, suggesting that much of the northern opposition to Museveni was based not on ethnicity but rather on shared grievances against the government's treatment of northerners.

The overwhelming support for Museveni in the central region (except for Kampala) and the strong support in the east also suggest that ethnicity is not the main factor in voter calculations and leads one to wonder about whether the strong support for Museveni in the western region is also less about ethnic identification and more about clientelism and patronage, which have been directed toward this region because there was an expectation that the returns could be counted upon. The lack of strong candidates from other regions surely must have also featured in voter inclinations, further strengthening the argument that ethnicity is not the only political factor at play.

Finally, the creation in 2009 of a broad-based coalition of parties, the Inter Party Cooperation (IPC), representing a wide range of political and ethnic interests as well as the election of northerner Norbert Mao to the leadership of the Democratic Party in 2010, further suggests the strengthening of crosscutting links and a loosening of the ethnic political grid that has shaped Ugandan politics since independence.

Thus, the tensions within the military and top leadership played out somewhat differently within the population, which, with the exception of the north, still largely supported Museveni even though his popularity had begun to dwindle. The support was not uncritical. At least 80 percent of the population approved or strongly approved of Museveni's performance at the time of the 2006 election, based on Afrobarometer survey findings.[8] And in spite of popular perceptions that westerners hold top positions in the military and government, ethnic tensions were not seen as a central problem in the country. The same Afrobarometer survey also found that people were fairly pragmatic in their concerns, naming political instability/political divisions/ethnic tensions as the ninth largest problem in Uganda, after poverty/destitution, unemployment, health, water supply, management of the economy, education, farming and agriculture, and crime and security.

These findings are important because they illustrate some of the ambiguities of Uganda as a semiauthoritarian country. Ethnicity still matters and has the power to create potentially explosive rifts within the elite. But at the local level, while the privileging of the west is an irritant, ethnic divisions are not foremost among most people's concerns, which are much more basic and developmental in scope.

Conclusion

The ethnic equation in Uganda is by no means a simple one and cannot be reduced simply to the west versus the rest, as will become even more clear in Chapter 3, which looks at tensions within the NRM fold. The political matrix in Uganda is fluid and constantly changing, resulting in a variety of alliances based on region, ethnicity, clan, caste, and religious denomination that intersect in complicated ways with party allegiances as well as military and other types of power. The tension inherent in a semiauthoritarian regime is between maintaining political control and allowing for freedom of political expression. The longer one remains in power, the more challenging it becomes to maintain alliances of loyalty, and the question becomes how best to pursue that loyalty.

Attempts to establish a broad-based government initially served the NRM well and won popular support. However, as the legitimacy of the NRM and Museveni waned, the president sought more expedient, narrower, and ever shifting alliances to ensure his own security and political future, as well as NRM dominance. He had to cater not only to the citizenry but also to the realities of remaining in power. As time wore on, these goals became increasingly incompatible and as a consequence, maintaining a broad base went by the wayside. Thus the rationale for political appointments seems to be not ethnic hatred, animosity, or sectarianism, but rather political expediency and survival.

In an authoritarian regime, it is generally irrelevant what the polity thinks about how political alliances are created. In a democracy, the leadership changes periodically, and with each election there is an opportunity to reconfigure political alliances. But in a semiauthoritarian regime like Museveni's Uganda, leaders need to answer to parliamentarians, civil society leaders, the media, political parties, and others, who question the composition of leadership. Charges of narrow ethnic promotion can be ignored, disputed, and suppressed for some time. But eventually the objective of inclusive governance comes into conflict with the imperatives of remaining in power.

Notes

1. Banyankole is the plural referent for the Ankole people, Munyankole the singular.

2. Buganda is the Ganda territory; Baganda are the people (plural); Muganda is a person from Ganda (singular); and Luganda is the Ganda language.

3. Museveni's colleagues from the Front for National Salvation included Eriya Kategaya, Amama Mbabazi, Kahinda Otafiire, Ruhakana Rugunda, Salim Saleh, and Ivan Koreta ("Museveni Doesn't Survive on War," 2006).

4. The DP's Paul Ssemogerere was appointed minister of internal affairs, while its treasurer, John Ssebaana Kizito, became minister of regional affairs; secretary general Robert Kitariko was minister of agriculture and another key official, Evaristo Nyanzi, became minister of commerce.

5. The commanders of the National Resistance Army (later Uganda People's Defence Forces) included Ahmed Seguya (from the central region) first commander of the NRA (1980–1981), Lieutenant Sam Magara (from Mbarara in the west) (1982–1983), Lieutenant General Elly Tumwine (from Kiruhura in the west) commander of NRA (1984–1987), Lieutenant General Salim Saleh (from Ntungamo in the west) (1987–1989), Major General Muntu Mugisha (also from Ntungamo) (1989–1998), Jeje Odongo (from Katakwi in the east) (1998–2001), James Kazini (from Kasese in the west) (2001–2003), and General Aronda Nyakairima (from Rukungiri in the west) (2003–present).

6. Commander in Chief General Y. Kaguta Museveni is from Ntungamo (in the west); Commander of Defence Forces General Aronda Nyakairima is from Rukungiri (west); Deputy Chief of Defence Forces Lieutenant General Ivan Koreta is from Mbarara (west); Joint Chief of Staff Brigadier Robert Rusoke is from Kabarole (west); Commander of Air Force Major General Jim Owoyesigire is from Kabale (west); Chief of Staff of Air Force Colonel Moses Rwakitarate is from Mbarara (west); Commander of Land Forces Lieutenant General Katumba Wamala is from Central Region; Chief of Staff of Land Forces Brigadier Charles Angina is from Teso (east); Chief of Military Intelligence Brigadier James Mugira is from Ankole (west); Chief of Special Forces Lieutenant Colonel Muhoozi Kainerugaba is from the west.

7. Commander in Chief is General Yoweri Kaguta Museveni from Ntungamo (west); Coordinator of Intelligence Agencies General David Tinyefuza is from Sembabule (central/west) and the historial High Command representatives include General Elly Tumwine, who is from Kiruhura (west); Major General (Retired) Kahinda Otafiire from Bushenyi (west); and General Salim Saleh from Ntungamo (west). Similar patterns are found in the defence ministry. Defence Minister Dr. Crispus Kiyonga is from Kasese (west); Minister of State for Defence Ruth Nankabirwa is from Kiboga (central), while Minister of Security Amama Mbabazi is from Kigezi (west).

8. Afrobarometer, http://www.afrobarometer.org/data.html. Accessed July 2, 2009.

3

A Troubled Household: Dissension Within the National Resistance Movement

The Jopadhola of my home Tororo District have a pungent proverb which says, "A pot of water breaks at the doorstep." Fetching water by the rural women is usually tedious. The women precariously balance the pots on their heads for a distance to the well and must carefully scoop clean water with a calabash until their pots are full. They then support each other, meticulously heaving the laden pots onto their heads to walk back. When they reach home to off-load the pot at the threshold of their low huts, the pot of water sometimes fatefully slips out of grip and breaks into pieces. The whole NRM war of resistance was concerned not simply with capturing power but with how the power ought to be used. This is why from the for-mation of NRA there was a deliberate inculcating of extraordinary exem-plariness and humility towards the people and their interests. Our NRM pot of water is now dangerously lurching. If we lose our hold, we shall drench ourselves wet and lose all, to start all over again.
— James Magode Ikuya, member of the National Executive Council, National Resistance Movement (Ikuya 2009)

Whereas the previous chapter discussed the challenges semiauthoritarian regimes such as Uganda's face in crafting national alliances to maintain those in power, an equally difficult problem is that of keeping one's own party in tow, as the experience of the National Resistance Movement (NRM) reveals. As it did while crafting the broader national political matrix, the NRM leader-ship experienced tensions between the contradictory needs of maintaining control and pressures for greater openness and democracy. Many within the NRM simply wanted the possibility for change in leadership institutionalized and did not have broader democratic aspirations. It is difficult for anyone in a party to remain in power for so long without others feeling that there should be an alteration in leadership, talent, and vision. In democracies, this alteration of power is institutionalized, ensuring that a rotation of power takes place. In authoritarian regimes, elections are fairly irrelevant, and there are few expres-sions of open dissent.

However, in a semiauthoritarian regime, most contenders for power find that there is only one game in town. Since the possibilities for reforming the dominant power configuration are limited, their only option is to make peace with the powers that be or leave and seek other more precarious options—for example, forming or joining a new political party. Unlike the ethnic tensions mentioned in the previous chapter, these internal conflicts are potentially the most challenging and disruptive, especially those involving the military.

This chapter discusses the growing concentration of power within the NRM itself and the ensuing battles between multipartyists and NRM loyalists. It discusses the shifts in the makeup of the army and government leadership, which, as we saw in the previous chapter, came to be dominated by western-ers. Dissension in the west is especially problematic, because the divisions between the Banyankole and Bahororo, the Bahima and Bairu, and even between older and younger generations within the NRM are creating divisions within the security forces. The chapter documents various splits within the NRM and analyzes their political consequences.

Dissension in the West

Although it is tempting to read Uganda's military and political power configu-ration in ethnic terms, doing so would mean overlooking the much more prob-lematic divisions within the military and within the western part of the country. One can find evidence of these splits within the government and parliament as well. Even strong electoral votes in the west cannot be assured, if recent elec-toral trends are any indication. In the 1996 election, Museveni won 98 percent of the vote in the western region against Democratic Party (DP) contender Paul Ssemogerere. In 2001, he won 90 percent of the vote against Besigye. But in 2006, he claimed only 79 percent of the vote in the region, if one accepts the official electoral outcome, which in itself is likely to overreport Museveni's gains. Nevertheless, this drop suggests a much stronger challenge for Museveni in 2011 in his home region. (Museveni won 76 percent of the national vote in 1996, 69 percent of the national vote in 2001, and 59 percent in 2006.)

Despite the numerical strength of the Banyankole in parliament (there are about twenty-seven MPs), they are the only ones without a formal caucus in the Assembly. Although efforts were made in 2003 to form an Ankole parlia-mentary group, they failed because of splits within the military and NRM.[1] There has also been opposition to the inclusion of the three Ankole army mem-bers in the Ankole parliamentary group since it is supposed to represent a national constituency rather than a local one. Museveni's bigger fear may be that if such a group did form, it might become interested in reviving the Ankole kingdom, which would have the potential to undercut his authority in the region ("Disagreements Rock Ankole MPs" 2007). Ankole is the only one of the traditional five kingdoms that was not revived after the government permitted the return of cultural and traditional leaders in 1993.

The divisions in the west involve power struggles between districts like Bushenyi (primarily Banyankole) and Rukungiri (primarily Bahororo and Kiga) that have plagued relations between the Internal Security Organisation (ISO) and External Security Organisation (ESO). Former ESO directors (for example, Minister of Local Government Colonel Kahinda Otafiire from Bushenyi) and former ISO directors (such as Major General Jim Muhwezi and Brigadier Henry Tumukunde from Rukungiri) continued to maintain their networks within the agencies. This resulted in a 2008 shakeup of the leadership of the organizations ("NRM Friction Spills to Spy Agencies" 2008).

Bahima-Bairu Conflicts

Underlying tensions between clans and castes also exist in the Ankole region and in the west more generally. Historically, there was a hierarchy in which the *omugabe* or king was at the top, followed by the royal clan or dynasty that stretched from Ankole into northwestern Tanzania. The pastoralist Bahima were associated with the monarchy and ruled the agriculturalist Bairu in a castelike system.[2] The Bahima were historically regarded as the aristocracy of the Ankole kingdom and were cattle owners. The Bahima are said to be related to the Tutsi in Rwanda and Burundi as well as to the Hema in the Democratic Republic of Congo. The Bairu, forming the majority of the population, are seen as agriculturalists, although they too own cattle. As a Muhima situated outside of the aristocracy, Museveni sought political alliances with the Bairu to broaden his political base (Mwenda 2008a).

The Iru-Hima conflict has shaped Ankole politics since the 1940s and continues to have implications for national politics. The Bairu-Bahima tensions intensified in the 1950s, according to the former Ankole *enganzi* (prime minister), James Kahigiriza, who describes these clashes in his 2001 book on Ankole history, *Bridging the Gap*. The Bahima held most administrative positions until the 1940s, but as more Bairu became educated, they resented the Bahima domination of the kingdom's administration and tussled over the leadership of the *enganzi*. The divisions became further entrenched when the Bairu Protestants joined the mainly Protestant Uganda People's Congress (UPC) party of Milton Obote, partly in defiance of the Bahima. The Bahima, who were mostly Protestant, joined the DP, a primarily Catholic party, and forged an alliance with Bairu Roman Catholics in the DP in the early 1960s (Kahigiriza 2001, 14–15). Under colonialism, with the introduction of Christianity into Uganda, most Bahima had become Protestants, whereas the Bairu were evenly divided between Catholics and Protestants (Doornbos 1978, 127).

When Milton Obote forced a constitutional crisis in 1966, he abolished the kingdoms, which had the effect of diminishing the Hima-Iru hierarchy. Four Ugandan kingdoms that were banned in 1967 were restored in 1993. However, the Ankole kingdom was not restored. It was widely believed that restoring the kingdom would give rise to latent tensions between the Bahima and Bairu that could only hurt Museveni at the ballot box, because the majority Bairu would have seen the move as an attempt to sideline them and further revive historic tensions. Efforts to revive the kingdom have met with harsh response. In 2009, some councillors in Ankole attempted to pass a resolution in the district councils demanding the restoration of Prince John Barigye as obugabe of Ankole; however, none of the district councils has managed to pass such a resolution (Wanambwa 2010). This effort met with angry response from people like Trade Minister Kahinda Otafiire, a longtime opponent of the institution.

Museveni needs the Bairu votes and has been eager to downplay these differences. In spite of his efforts to keep these tensions at bay, however, they have reemerged, most notably in the contestation between Museveni, a Muhima, and Kizza Besigye, a Mwiru, in the 2001 and 2006 electoral races. The firing of Eriya Kategaya as deputy prime minister in 2000 together with other Bairu who opposed Museveni's bid for a third term—including Miria Matembe, who had been minister of ethics—may have reflected these tensions, as did the sidelining of Mugisha Muntu, Richard Kaijuka, and Amanya Mushega (Mugisha 2003). They also played out in the 2006 elections insofar as the old Protestant Bahima alliance with Bairu Roman Catholics was believed to have resurfaced. Museveni's opponents believed that Bairu Catholics in the NRM primaries were given support to defeat the Bairu Protestants in Mbarara, Kiruhura, Ibanda, and Isingiro, thus dividing the loyalties of the Bairu, who predominate in Ankole (Mugisha 2006). Similarly, all the chairmen of the six Ankole districts are Bairu Catholics. Anne Mugisha has argued that Museveni sought the support of Bairu Catholics, taking advantage of divisions between the Protestant and Catholic Bairu to lessen the possibility of a unified Bairu challenge to Bahima dominance. Without political manipulation, these differences might have remained latent and inconsequential, especially given generational changes. Instead they gained new salience and became mechanisms for structuring patronage and loyalty.

Ankole-Rukungiri Tensions

In addition to the Bahima-Bairu split, there were other conflicts among westerners, such as that between the Banyankole from Ankole and the Bahororo from Rukungiri and Kigezi. Some have argued that the splits in the army and the NRM have fallen between the Banyankole and those who would like to see power decentered from Ankole but still based in the west. Although the conflicts are primarily behind the scenes, occasionally they surface, especially now that so many past and present Bahororo NRM leaders from Rukungiri have been sidelined or have left the fold, including Kizza Besigye. Major General Jim Muhwezi and Brigadier Henry Tumukunde, both former heads of the Internal Security Organisation who have been publicly sidelined, have lashed back at Museveni. At the 2008 funeral of Tumukunde's mother, Muhwezi publicly stated, "We Bahororo, we are closely related and if you attack one, we all react" ("Tumukunde, Muhwezi Attack Gen. Museveni" 2008).

The Historicals and Young Turks

Other divisions can be found within the NRM itself that are based primarily in the west. They involve the thirty-eight men and women who formed the interim parliament from 1986 until it was expanded to include elected members of parliament. A large contingent of them were the historicals, or NRM members who were given parliamentary seats and other forms of recognition for their role in the guerrilla war that brought Museveni into power. These same historicals were well represented in the army as well. At the time of the 1986 takeover, the army High Command was made up primarily of westerners like Museveni, Salim Saleh, the late Fred Rwigema, David Tinyefuza, Jim Muhwezi, current Rwandan president Paul Kagame, Moses Kigongo, Kizza Besigye, Kahinda Otafiire, and others. Some of the historicals have broken with Museveni and joined the Forum for Democratic Change (FDC) camp. Others reflect divisions within the Movement, such as the Norfolk Group (so named because of a meeting they were alleged to hold at the Norfolk Hotel in Nairobi in 2008).

There have also emerged tensions between the older NRM loyalists and the young Turks, led by people like Moses Byaruhanga, Charles Rwomushana, and David K. Mafabi, who felt sidelined (Mpagi 2007a). Henry Banyenzaki from Rubanda West in Kabale served as the unofficial leader of the young revolution within parliament and became leader of the Young Parliamentarians Association (YPA) in 2007, made up of both NRM and other party members. The YPA focused on issues of parliamentary reform, privatization, and corruption and were especially active in challenging the expansion of executive power within parliament. The YPA was hijacked by the Parliamentary Advocacy Forum (PAFO), which opposed the Movement for some years, but returned in 2007 to work across party lines ("Amama Glossed Over Issues Raised by Four NRM Party MPs" 2007; Kasfir and Twebaze 2005).

In addition to such differences, some have pointed to splits between the educated and uneducated members of security agencies and the military—for example, between Salim Saleh and the better educated Mugisha Muntu, Jeje Odongo, and Aronda Nyakairima (Mwenda 2008a; Onyango-Obbo 2002).

Museveni responded to charges of dissension at the Movement's National Executive Committee (NEC) meeting at Kyankwanzi in the Kiboga district on March 26, 2003:

Certain leaders from Ankole, sometimes in concert with other elements from other areas, carry out a whispering campaign against the leadership of our Movement and the state. Sometimes, they take overt acts that are at variance with the previously, collectively agreed positions. . . . Trying to revive sectarianism in Ankole along the lines of castes (Bahima versus Bairu) and religious denominations (Catholics versus Protestants). There was an attempt, for instance, to say that Bahima are "dominating" the public service. ("Museveni Warned Ankole in 2003" 2003)

These divisions among westerners have involved military and government leaders at the highest levels. It would seem that they have greater potential to destabilize the country than do any threats posed by the war-weary north that has been weighed down by its own challenges of reconstruction since 2009. Buganda, in spite of increasing unrest after 2009, similarly seems unlikely to challenge the government politically or militarily, even though it has been unable to reach any kind of accord with the NRM government around key issues of concern.

Dissension in the Military

Some of the sharpest criticisms of the lack of democracy have come from those who were once Museveni's staunchest supporters, closest confidantes, and political appointees. These fissures within the military and political elite have revealed the extent of corruption in the government and of human rights abuses by security forces, as well as the limits of political reform. But they also show how the demise of the broad-based government has drawn some of its strongest reactions from the individuals who were to benefit the most from the no-party Movement system. The splits reveal that the biggest threats to the NRM's power emanate from those closest to Museveni and not from the north, east, or any other region.

Although there has been an active opposition movement led by the DP and the UPC from the outset, the first public rumblings of discontent within the NRM and the military were evident during the Constituent Assembly debates over opposition to the Movement system. At this time, the late Lieutenant Colonel Sserwanga Lwanga, Colonel Kizza Besigye, and General David Tinyefuza began to express their frustration with the NRM (Nganda 2006). All the concerns raised by these initial spoilers have continued to plague the Museveni regime: corruption, the nature of the political system, the role of the government in the north, and the lack of democracy and rule of law. They argued, for example, against the entrenchment of the Movement system in the constitution, pointing out that the Movement had become a government, not a system. The fact that these criticisms came primarily from within the NRM and the military is all the more significant, but the return to the fold by

Tinyefuza, Kategaya, and others suggests that there are few options for Museveni's critics, who have watched those compatriots who left the NRM endure vicious persecution, bodily harm, political isolation, and even exile in some cases.

The most vocal military leader and critic at the time of the Constituent Assembly was Lieutenant General David Tinyefuza, special military adviser to Museveni and the coordinator of Intelligence Services ("Uganda in the Front Ranks" 2007). He joined the National Resistance Army (NRA) in 1981 and rose to the rank of major general in 1990. Tinyefuza was one of ten army representatives within the Constituent Assembly. At one point during the Constituent Assembly proceedings, Tinyefuza ignored Movement discipline and expressed his criticism of the extension of the Movement system through the period leading up to the referendum. He called for a rapid return to multiparty politics, claiming, "It is almost immoral to want another free extension of five years to make it twenty" years of NRM rule (Kabushenga 1999). In response, Museveni convened the Army Council, which resolved that army representatives should not take public positions on controversial issues. The NRM forced Tinyefuza to make an apology, retract his comments, and promise to seek guidance from the army before expressing an opinion on the constitution.

Soon after, in 1996, Tinyefuza had another falling out with Museveni over the way in which the war in the north was being waged. Tinyefuza had been responsible for suppressing a rebellion by ex-Uganda National Liberation Army (UNLA) forces, carrying out a fierce counterinsurgency mission named Operation North (1991–1993) that by all accounts involved massive human rights violations against citizens in the north and was perceived by northerners as payback for atrocities committed by northern troops during the Luwero war (1981–1986) when the NRA was fighting Obote's forces. Tinyefuza also ordered the humiliating arrest of eleven northern Uganda politicians, including ministers, on the grounds that they were collaborating with the rebels.

Tinyefuza felt that the war should have been brought to an end earlier and that the government should have stepped down, given its failure. Army Commander Major General Mugisha Muntu told him to resign if he could not submit to army discipline. The army High Command demanded that he submit his resignation to the Army Commissions Board, whereupon he took his case to the Constitutional Court, which ruled in his favor. Five years later, in 2001, he was persuaded to return to the NRM and was brought into the High Command of the army ("Like or Hate Him, You Can't Ignore Tinyefuza" 2008). By 2005, he was back in the limelight as coordinator of internal and external security and was behind the arrest of his erstwhile colleague Colonel Kizza Besigye when the latter returned from exile in South Africa to run for the presidency the following year.

Another significant break with the Museveni regime came in 1999 when Besigye wrote an open letter criticizing Museveni's government for corruption, lack of democracy, and tribalism. Besigye had been part of the NRA rebellion from 1980 to 1986 and was Museveni's personal physician during the bush war. He held several key positions, including minister of state for Internal Affairs, national political commissar, and senior military adviser to the Ministry of Defence. He was unceremoniously discharged from the army prior to running against Museveni.

In 2001, Besigye garnered 26 percent of the vote as a leader of the Reform Agenda. After witnessing the continued torture and intimidation of his supporters and enduring harassment himself prior to and after the election, he fled the country and lived in self-imposed exile in South Africa for four years. No sooner did he return to run in the 2006 presidential elections than he was charged with treason, illegal possession of firearms, and rape. The government alleged that he was linked to the Lord's Resistance Army (LRA) and the People's Redemption Army (PRA), which was supposedly made up of ex-army officers and which the government claims has been based in the eastern part of Democratic Republic of Congo since 2004.

Besigye ran for president in 2006 as the candidate of the FDC, which had formed in 2004 as a merger between the National Democratic Forum, PAFO, and some members of the Reform Agenda. The FDC sought to rally prodemocracy and antidictatorship forces to challenge the Movement and Museveni, uphold the constitutional presidential two-term limit, build strong professional security agencies, eliminate the militaristic motivations of Uganda's foreign policy, and eliminate corruption and political patronage. In the 2006 election, 59 percent voted for Museveni and 37 percent for Besigye, who challenged the results. Although the Supreme Court ruled that the election was flawed, it nevertheless voted to uphold the results of the election in a 4–3 vote. Complicating Besigye's bid for power was the well-known fact that his wife, Winnie Byanyima, a politician in her own right, had at one time been a girlfriend of Museveni's. Earlier she had been removed from her position in the NRM Secretariat as a result of her criticisms of Movement corruption. Besigye denies that his wife's prior relationship with Museveni has influenced his critique of the Movement.

On November 16, 2005, Besigye and fourteen of his twenty-two codefendants were to be brought to the High Court to be released on bail. At least thirty armed security members of the Black Mamba squad were deployed at the court to rearrest him in full view of the journalists, judicial personnel, and foreign diplomats who were observing the proceedings. The presence of these extralegal forces in the courthouse was bitterly protested by the judiciary, judges, and lawyers alike, who felt the independence of the judiciary threatened. The principal judge of Uganda, Justice James Ogoola, called the action "unprecedented," marking a "day of infamy" (Mulondo 2005). The government issued the ban on free speech and demonstrations on November 22, saying that they would "interfere" with fair trial rights. Besigye was returned to prison because of military charges against him in a court-martial, but the High Court ordered his release a month later. The Constitutional Court ruled that he could not be tried for terrorism and the courts also dropped the rape charges, although the treason charges remained as of May 2010. President Museveni allegedly had personally ordered police to investigate the case. The FDC asked that the charges be dropped before the 2011 elections lest they sabotage Besigye's ability to run, expressing concern that he might be arrested again. Besigye's break with Museveni was one of the first in a long line of schisms that were to come.

The period leading up to the 2001 election resulted in a purge of top military brass, who were told to support Museveni and that support for Besigye would be considered treasonous. After the election, Museveni promoted a large group of military personnel, including many who were no longer in active service. With a few exceptions, those promoted were from the west, which was seen as highly unusual. They included Elly Tumwine, Salim Saleh, and David Tinyefuza, who were promoted from the rank of major general to that of lieutenant general; James Kazini, who was promoted from brigadier to major general; and Aronda Nyakairima, Levi Karuhanga, and others, who moved from colonel to brigadier ("Did Saleh, Tinye, Jeje, Elly Deserve Promotion?" 2001). Given the ethnic basis of this large number of promotions, it is more than likely they were aimed at shoring up support for the NRM within the military.

At this time, Colonel Samson Mande, one of the historicals, was apprehended and allegedly tortured in Uganda after aligning himself with the Reform Agenda and, later, its successor FDC. He fled to Rwanda in 2001 and then to Sweden. The Ugandan government alleged that he, Colonel Anthony Kyakabale, Colonel Edison Muzoora, and some other officers were leaders of the rebel PRA, which was said to have been based in eastern Democratic Republic of Congo (Ahimbisibwe 2007). All three are from the west: Mande from Rukungiri, Muzoora from Bushenyi, and Kyakabale from Kabale. Muzoora had been one of the up-and-coming officers in the army. These colonels denied any connection to the PRA, and there has been no independent confirmation of its existence to date. There have been no reports of PRA camps, attacks, or statements issued since its first mention in 2001. Unbelievably, after they went into exile, Tinyefuza said, "These comrades are always welcome. We have always told them there is no problem with their return" (Atuhaire 2008b).

In 2003, a government commission of inquiry led by Justice David Porter resulted in the first major divisions within the military, implicating those who provided detailed accounts of corruption in eastern Congo involving the country's mineral resources. Porter's report named top military officers and associates of Museveni—including Major General James Kazini; Jovia Akandwanaho, the wife of Lieutenant General Salim Saleh; Major General Kahinda

Otafiire; and Brigadier Noble Mayombo—for taking part in the plunder ("Colonel Kizza's Story" 2003). With the exception of Kazini, no action was taken against the individuals implicated in the scandal.

Another major fissure within the military and the NRM in general erupted in 2004, when Museveni began to press for the lifting of constitutionally imposed term limits on the presidency, otherwise referred to as *kisanja* (which in Luganda literally means "dried banana leaves"). There was yet another fall-out from the military that included Major General Mugisha Muntu, Major Ruranga Rubaramira, and Major John Kazoora, new military officers who joined the FDC at this time over the *kisanja* issue. Mugisha Muntu was the former head of military intelligence in 1986 and later commander of the NRA (1989–1998). Brigadier Henry Tumukunde was forced to resign from parliament, placed under house arrest, and court-martialed because he spoke out against the lifting of term limits and against open voting in parliament when related constitutional amendments were being considered (Obore 2007). In the end, the Supreme Court ruled that his resignation and subsequent prosecution in the Military General Court Martial was unconstitutional. Tumukunde had once been a loyal NRM cadre from Rukungiri; he joined the NRA in 1981 and became its chief of personnel and administration from 1996 to 1998. He headed up the Internal Security Organisation and is said to have secured Museveni's 2001 election victory through legal and extralegal means. Nevertheless, he was charged with spreading harmful propaganda and breaching army conduct. In a separate (but no doubt related) development, he was charged with the creation and maintenance of ghost soldiers (nonexistent soldiers who were listed on the army payroll so that someone else could garner their paycheck) and the misappropriation of funds for personal gain. The fact that he was a relative of the president's wife may have saved him more extreme recrimination (Nganda 2005b; Obore 2007). However, Tumukunde is also rumored to have harbored presidential aspirations, which may have also contributed to his premature and forced departure from politics.

More Dissension in the NRM Family

A group of loyal supporters of the NRM known as the Malwa Group resisted these aforementioned efforts to change the constitution in order to lift presidential term limits. Their break with Museveni was especially surprising given how unwavering they had been in their support for the NRM up to that time. Led by the former inspector general of government, Augustine Ruzindana, the group included Eriya Kategaya, the former first deputy and foreign affairs minister who had once been one of Museveni's closest political associates, as well as the former minister for ethics and integrity, Miria Matembe, who was a leader in the women's movement and had helped build support among women for the

NRM by claiming that it was strongly backing women's rights. She became deeply disillusioned when the 1998 Land Act amendments failed to include the co-ownership clause she had worked hard to gain approval for, only to watch Museveni personally withdraw it after it had been approved by parliament. Both Matembe and Kategaya were fired allegedly for their opposition to *kisanja*. The Malwa Group also included an MP for Bunyole, Emmanuel Dombo, and Secretary-General of the East African Community, Colonel Amanya Mushega, a historical and former education minister. Another NRM historical in whose home the NRA armed struggle was launched, Matthew Rukikaire, spoke out against the third term at this time (Nganda 2004). Jaberi Bidandi Ssali was yet another NRM die-hard who broke with Museveni during this period. Bidandi Ssali, who was the first secretary-general of the Uganda Patriotic Movement (predecessor of the NRM), had been founding vice chairman of the NRM and served as minister of local government. He opposed the lifting of presidential term limits and was thrown out of the cabinet as a result in 2003. Unlike most of the other top officials who left the NRM in 2002 to join the PAFO or the Reform Agenda or, later, the FDC, Bidandi Ssali formed his own party, the People's Progressive Party.

As with members of the military, civilians exhibiting presidential aspirations risked being sidelined. The late and popular James Wapakhabulo, one-time foreign minister and Speaker of Parliament, was undercut for these reasons. During the Luwero war, Tom Butime had served on the NRA political High Command; later, under the NRM, he served in top cabinet positions as minister of lands, housing, and urban development and minister of internal affairs (Nganda 2006). When it was perceived that he had higher ambitions, his political opponents received what was believed to be state support to run against him. He was able to retain his parliamentary seat in 1996 but lost in 2001. He was then given minor ministerial positions, and in 2006 finally resigned as minister for Karamoja.

The Transition to Multipartyism

Eventually it became too costly, politically speaking, for the NRM to continue its merger with the state, given the continuing hemorrhaging of top political and military leadership. Divisions within the top military leadership were particularly important in shaping outcomes. The NRM leaders came to the conclusion that they would be able to stay in power more effectively by opening up the political system. The same decision was made by other hybrid states in Africa, but Uganda was one of the last to transition to a multiparty system.

When, in the early 1990s, the Tanzanian government and ruling party initiated measures to liberalize their country politically, they were not being propelled by a massive popular movement. Instead, the leaders were responding to their reading of the political tea leaves. In 1994, I asked Cleopa Msuya (former Tanzanian prime minister, economic affairs and planning minister, industry minister, and finance minister), why the ruling party, Chama cha Mapinduzi (CCM), had adopted multipartyism in 1991 when there weren't any particular pressures to do so. He said that the political authorities had taken note of the democratizing winds sweeping Africa and sensed that the process would inevitably take hold in Tanzania. By jumpstarting political liberalization, they hoped to be able to manage the process without risking their own political standing. The leaders also wanted to stay in the good graces of foreign donors, who were beginning to exert pressure to democratize. And finally, the CCM thought that by injecting an element of competition into the process, they would be able to reinvigorate their own party. They launched the liberalization process only because they believed that they would be able to manage the transition and stay in power and that taking the initiative would enhance CCM credibility. Their inclinations were correct; to this day, the CCM remains the dominant party in Tanzania.

A similar logic drove the NRM's decision to open the country to multipartyism, as is evident in the recommendations of the ad hoc subcommittee of the National Executive Committee of the NRM, which argued that the NRM would be able to purify itself of those who were in the Movement because of its principle of broad basedness; it would deprive opponents of a weapon with which they could attack the NRM for being undemocratic; and it would improve Uganda's relationship with its development partners and thus facilitate access to world markets and foreign aid (Makara, Rakner, and Svåsand 2009). Sabiti Makara, Lise Rakner, and Lars Svåsand (2009) argue that the shift to multipartyism was never a condition for continuing support from the international donor community. Rather, they claim, the main consideration had to do with political tensions within the NRM coming from the president's family and loyalists from his home area. In particular, they single out internal conflicts within the army and police force, among the Movement historicals, and between the Young Parliamentarians Association and the veteran NRM group.

Conclusion

The fact that so many of the departures from the NRM family occurred within the highest ranks of the military must surely have been troubling to those in power, given the dangers inherent in military dissension. However, it may also have been these tensions that made the later transition to multipartyism virtually inevitable, especially given the loss of some of the strongest military leaders to the opposition.

What these comings and goings from the NRM household suggest is that even though the NRM has primarily drawn on westerners for top military and political appointments, the biggest threats to NRM dominance do not emanate from the north or from Buganda. In fact, they are from westerners themselves, especially those within the top military brass. Museveni's own appointments in the military seem to be intended to stave off the increasing erosion of support from his former colleagues in the guerrilla war and other long-standing NRM stalwarts within the military. The appointments of westerners in the military, the cabinet, and other top positions have been a defensive move rather than an assertion of ethnic supremacy. In order to prevent further dissension among the very people he needs to rely on and trust the most, Museveni has not only made more appointments of westerners but also sought support from the groups in the west that feel the most alienated by his government. While these appointments have a western bias, which has aroused considerable criticism throughout the country, the divisions among leaders from the west and the willingness of northerners and others to vote and form party coalitions across ethnic differences (see Chapter 2) suggest that there are countercurrents that mitigate against ethnic polarization.

Some of Museveni's closest associates and strongest allies at one time were from Rukungiri, Kigezi, and Toro; some were Bairu, others Bahima; some were Protestant, others were Catholics and Muslims; and many were from other parts of the country. Just as, according to Stathis Kalyvas (2006), local conflicts often have nothing to do with ethnicity yet are situated within an ethnic matrix, so ethnicity at the top levels can also be about holding on to power, finding scapegoats for corruption and military misadventures, failing to control the actions of top military commanders, and maintaining control at the cheapest price when the cost of power no longer rests on ideology, faith in the party, or other abstract ties.

Although the hybrid nature of the Ugandan regime meant that power became overly concentrated on the one hand, divisions within the elite from the western part of the country eventually resulted in pressures to further liberalize and open the country up to multipartyism on the other. This seemingly put Uganda on a trajectory more compatible with changing African and international norms. The NRM's goal in opting for multipartyism was to quiet its critics while at the same time allowing for a new strategy of NRM and executive dominance, as will become evident in the next chapter. This strategy perfectly embodies the dual nature of semiauthoritarianism, which is the product of oppositional pressures for both political liberalization and the centralization of power.

Leonardo Villalón and Peter VonDoepp (2005) have highlighted the important role of elites in shaping democratic outcomes in Africa. They argue that this happens in a number of ways: democratically elected governments may control income streams and rent-seeking opportunities that give them political advantage as incumbents, leading at times to resistance from the opposition and in other instances to incumbent victory. The types of resources available determine the kinds of patronage networks that are formed, as peasant economies lead to the development of rural-state institutions, while plantation or extractive economies lead to other formations. The authors also touch on the role of elites as mediators of donor funds and of political culture.

It has been observed that in those semiauthoritarian countries where the opposition is able to build party coalitions and jointly run candidates to challenge the incumbent, this significantly raises the cost of repression, manipulation, and intimidation. This triggering of some of the inherent contradictions of a semiauthoritarian regime makes further democratization more likely and can result in regime change that is both rapid and dramatic. The example of Kenya in 2002 is often cited in the literature as an example of how this dynamic comes into play (Howard and Roessler 2006). Until recently, the Ugandan opposition has united only temporarily and partially around boycotts. This may change with the new party coalition formed to oust Museveni in the 2011 elections.

In Uganda, the military leadership is the most important elite grouping shaping political liberalization. The main opposition party, the FDC, draws heavily on the top military brass who have left the NRM. Museveni has spent much of his energy trying to shore up support for his government within the military, cultivating loyal, nonpolitical military leaders, overlooking corruption in the military, and trying to head off further splits. The military leaders are placated through various forms of patronage and promotions, the strengthening of ethnic ties within the Uganda People's Defence Forces (UPDF) command structure, and paramilitary formations.

Some concessions nevertheless have been made to the reformists within the NRM and to those who left as the government moved toward multipartyism, gave the judiciary more room to maneuver, and lessened the harassment and intimidation of opposition parties at various junctures. Some—like Lieutenant General Tinyefuza, who left the NRM initially because of differences with Museveni—later returned to the fold to high posts, perhaps realizing that this was, for the time being, the only game in town.

Placating the military has come at a high price, but it is the one elite constituency that cannot be ignored so long as power is maintained through patronage and violence. Uganda's ventures in the Democratic Republic of Congo (see Chapter 7) have resulted in violent conflict, destabilization, countless lost lives, rape, displacement, the conscription of child soldiers, and other horrors of war. They have also cost Uganda in terms of its international reputation. Appeasing the military has led to impunity for military leaders. It has also resulted in violations of the rights of military personnel. Because of the way in which the military leaders are recruited, it has led to the perception of ethnic favoritism toward the west, which, given Uganda's legacy of politicized and militarized ethnicity, has potentially explosive consequences.

The fact that the military is split in its allegiances makes the process of democratization potentially treacherous, particularly where changes at the top or in party dominance in the legislature are involved. At the same time, these splits may also have laid the groundwork for further liberalization.

Notes

1. The Ankole districts include Mbarara, Ntungamo, Kiruhura, Ibanda, Bushenyi, and Insigiro. Ankole has the second-highest number of MPs in the House. *The Monitor,* http://www.monitor.co.ug/artman/publish/news/Gen_Aronda_answers_Tumukunde_on _UPDF_67939.shtm.
2. Bahima (pl.) refers to the Hima people; Muhima (sing.) is one Hima. Bairu (pl.) refers to the Ira people; Mwiru (sing.) is one Ira.

4

The Quid Pro Quo
of Political Liberalization

*Some of us chose to be journalists because we were searching for meaning
in life. And even when adversity strikes . . . we remind ourselves that worse
things can happen to us. The worst thing that can happen to us now is to
allow our collective spirit to be crushed, to bail out for comfortable lives in
exile, talking about our persecuted little experiences at small colleges in
Europe and North America. But because we know we are not the enemy, we
must weather this storm.*
    — Simwogerere Kyazze (1999), reflecting on the shooting of the
    lawyer of one of three senior *Monitor* editors charged with sedition

One of the central dilemmas for semiauthoritarian regimes is how to maintain
the status quo while opening up space for civil and political society, which
may press for greater liberalization. Their solutions often amount to subver-
sions of what in form appear to be democratic institutions. The extent to which
the National Resistance Movement (NRM) sought to enshrine nondemocratic
provisions in laws and in the constitution illustrates both its need to legitimize
its practices through formal mechanisms and its impulse to monopolize power.
Basic institutions in hybrid regimes are strongly contested because the means
exist for those in power to subvert their democratic aspects; likewise, the
means exist for those seeking greater judicial, legislative, associational, media,
and other forms of autonomy to achieve their ends.

When he came to power in 1986, President Yoweri Museveni envisioned
that the National Resistance Movement (later known as the Movement) would
encompass all political interests and parties in Uganda as a way of suppressing sectarian tendencies and garnering legitimacy for himself. By the mid-
1990s, however, rather than ushering in a period of greater inclusiveness in the
political process, the country appeared to have experienced the shrinking of
political space, as Museveni eliminated the non-NRM multipartyists from his
cabinet and other key positions (as described in Chapter 2). Ironically, as is
common in nondemocratic regimes, the shrinking of political space necessi-
tated the expansion of what was considered the political sphere to restrict certain nongovernmental organization (NGO) activities, civil society advocacy,

75

and standard newspaper investigative reporting when these societal actors became too outspoken against the government.

The constitution-making process of 1995 and subsequent legislation further tightened the grip of the Movement. Even the opening to multipartyism in 2005 prior to the 2006 elections was overshadowed by the expansion of executive powers, insofar as multipartyism became a quid pro quo for the lifting of presidential term limits. It was widely acknowledged that 70 percent of parliamentarians were openly bribed to give President Museveni the two-thirds vote needed to alter the constitution to allow him a third term.[1] Museveni had already purged some of the staunchest NRM supporters from the cabinet, military, and security agencies after they opposed his bid for a third term (see Chapter 2). Meanwhile, Museveni strengthened his reliance on Uganda's military and extralegal security units. Thus, the opening to multipartyism in 2005 needs to be seen in the broader historical context of continued repression of the opposition.

This chapter looks at the way in which the NRM established a no-party system in Uganda, which became a de facto one-party system. It shows how this imperative to create a no-party system permeated the constitution-making process, including the proceedings of the Constitutional Commission, the Constituent Assembly (CA) elections and deliberations, and the actual constitution itself. It documents the introduction of legislation to further the goal of institutionalizing the Movement system, and it also explores the resistance against efforts to expand executive powers by the judiciary, the legislature, political parties, the media, women's movements, and other groups. Finally, it looks at the impact of the constitution and legislation on the actual exercise of political rights by parties, on freedom of speech as it has affected the media, on freedom of association as it has influenced advocacy organizations—particularly one of the most active sectors, the women's movement—and on the independence of the legislature and judiciary.

The Evolution of a No-Party System

When the NRM first came to power in 1986, it had not yet taken an antiparty line. In fact, it brought the leaders of opposition parties into its ruling coalition so as to gain legitimacy as a broad-based movement representing the interests of all and to promote its opposition to sectarianism. It sought, as did all prior governments, to create a coalition broad enough to consolidate its rule. The NRM gradually found that maintaining such a coalition came at the price of a level of openness to political mobilization that it found too threatening. As it sought to further consolidate power, the NRM edged out certain members of its coalition, as we saw in Chapter 2, while limiting political activity.

The NRM instituted a hierarchical system of local government called Resistance Councils (RCs), renamed Local Councils (LCs) with the 1995 constitution. Council officers were elected based on their individual merit rather than party allegiance. Although initially heralded as a form of grassroots popular participation, the system was, as soon became clear, being used as a party machine to advance the interests of the NRM at the expense of other political parties; the NRM was acting as a de facto political party as it sought support through the LC system. (Chapter 5 explores the role of the LCs in greater depth.)

As we have seen, the NRM initially advocated a no-party system called the Movement system. The rationale for the Movement system was tied to Uganda's postindependence experience. The Movement blamed parties for fostering sectarianism and for the ills of the preceding regimes (Carbone 2003). Museveni argued that preindustrial countries like Uganda were not ready for parties because of the persistence of sectarian tendencies; moreover, he saw parties as elite institutions that believed they could represent popular interests, whereas the Movement and its LCs were vehicles for direct grassroots political participation by the masses. Opponents of Museveni said his antisectarian stance was simply populist rhetoric and that he was politicizing ethnicity just like his predecessors (see Chapter 2).

The NRM also advanced its objectives by carrying out political education throughout the country. It created a National School of Political Education for local leaders and promoted *mchakamchaka,* or military and political education programs, throughout the country. Early every morning, hundreds of thousands of Ugandans could be seen marching with wooden guns in formation and chanting pro-NRM slogans. These programs were bitterly criticized by political parties as being antidemocratic. To this day, these programs continue, although in modified form, and they are not a requirement for all citizens as they once were. The NRM attempted to suffuse every aspect of society, directing all civil servants to have an NRM manifesto even though the constitution stipulates that civil servants are not to engage in political activity ("NRM Policy a Must for Civil Servants" 2007).

In 1989, sensing that it had not consolidated its rule, the National Executive Council of the NRM decided to extend the NRM administration for another five years, starting in 1990, before popular elections could be held. Meanwhile, political parties, although not outright banned, were not permitted to hold public rallies, create local party branches, or organize delegate conferences. They could run for RC positions and for parliament, but not as party representatives. Not surprisingly, this resulted in elections that focused on individual personalities rather than on party platforms, which was characteristic of the no-party system and also of emerging multiparty systems in Africa (van de Walle 2003). This damper on political activity not only made it difficult for existing parties to operate, but it prevented the creation and institutionalization of other parties. In 1992, the legislative body, known then as the National Resistance Council (NRC), adopted a resolution suspending political activity. These developments were all precursors to the 1995 constitution, which was an attempt to institutionalize the Movement and its no-party system.

Constitution-Making and Political Parties

Throughout the process of constitution-making, including the deliberations of the Constitutional Commission and the CA, political parties were unable to organize freely, and therefore the framework of the debate did not adequately allow for alternate views to be fully aired (Tripp 2010).[2]

The Constitutional Commission

Many of the undemocratic characteristics of the 1995 constitution can be traced back to undemocratic aspects of the constitution-making process itself. Even though the Constitutional Commission was regionally balanced in its composition and one Democratic Party (DP) member sat on it, it did not include even one member who openly opposed the Movement system (Furley and Katalikawe 1997, 248). Moreover, it included both the political commissar of the NRM and his counterpart in the National Resistance Army (NRA). This left the commission open to criticism that the process of selecting members was not carried out in a sufficiently democratic fashion (Barya 2000, 17; Oloka-Onyango 2000, 45). The commission was headed by Justice Benjamin Odoki and was under the direction of the minister of constitutional affairs. It was financed by the government (with donor support), which gave the executive branch additional leverage in the operation of the commission.

Rarely in Africa has one seen the level of popular engagement in education seminars, debates, media discussions, and submission of memoranda such as was evident during the Ugandan constitution-making process. According to Devra Moehler, "In Uganda, a higher percentage of individuals participated in a larger variety of activities over a longer period of time than in any other participatory constitution-making process worldwide" (2006, 282).

At least 25,547 separate submissions of views were sent to the commission (Uganda, Constituent Assembly 1994). The fact that there was such wide consultation with the public through formalized methods may itself be seen as a major achievement. The submissions to the commission took the form of LC memoranda (10,134); essay competitions (5,844); seminar reports from district, subcounty, and various other institutions (899); newspaper opinion articles (2,763); individual memoranda (2,553); group memoranda (839); and position papers (290) (Mukholi 1995, 30). The level of involvement of women in the process was unprecedented in Africa and perhaps globally. No other sector of society sent as many memoranda to the commission as did women's groups.

Members of the commission also toured the country, holding seminars and gathering the views of opinion leaders and the representatives of key organizations in each district. A draft constitution in the form of a document called "Guidelines and Guiding Questions" was prepared to elicit further commentary. Massive numbers of people attended the seminars and participated in debates. The late Father John Waliggo, one of the members of the commission, indicated that about 30,000 community leaders were engaged in seminars regarding the constitution. The tour was followed by the holding of seminars in 870 subcounties around the country in which commissioners gave an introduction and explanation of the constitution-making process and then let people air their views. These seminars were in turn followed by the solicitation of memoranda (Waliggo 1995, 18–40, 26–27).

The Constitutional Commission claimed that the draft constitution it produced was based on people's views. Critics have been skeptical about how much of the constitution reflected popular views, especially since the emphasis of the commission's tour was on educating people about the constitution rather than consulting with them. Opposition leaders accused the commission of ignoring memoranda that raised contentious issues. Moreover, memoranda written at the subcounty level were vetted by NRM leaders before submission to the commission. Critics also have argued that the commission was part of the NRM's design to persuade the public to support the NRM. This is because, while the so-called guiding questions that set the framework for the debate allowed for either a multiparty, one-party, or no-party system, the advantages and disadvantages of the former were listed, while only the advantages of the other two options were presented.

The commission determined that a referendum would be held over the nature of the political system in Uganda, but it did not address issues relating to the context in which the referendum would be held. Its proposals did nothing to ensure that the supporters of a multiparty system would be able to freely articulate their views at any stage in the process of instituting a Movement system. Instead, those party activities that were defined in the commission's draft constitution as incompatible with the Movement system were to remain suspended during the period the system was in place—in other words, in the period leading up to the referendum. This put those who did not want a Movement system at a serious disadvantage.

The Constituent Assembly

In 1993, the CA statute prohibited parties from running candidates in the elections for the Assembly, thus giving the NRM a clear advantage. The constitution itself, in spite of its many progressive provisions, especially regarding women, ended up being a mechanism to keep political parties in limbo while the Movement system was being institutionalized (Oloka-Onyango 1997, 213). The CA elections were the first popular elections since 1980 in Uganda and proved to be an important harbinger of things to come. The original intent of the NRM was to have the National Assembly serve as the CA, as had been the case in the 1967 constitutional deliberations. However, many questioned the representativeness of the existing parliament, given the large number of historicals, presidential nominees, and army representatives, in addition to the women who were elected by an electoral college that was closely associated with the NRM (Mukholi 1995, 35).[3] As a result of pressure from political parties to have delegates elected freely from all parts of the country, the idea of using the National Assembly was dropped. But other crucial efforts to keep the playing field tilted toward the Movement succeeded.

The CA statute of 1993 provided for the special selection of seventy-four of the delegates, in addition to the 214 directly elected from the districts. Of those, ten were to be appointed by the president, ten by the NRA, two by the National Organisation of Trade Unions, two by each of the four political parties, four by the National Youth Council, and one by the National Union of Disabled Persons of Uganda. In addition, thirty-nine women were elected by an electoral college of subcounty counselors and members of the subcounty women's councils within the district. The actual number of special delegates seated in the CA was only seventy, since the Uganda People's Congress (UPC) refused to send its two delegates in protest against the ban on party activities. The Uganda Patriotic Movement (UPM), which had been formed by Museveni in 1980, also did not send delegates because it argued that the NRM was already representing its views (Mukholi 1995, 37).

This meant that at least sixty-six of the CA's delegates were institutionally beholden to the NRM for their positions. Although they did not compose a majority, these delegates formed a major block of NRM supporters who could be counted on to adopt pro-NRM positions in addition to the chair and vice chair, who were to be elected from among five presidential nominees. Despite the insistence of political parties that they be consulted on these five nominations, no such consultations took place. Movementist James Wapakhabulo became the chair of the CA, and the vice chair went to Professor Victoria Mwaka, presumably with the intent of helping mobilize the support of women and the Baganda. With one exception, Movementists also headed the four CA committees that were established.

The Constituent Assembly Election Act of 1993 was the first opportunity for the NRM government to translate its implicit ban on political party activity into a legal ban at the national level. Under the act, candidates were not allowed to use a political party affiliation in running for the CA. They were allowed to participate in only those campaign rallies or meetings that were organized by the government; no other rallies or form of public demonstration in support of or against a candidate were allowed (Barya 2000, 22). Political party membership recruitment, establishment of branch offices, party member conferences, and campaigning under party banners were forbidden. Candidates simply had to run as individuals. These provisions of the act violated the 1967 constitution's guarantees of freedom of association and of assembly. They also served to suppress public debate, especially on the draft constitution's more controversial aspects.

Meanwhile, NRM candidates continued to use the media to assert their views, an opportunity not as available to non-NRM candidates. Candidates participated in the CA elections as though they were contestants in a struggle for political power, rather than as participants in a constitutional debate. This is evident, for example, in Museveni's proclamation after the CA elections: "We have won!" Who were "we," if everyone was running individually? By directly and openly supporting Movement candidates, the NRM, in effect, behaved like a political party while disallowing other political groups to operate in the same fashion. Not surprisingly, the CA elections became a turning point at which the Movement emerged as a de facto single ruling party.

The 1993 CA statute adopted by the National Assembly was challenged in the Constitutional Court by a petition from the UPC, which argued that the ban on party activity suppressed constitutionally guaranteed rights of free assembly and association and that the provisions governing campaigning adversely affected the right to free expression. In a blatantly political decision, the court dismissed the petition on the grounds that the suspension of party activity was a temporary measure and that such a measure was necessary in order to prevent a reversion to the chaos of the past.

The effect of the regulations governing the CA elections was to drive parts of the electoral process underground, with campaign events being held at funeral meetings, in churches, and at fundraising events with limited impact. It also shifted the debate from a focus on the issues to a focus on personalities and their relationships to the president. In light of the restrictions on campaigning and organized political activity, the electorate was not able to consider viewpoints that were effectively excluded from the public debate. As a result, the election process suffered from the lack of effective representation of differing positions on issues that lay at the heart of Uganda's political conflicts.

All in all, the elections gave every advantage to the NRM. The fairness of the elections largely depended on the impartiality and integrity of the commissioner running the elections. Museveni appointed his friend Steven Akabway as commissioner. Many regarded him as a political flunky and were critical of his appointment (Furley and Katalikawe 1997, 252).

There were complaints that government ministers were holding public rallies prior to the date that was set for campaigning to begin on the pretext that they were conducting government business. Police were called in, but no one was prosecuted for holding such events. In many cases, large sums of money and goods were donated to local schools and hospitals before and during the election campaign by government ministers who were standing as candidates while they were on so-called official tours. This gave them undue advantage over their rivals. Indeed, ministers had many advantages others did not have, including access to the trappings of state power for their campaigns. For example, almost every minister was accompanied by convoys of ministerial vehicles, which they used for transporting themselves and their supporters to polling stations. One even traveled from his home less than half a mile from the polling place in an official helicopter.

In some cases, NRM candidates bestowed gifts, including money, alcohol, food, and promises of future gains to voters. In other instances, the electorate became extortionists (Geist 1995, 97). Longtime MP Adoko Nekyon said at the time that in the forty-three years since the National Assembly had been formed, he had never seen such extensive buying of votes as he witnessed in the CA elections ("Museveni Rigging Worse than Obote" 2001). Such charges are hard to prove, but there was ample anecdotal evidence to support them.

Voter turnout in the CA election was very high, ranging from 66 percent in Karamoja to 97 percent in Kabale (Geist 1995, 99; Katorobo 1995, 131). In the election, 84 percent of the National Assembly members ran in the CA elections, and—despite the NRM's many advantages—51 percent of the parliamentary candidates who ran for the CA lost. The largest number who lost were in the east (60 percent of parliamentary candidates) and the north (67 percent), both centers of opposition where citizens were frustrated by continued conflict and the lack of development in their regions (Katorobo 1995, 121).

Since political parties could not field candidates or carry out campaigns, it is difficult to know to what extent the outcome of these elections reflected real political sentiments as opposed to the capacity of candidates to hand out material inducements. Ethnic allegiances were an additional factor in many of the races. The elections reflected support for the NRM among the Baganda in the south, who by this point had been persuaded to endorse the Movement after the restoration of their kingship in 1993 (Kasfir 1994, 171–176).

Deliberations over the Political System

One of the most controversial issues addressed in the CA deliberations was whether the country should adopt a no-party Movement system, a multiparty system, or some other type of democratic and representative system. There were several dramatic standoffs in the CA between the Movementists and supporters of a multiparty system around this issue.

The multipartyists wanted the constitution to provide for freedom of association and the creation of an interim government composed of all political parties that would govern the country for three years until the new constitution came into force. The Movementists felt that Uganda was not ready for multi-partyism and that it would fracture the country irreparably. In the end, the CA's decisions reinforced the recommendations of the Constitutional Commission, namely that the Movement system should continue in power for another five years, after which a referendum would be held to determine whether to transition to a multiparty political system. Its advocates deemed the Movement system to be broad based, inclusive of all people, and nonsectarian, hence nonpartisan. The use of a referendum was seen as enhancing democracy and popular participation, allowing people to have a say in the formation of their political system.

Ultimately, the CA reaffirmed the monopoly on political power held by the NRM and banned "any activities" that might "interfere with the Movement political system" (Article 269 of the 1995 constitution). The crucial debate over the future of multipartyism in the CA was resolved in July 1995, after four days of deliberations and a walkout by multiparty forces. The NRM prevailed with 199 votes in favor of continued no-party rule, sixty-eight opposed, and two abstentions. Multipartyists argued against enshrining the Movement political system in the constitution because it would constrain Ugandans' ability to alter their own political system. Multipartyists also argued that the use of periodic referenda to change the political system would create instability and could be easily manipulated by whoever was in power. The CA rejected these arguments and voted down the multipartyists' proposals.

The no-party Movement system not only circumscribed the activity of opposition parties but, because it was theoretically to be a movement representing the entire citizenry, it also gave the NRM a rationale not to institutionalize itself as an internally democratic political party. This left key elements of political control highly centralized within the NRM. Power within the NRM continued to be concentrated at the top; the NRM did not hold elections for any of its leaders, nor did it convene any popularly elected body to vote on policies during this time (Kasfir 1994, 61). This later led to disaffection within the Movement, although signs of such dissatisfaction were already evident during the CA deliberations (see the discussion about Major General Tinyefuza and the CA in Chapter 3).

Multipartyists and Movementists clashed on other points as well. Dick Nyai, a UPC CA member, wanted presidential and parliamentary elections to be held on the same day on the grounds of expense, logistics, and practicality. Even though it seemed reasonable to many, his proposal was rejected purely on the grounds that a multipartyist had presented it. Many observers were incredulous that this move was defeated. Many multipartyists felt that if the elections were split and the presidential elections held first, a large victory for Museveni would demoralize supporters of the multipartyists and would convince some of those who were wavering to join the Movementists. Similarly, the Movementists reasoned that a presidential victory would guarantee them a victory in the upcoming parliamentary elections as well.

Legislative Acts to Entrench the NRM

After the constitution was adopted, a series of legislative acts were pursued to seal Movement dominance, which had begun to look increasingly like an old-style, hegemonic single party. In 1997, amid controversy, parliament passed the Movement Bill, an act that required all adult Ugandans to belong to the Movement system, even those who opposed it. Multipartyists and many prodemocracy advocates opposed the bill because, they argued, it was unconstitutional. They feared that making membership in the Movement mandatory would destroy freedom of association. The bill was seen as enhancing the executive's authority while reducing the already limited powers of the legislature. It was also seen as a ploy by the Movement to formally turn the five-tiered Local Council system into branches of the Movement.

At the eleventh hour in 1999, the NRM brought to parliament another proposal, the Referendum Bill, with little time for debate. The act paved the way for a constitutionally mandated referendum in 2000, with a second referendum to be held in 2005. These referenda would determine whether Uganda would have a Movement, multiparty, or some other kind of system. The bill was steamrolled through parliament, and Museveni signed it, even though the required ninety-member quorum was not reached (only fifty members of parliament voted on the bill). The overwhelming lack of parliamentary support for the referendum indicated growing divisions within the Movement.

The first referendum was held July 1, 2000, and the Movement system won by 94.3 percent. The major opposition parties, the UPC and the DP, boycotted the referendum, refusing to lend legitimacy to the process on the grounds that, given all the restrictions on party activity, there was no way multiparty perspectives would be given a fair hearing.

A study based on a survey of public attitudes found that people shunned the 2000 referendum not so much in response to the DP-UPC boycott but because they disliked the choices: the referendum made them choose between the hegemony of the NRM and a return to old-guard parties, which they associated with violent conflict, war, hatred, and death (Bratton and Lambright 2001, 446, 451).

In August 2000, the DP got the Constitutional Court to rule that the law governing the 2000 referendum on political systems was null and void because its passage violated parliamentary rules. This ruling has implications for other acts passed by parliament in a similar fashion without the required quorum (as will be discussed later in the chapter with respect to the role of the judiciary).

Yet another controversial piece of legislation, the Political Parties and Organisations Bill, was introduced and withdrawn numerous times in parliament as a result of sharp disagreements over its content. It was a highly restrictive bill, curtailing party and associational activities, but was nevertheless passed on June 7, 2002. It was contested in the Constitutional Court by the DP, which in 2003 got its most restrictive clauses overturned: the court nullified the sections on using party symbols, colors, and slogans in campaigns; banning political parties from sponsoring platforms; campaigning for candidates in presidential and parliamentary elections; and performing any activity that might interfere with the Movement system. The court ruled that political parties could organize not only at their headquarters at the national level but also in their constituencies. It ruled that the Movement was not a political system as it claimed but a political organization. The attorney general announced that political parties could operate so long as they were registered.

The fact that the 2002 bill restricting parties and associations was even brought to the floor of the National Assembly is telling of the Movement's agenda. However, the subsequent Movement retreat from this agenda can be seen in part as a response to changing popular sentiments. The sharp restrictions on political activity came at a time when a poll taken by the Nairobi-based firm Strategic Public Relations & Research indicated that 67 percent of the population supported multipartyism and that the numbers of supporters were rapidly increasing. At the same time, the largest percentage (38 percent) believed the Movement was the "party" best equipped to address issues that mattered to them. Most (63 percent) thought of the Movement as a party, even though it was still claiming to be a system at the time. According to the 2002 poll, the UPC claimed 20 percent support, the DP 19 percent, and the Reform Agenda 8 percent (Nakazibwe 2002).

After resisting multipartyism for two decades, in an about-face, multipartyism all of a sudden became acceptable to the NRM in 2004. This was largely due to pressure within the NRM, as discussed in Chapter 3. However, allowing parties to operate was seen by many as a relatively small price for Museveni to pay in order to accomplish an even more important objective: that of staying in power. This is illustrative of the practice commonplace among semiauthoritarian regimes of using democratic institutions to achieve undemocratic objectives. Museveni sought a quid pro quo arrangement that allowed him to remain in power for yet another term. In December 2004, the government presented parliament with 119 constitutional amendments, including amendments that lifted limits on the president's service of two terms, ended parliament's ability to approve ministerial appointments and censure ministers for incompetence or corruption, and gave the president the right to dissolve parliament. The amendments also provided for the closure of the Human Rights Commission, limited the authority of the inspector general, and imposed sanctions on cultural leaders (kings and chiefs) who violated the constitution. In exchange, Museveni lifted restrictions on political parties and changed the political system to a multiparty system. At the same time, Museveni openly bribed 213 of the 305 members of parliament with 5 million shillings (US$3,000) each in exchange for supporting the lifting of term limits.

Museveni ultimately succeeded in lifting term limits in a 2005 parliamentary vote, paving the way for him to run for president in 2006. The move represented an attempt to expand executive power at the expense of the legislature. Although the legislature had challenged presidential authority sporadically around corruption scandals involving his close associates, it completely succumbed to presidential pressure on lifting term limits. Even Supreme Court judge George Kanyeihamba sharply criticized the MPs involved in amending clauses of the constitution without consulting the people, saying: "Someone had to pay MPs Shs 5 million to change the provision" ("Kanyeihamba Criticises MPs" 2008). Five years later, opposition parties met with the NRM and unsuccessfully demanded the restoration of presidential term limits as evidence that the NRM was committed to democratic reforms prior to the 2011 elections (Mugerwa 2009).

The NRM had already been registered as an organization in 2003. A referendum on multipartyism was held amid opposition protests in July 2005. Nevertheless, with encouragement from Museveni, the "yes" side won with 93 percent of the vote against the 7 percent cast by the "no" side.

A flurry of legislation was then quickly passed, including a new Political Parties and Organizations Act, which allowed for free party mobilization; the Presidential Elections Act; the Parliamentary Elections Act; and the Local Governments Amendment Act. They all came into force in November 2005, only one month before the presidential and parliamentary election campaigns got underway. This meant that many political parties had only three months to form and establish a grassroots presence, hold primaries, and campaign prior to the 2006 election. The situation was challenging for both new and old political parties. Years of restrictions had weakened the older parties (namely the DP, the UPC, and the Conservative Party, or CP). The NRM, with its Movement machine in place, was therefore better poised to take advantage of the abrupt shift in policy. This meant that even though there were over thirty registered parties, only four were able to effectively participate in the elections. Thus it was no surprise that the NRM won both the parliamentary and presidential elections (see Tables 4.1 and 4.2).

The Independence of the Judiciary

The judiciary has played a central role in Uganda under Museveni, and its experiences in defending its independence reflect some of the central tensions in a semiauthoritarian regime, which have to do with countervailing impulses

Table 4.1   Presidential Election Results, 2006

Candidate (Party)	Number of Votes	Percentage of Votes
Yoweri Museveni (NRM)	4,109,449	59.26
Kizza Besigye (FDC)	2,592,954	37.39
John Ssebaana Kizito (DP)	109,583	1.58
Abed Bwanika	65,874	0.95
Miria Obote (UPC)	57,071	0.82

Source: Inter-Parliamentary Union, http://www.ipu.org. Accessed June 19, 2009.

Table 4.2   Parliamentary Election Results, 2006

Party	Number of Seats (319)
National Resistance Movement (NRM)	205
Forum for Democratic Change (FDC)	37
Uganda People's Congress (UPC)	9
Democratic Party (DP)	8
Conservative Party (CP)	1
Justice Forum (JEEMA)	1
Independents	36

Source: Inter-Parliamentary Union, http://www.ipu.org. Accessed June 19, 2009.

to restrain and expand executive power. The judiciary was never able to assert its independence under any of the previous governments in Uganda, but under Museveni's government, one began to see changes in this area. At the same time, because the judiciary has been so active in pushing back against executive encroachments, its experience is a good measure of both the possibilities for and the limits of democratization, a process that seemed to become especially challenging in Uganda after the 1995 constitution was adopted and during the 2001 elections. While legal scholars are prudently tentative about the possibilities for reform driven by the judiciary, some are beginning to argue that the momentum shifted to the courts after 2000 in a way that it did not within the legislature and other institutions. This occurred as the Movement was forced by the judiciary to justify its limitations on rights and on the political process (Bussey 2005, 23).

Right from the outset there were tensions between the judiciary and the executive branch. The judiciary has consistently resisted government meddling in verdicts, efforts to ban the right to bail, and countless other attempts to limit its authority (Ellett 2008, 431). There have been at the same time concerted efforts to rein in the judiciary ever since the passage of the 1995 constitution, which expanded judicial powers and protections but also dramatically expanded executive privilege. The courts ruled against the government in several notable cases, including *Ssempebwa v. Attorney General* (1986) and *Ontario Lt v. Crispus Kiyonga & Ors* (1992).

The courts even struck at the military in one case, *Attorney General v. Major General David Tinyefuza* (see the discussion of the 1997 case in Chapter 3). The ruling in favor of Tinyefuza and against military intimidation was hailed by lawyers as vindication of the judiciary's independence. Tinyefuza, a member of parliament and an army general, had criticized the government's handling of the war in northern Uganda to a parliamentary committee. He had submitted his resignation from the army and had taken up a post as presidential adviser on military affairs. His resignation was rejected by the minister of defense and he was about to be court-martialed when he filed a petition in the Court of Appeal. The court ruled in his favor, stating that threats by the military and executive were unconstitutional (Ellett 2008, 431–433).

Three cases filed by Paul Ssemogerere, former president of the DP, were also seminal in Ugandan jurisprudence. In the first case in 1999 Paul Ssemogerere and two parliamentarians petitioned the Constitutional Court to nullify the Referendum and Other Provisions Act of 1999, alleging that the act was passed without a sufficient quorum in parliament to transact business. The court claimed that it did not have sufficient jurisdiction to hear the claim based on the attorney general's argument that the parliament was a sovereign body. Ssemogerere and his colleagues appealed to the Supreme Court, which ruled that the Constitutional Court did, in fact, have jurisdiction to rule on the case.

This was the first time the Ugandan courts challenged parliamentary sovereignty and the attorney general, thus challenging de facto executive authority over parliament. Ellett (2008) argued that this ruling was extremely important for Uganda and the rest of East Africa because it spelled out the supremacy of the constitution and the prerogative of the judiciary to uphold it. The Supreme Court had taken the lead, proving more assertive than the Constitutional Court. Supreme Court Justice George Kanyeihamba wrote the lead judgment in this case, stating, "If Parliament is to successfully claim and protect its powers and internal procedures, it must act in accordance with the constitutional provisions which determine its legislative capacity and the manner in which it must perform its functions" ("Part III: The Act Held No Substance" 2004).

While the case was pending in Constitutional Court, the parliament passed another Referendum Act within two hours of deliberation. Paul Ssemogerere and Zachary Olum then filed a second petition with the Constitutional Court, testing the constitutionality of the Referendum Act of 2000. James Rwanyarare and Badru Wegulo also sought a temporary order to prohibit the holding of the referendum until the first Ssemogerere case was resolved; however these petitions were not heard until after the referendum (Ellett 2008, 439). The government went ahead with the referendum on June 29, 2000. As predicted, the referendum resulted in a 94.3 percent vote overwhelmingly in favor of the Movement system.

When the Constitutional Court finally heard the first Ssemogerere case in 2004, it declared the referendum and the political system to be unconstitutional because it could not be established that the parliamentary vote was taken by a quorum. The speaker of the legislative body had not actually counted the votes but had relied on his own observation.

Parliament responded to the Constitutional Court decision by amending the 1995 constitution to enable bills to be passed without a two-week waiting period and without going through committee. No quorum was required during the debate, only during the vote. This validated the 2000 Referendum Act, thus annoying the courts, which felt it was a direct challenge to their authority and independence (Ellett 2008).

Unhappy with the astounding ruling that threatened to bring Uganda to the brink of a constitutional crisis, Museveni came out and said,

> A closer look at the implications of this judgment reveals an absurdity. It shows that what these judges are saying is absurd, doesn't make sense, reveals an absurdity so gross as to shock the general moral of common sense. The court has declared that the Movement system doesn't exist. . . . This is not acceptable, it simply will not work, and I would like you the people to know this and simply don't get unduly worried about such irrational decisions. . . . We restored constitutionalism and the rule of law; that is why the judges can even make decisions against the government. . . . However, some of them take the people of Uganda for a ride and this is what we can't accept, because some of them think that they can usurp the power of the people— that they can more or less nullify the NRM system with means other than the popular vote; that will not happen.
>
> I was looking at this article of the administration of justice, article 126(1)—judicial power is derived from the people and shall be exercised by the courts established under this constitution in the name of the people and in conformity with law norms and values and aspirations of the people. Norms and aspirations of the people, in conformity with—not in contradiction to—and the people vote in a referendum. That is not an aspiration. It is a decision.
>
> It is a decision and now we have decided and you the courts who should be working on behalf of the people, you nullify what the people have decided; that is not acceptable. ("Museveni Mad with Judges over Nullifying 2000 Referendum Act" 2004)

The government threatened to dismiss the judges involved in this ruling for being corrupt, sectarian, partisan, and political. The chief justice responded by telling the government to leave the judiciary alone. The Supreme Court agreed with the Constitutional Court regarding the legality of the Referendum Act of 2000 but did not regard the referendum itself as having violated the constitution. Thus the referendum outcome was sustained and the government was to be regarded as legal. Since this time, the judiciary has come under greater pressure from the government and has at times retreated.

The DP and UPC also challenged the 2002 Political Parties and Organizations Act through the courts. The constitution had restricted political party activity only temporarily, but the act institutionalized the ban on national-level activities, the holding of public rallies, and the sponsorship of electoral candidates. Ssemogerere petitioned the Constitutional Court on behalf of the DP, and Dr. Rwanyarare did the same for the UPC, contesting the constitutionality of the act. They succeeded in getting the ban on local-level campaigning overturned. Under the act, parties could only campaign at the national level.

Relations between the executive and the judiciary have also become strained as a result of other attempts to expand executive powers. They reached their all-time low on November 16, 2005, when key opposition leader Kizza Besigye of the FDC was arrested on charges of treason and rape. The day he was to be brought to the High Court to be released on bail, members of the Black Mamba squad were deployed at the court to arrest him in an extralegal action. This prompted protests from the High Court judges, Chief Justice Odoki (former head of the Constitutional Commission), the inspector general, leaders of the Uganda Law Society, the government's Human Rights Commission, and many others who condemned the siege of the courts as undermining the rule of law. More than three hundred lawyers went on strike to protest military interference in the independence of the judiciary.

The Supreme Court has continued to assert itself in limiting executive powers. In a landmark case, *Brigadier Henry Tumukunde v. Attorney General and the Electoral Commission (Constitutional Petition No. 6 of 2005)*, the Supreme Court overturned a court-martial ruling against Tumukunde, who argued that he had been forced to resign from parliament because of his statements to the press regarding presidential term limits and open voting in parliament. He claimed he wrote his resignation letter under "immense fear and undue coercion," making his resignation unconstitutional. The court noted that neither the commander in chief nor members of the High Command could force a member of parliament to resign from parliament. As one anonymous Ugandan advocate reflected in *The Monitor*:

> The doctrine of separation of powers is very important for our fragile democracy because as it were, there is a constitutional desire to protect citizens of this country from the excesses of the executive and stop it from abusing state power. That's one of the roles of the judiciary and parliament, and the former needs to be commended for standing up to this high ground. ("Tumukunde Case a Test of Court's Boldness" 2008)

Similarly, when asked by a reporter whether he and his colleagues feared that the "constant Executive bashing" was "likely to scare the judiciary into giving compromised judgments," Supreme Court Judge G. W. Kanyeihamba insisted on judicial independence, replying,

No, not at all. The mood is one of professionalism. . . . At the Court of Appeal and the Supreme Court where I am a member, we've never wavered. We were appointed to serve without fear or favour and we'll continue to do so. We have on the bench very courageous and very dedicated Judges who won't succumb to threats. So we have no fear at all. (Jabweli 2003)

Thus, the judiciary has in general been less prone to manipulation than the legislature and has fiercely sought to defend its independence. The Constitutional Court, through a series of rulings, has helped overturn some of the most restrictive clauses within the constitution regarding political parties and freedom of association. But these rulings have brought it directly into confrontation with the president and the executive branch and to the brink of constitutional crisis. The Supreme Court and Constitutional Court have stood their ground, but they have continued to face assaults on their integrity and have had to pick their battles carefully.

The Independence of the Legislature Threatened

The legislature has not fared as well as the judiciary in the face of executive pressures. The 1995 constitution expanded the powers of parliament and potentially allowed it to check executive excesses. Yet in reality, since 1996, the executive branch has been able to push undemocratic legislation through parliament, often without a quorum, in spite of the constitutional limitations on executive powers. Museveni had also expanded executive influence in the legislature by increasing the numbers of executive-appointed cabinet members, who, together with the military representatives, make up almost one quarter of parliament. The Seventh Parliament (2001–2006), according to Kasfir and Twebaze (2005), took an even lower profile than the Sixth Parliament had and made even fewer efforts to curb the executive. Both Movement and non-Movement parliamentarians who disagreed with the president had a harder time passing legislation.

When in 1998, parliament began to show some independence, it was soon beaten into submission, sometimes quite literally. In 2004, the military arrested and brutally beat four northern members of parliament for organizing a rally in their constituencies. Even after a 2008 Constitutional Court ruling that permitted people to freely organize rallies, opposition parliamentarians were harassed and arrested when they tested the law by organizing rallies in their constituencies. Internal Affairs Minister Ruhakana Rugunda came to parliament after the incidents to defend the actions of the police, but parliamentarians booed him, accused him of peddling rumors, and told him to withdraw his statement (Naturinda 2008).

In the late 1990s, parliamentarians began to confront Museveni about his ties to corruption scandals involving his close associates and relatives. Criticism was not limited to opposition-party legislators. Even the Movement Caucus in parliament was openly critical of the president regarding these scandals and called on him to distance himself from the individuals involved. However, over time, the number of bills passed began to fall and parliament played less of a role in checking graft, particularly when one compares the Sixth with the Seventh Parliament (Kasfir and Twebaze 2005, 18).

The legislature generally wanted inquiries of abuse to be taken up by its select committees rather than by presidentially appointed judicial commissions, because the latter rarely made their reports public; even when they did, the recommendations were not implemented. Commissions were seen as a way of stalling and sliding issues under the rug, as was the case with the investigation of a junk helicopter purchase involving Museveni's half brother. Members of parliament also challenged the president over the sale of the Uganda Commercial Bank and attempted to halt it, but the government went ahead and sold it to Stanbic anyway (Ouma Balikowa 2002).

Parliamentarians, including Movement supporters, resisted pressure from the executive branch to speed up the passage of controversial bills and accused the president of trying to rig the legislative process. In November 1999, parliamentarians and the president hurled accusations and counteraccusations against one another over the speed of deliberation on various bills. Many parliamentarians were critical of the way controversial bills (such as the 1997 Movement Bill and the 1999 Referendum Bill) had been passed without the required parliamentary quorum.

In spite of such challenges to the executive branch, parliament was not beyond manipulation. As mentioned, in 2005, it succumbed to executive pressures to lift presidential term limits and to a series of constitutional amendments that undermined its own authority. Parliamentarians critical of excessive executive power have been on the losing end of most battles, and it has cost them politically to challenge the executive branch. They have often found themselves being publicly decampaigned and pitted against candidates with generous financial backing.

The stick is not the only weapon in the NRM arsenal when it comes to parliamentarians. Another approach has been to lure opposition leaders from their parties with promises of financial rewards, positions, and other enticements. The NRM has been especially eager to win over northern and eastern politicians and has succeeded in winning over Alex Onzima, an MP from Maracha County in West Nile who was once FDC vice chairman, as well as UPC leaders Aggrey Awori, Jacob Oulanyah, Omara Atubo, and the former state minister for finance under the Obote II government, Makmot Okello ("Onzima Tests FDC's Resolve" 2008; Maseruka 2007; Kiggundu and Tash Lumu 2006). "For us in the Movement, we do not catch the smaller fish; we target the bigger ones like Omara Atubo [and] Makmot Okello among others," Museveni said in a visit to Lira ("Makmot Joins NRM" 2006).

Thus, the legislature has been generally weak and vulnerable to executive carrots and sticks in the form of threats to withdraw campaign support, decampaigning, and support for political opponents in electoral contests. They have been bribed by the executive branch before crucial votes and have even suffered physical intimidation. Nevertheless, they have also mounted important challenges to government corruption and the overstepping of executive bounds. They have succeeded in not granting the executive branch the power to dissolve parliament, and they have been able to decide when to convene and for how long. They still have the authority to approve presidential appointments and impeach the president. These are all improvements on the 1967 constitution.

Human Rights and Political Rights

The treatment of political opponents is indicative of how the government feels about political freedom. Although the human rights situation in Uganda improved considerably after Museveni came to power and has continued to improve overall, it eroded in 2000 and particularly during the 2001 presidential campaign. Elections remain particular periods of concern, although the 2006 election did show fewer signs of repression than the 2001 election.

Until Uganda became a multiparty state in July 2005, political candidates could run only as individuals and were forbidden from running on a party ticket. It was not until a constitutional court ruling in 2008 that political parties could legally hold workshops, conferences, and party congresses and organize rallies. Even after the lifting of the ban, as mentioned earlier, the first rallies held were suppressed.

In the past, it was only UPC and DP activists who feared sporadic repression. However, politically motivated repression escalated during the 2001 elections, in which Kizza Besigye was the main contender against Museveni. Members of Besigye's Reform Agenda, a pressure group formed by former Movementists, stated that about 4,000 of its supporters were arrested and that an army-sponsored paramilitary group had killed some and tortured others. The group also protested the government's characterization of the Reform Agenda as supporting rebel organizations, a characterization that provided a pretext for harassment directed at them (Nganda 2003). There were police reports of election-related violence that included attempted murder, assault, and robbery as well as beatings, harassment, and intimidation (US Department of State 2002). Some attacks were carried out in broad daylight. It was widely reported that Major Rabwoni Okwir, who headed Besigye's youth desk and was also the brother of Nobel Mayombo—one of Museveni's closest confidants and his head of internal security—was arrested at Entebbe International Airport by military police. Although accompanied by Besigye, he was violently grabbed, assaulted, and thrown into a pick-up truck by personnel from various security agencies at the airport.

The July 19, 2002, report by the Parliamentary Committee on Election Violence, noted that violence had increased since 1996, moving from "primarily spontaneous eruptions of fighting, which resulted in only injuries and destruction of opponents' property" to violence that was "highly planned and organized . . . resulting in loss of lives, serious and fatal injuries and massive loss of property." Police reports indicated that seventeen people were killed in election-related violence in 2001 (Mufumba 2010). Many scholars and lawyers in the United States were inundated with a flood of requests for assistance in asylum cases involving detention, torture, and threats made to people active in the 2001 election campaign, particularly after the elections. Given how similar the asylum seekers' experiences were, there can be no question that such torture went on. Other political activists disappeared. In August 2003, for example, Reform Agenda activist Santo Okema went missing in Gulu. Another FDC member, Robert Mugyenyi, went missing in 2006 and has yet to be found.

Presidential candidates and their close associates received death threats following the election; Besigye went into exile, along with some of his supporters. Museveni said he was free to return but then publicly accused Besigye of being a terrorist and threatened to capture and kill all terrorists. When Besigye returned, he was indeed arrested and charged with treason and rape. Besigye filed a petition with the Supreme Court in 2001, alleging corrupt practices during the election that included chasing election observers from polling stations, stuffing the ballot boxes, allowing for underage voting, intimidating and kidnapping Besigye supporters, using the military in elections, and making slanderous accusations, such as that Besigye had contracted AIDS (Ellett 2008, 462). Besigye lost his petition, but the dissenting opinion by Justice Oder revealed possible culpability of the president in some of these practices. He said that "if he [Museveni] did not approve what the UPDF and the PPU [Presidential Protection Unit] were doing he would have made an order to stop it. . . . His approval was not express, it was tacit" (cited in Mufumba 2010).

There have been many unofficial reports of arbitrary detention and torture in safe houses. Some of those tortured were accused of being members of the People's Redemption Army (PRA), the existence of which has been questioned; others were accused of associating with a rebel group in the west, the Allied Democratic Forces (ADF), and still others with the FDC and the Reform Agenda.

But some of the torture took place in regular prisons. The Uganda Human Rights Commission (UHRC), which has been notably vocal and active around human rights issues, visited Makindye Military Barracks in July 2004 unannounced and found that people had been arrested and dumped there without charge. They found people with wounds indicative of torture. Commissioner

Omara Aliro told the Parliamentary Committee on Legal and Parliamentary Affairs that the suspects claimed they were illegally arrested and tortured by the paramilitary Violent Crime Crack Unit (VCCU) and Operation Wembley. They had scars on their bodies and some had had their teeth extracted.

Similarly, members of parliament on the Defence and Internal Affairs Committee compiled a report in 2003 on detainees allegedly tortured by state security agents at Kigo prison. They had received over twenty memoranda from torture victims captured by agents of Operation Wembley, the Chieftaincy of Military Intelligence (CMI), and other state security organs. A parliamentary delegation to the prison said that they were stunned and overwhelmed by the level of torture. Inmates showed them their crushed testicles. Some claimed heavy stones had been suspended from their private parts. Crocodiles, snakes, and red ants were used to threaten and torture their victims ("MPs Compile Torture Report" 2003).

In June 2004, the High Court ordered the government to pay Pascal Gakyaro 30 million shillings (US$17,000) as compensation for unlawful arrest, detention, and torture. He was arrested for campaigning in the 2001 elections. Other such compensation cases have been reported.

The UHRC submitted annual reports to parliament, but for ten years not even one report was discussed ("Parliamentarians Ignore Debates on Human Rights Abuses" 2007). They were especially concerned about the situations in which innocent people had been killed, harassed, tortured, and forced into exile, all without recognition by parliament. Half of the 729 inmates being held in Kigo Prison have not been on trial. In response to the seriousness of the situation, the Coalition Against Torture initiated a bill to criminalize torture in Uganda.[4]

Nevertheless, there has been a drop in the number of complaints brought to the commission, which may be indicative of the overall improvement in human rights. Since 1998, the UHRC has logged more than 7,500 complaints ("Torture in a Safe House" 2008). The highest number of complaints (1,429) was received in 2002 (15 percent of them related to torture). In 2008 there were fewer complaints (1,060), but 30 percent had to do with torture or inhuman or degrading treatment or punishment (Uganda Human Rights Commission, 2008). There has been continued improvement in the police and prison systems as a result of education.

Not all repression has been directed at political party activists. Uganda, which bans homosexuality under a colonial antisodomy law, has seen increased advocacy for gay rights in response to increased violence and intimidation directed at gays as well as arbitrary arrests and detentions. For example, Kampala police arrested three gay rights activists during a peaceful June 2008 protest that was staged to draw attention to the vulnerability of the gay community to HIV/AIDS issues. The protesters were responding to a public statement made by the chairman of the Uganda AIDS Commission, who said that even though gays were one of the drivers of HIV in Uganda, the country's limited resources could not be allocated to them at that time. Earlier, in 2004, a radio station had been fined for hosting a lesbian and two gay men on a talk show, and there were growing numbers of antigay comments made by public officials, religious leaders, and news media figures, creating a hostile environment for gays and lesbians. Two films said to be promoting homosexuality were banned by the Media Council from a Kampala film festival in 2008.

Sexual Minorities Uganda (SMUG), a coalition of four organizations—Freedom and Roam Uganda, Spectrum Uganda, Integrity Uganda, and Icebreakers Uganda—formed in support of gay rights launched a 2007 campaign called "Let Us Live in Peace." In response, Deputy Attorney General Fred Ruhindi called for using the penal code against gays and Pastor Martin Ssempa organized large rallies demanding government action against homosexuals (Human Rights Watch 2007).

Tensions between antigay and human rights activists came to a head in 2009, when an NRM parliamentarian from Ndorwa West, David Bahati, introduced a draconian Anti-Homosexuality Bill that proposed life imprisonment for acts of homosexuality. Offenders caught having sex with minors or disabled persons or found to have infected their partners with HIV would face the death penalty. The proposed law would also punish the failure of a third party to inform the authorities of homosexual activity. The bill drew immediate international condemnation from the United States, Britain, Sweden, Canada, and Uganda's other major donors as well as from prominent individuals like South African Nobel Laureate Archbishop Desmond Tutu (2010). It also drew protests from international human rights organizations and civil society organizations within Uganda, such as the Civil Society Coalition on Human Rights and Constitutional Law, which represents nearly twenty Ugandan advocacy groups who saw the bill as an unprecedented threat to the fundamental human rights of Ugandans. Other resistance to the bill came from the Uganda People's Congress, opposition leaders like FDC's Anne Mugisha (2010), and an outspoken advocate of gay rights and Makerere law professor, Sylvia Tamale (2010).

The most vocal supporters of the antigay bill were conservative Christian religious groups in Uganda, who claimed that homosexuality in Uganda was a product of Western influences. Nevertheless, some of their strongest support and encouragement came from US fundamentalist Christian organizations.

Freedom of Speech

A central part of the strategy of ensuring Movement dominance has been control of the media, which has been one of the most important forces exposing government corruption and repression. When Museveni first took over, there appeared to be a flowering of independent media, and even to this day a remarkable amount of open political discussion takes place in the media. Nevertheless, the vibrancy of the coverage and debates soon met with resistance from the Movement, which harassed media workers and found legal ways to suppress the media. Various key pieces of legislation have been enacted that restrict the media, and their enforcement has evoked strong responses from media workers. Under Amin, such commentary never would have been tolerated and would have resulted in certain death in many cases. The difference under the semiauthoritarian regime of Museveni is that there is pressure from the media itself to maintain openness and the freedom of the press.

In January 1986, Museveni had assured journalists of press freedom. Overnight, the streets were inundated with independent newspapers eager to feed a population starved of alternative points of view and genuine news coverage. Between 1986 and 1990, nearly thirty newspapers and magazines were started (Onyango-Obbo 1999a). The press visibly felt freer since Amin's time, when bold investigative journalism earned reporters a trip to the Nile in the trunk of a car. The situation was not much better under the second Obote regime, when, in 1984, eight journalists were arrested and spent nineteen days in Makindye Barracks, where they were tortured and forced to watch killings (Mutono 1994).

Museveni's initial policy of tolerating a relatively free press was a break with such strong-arm practices. A free media flourished, and papers openly criticized the regime. Even government papers were often among the first to break the news about corruption scandals involving government officials—something unheard of during the Obote and Amin regimes. The government-owned *New Vision* under the editorship of William Pike from 1987 to 2006 was a fairly credible source of coverage that provided a range of alternative viewpoints. *New Vision* frequently broke stories involving government scandals but did not always cover the full story, leaving out crucial facts or observations.

However, since the mid-1990s, the number of newspapers has declined considerably and the environment has become more constrained. Whereas Uganda ranked ninth in Africa in press freedom according to the Press Freedom Index in 2002, by 2009 it had fallen to eighteenth place.[5] Increasingly, editors, journalists, photographers, and publishers have faced harassment and detentions, and some publications have been banned, especially in those outlets that do not enjoy the protection of political "godfathers," as one seasoned Ugandan journalist put it (Onyango-Obbo 2008a).

It is not uncommon for journalists to be charged with sedition and later have the charges dropped. Andrew Mwenda, for example, along with two of his colleagues, was arrested in April 2008 and charged with sedition for publishing in his news magazine *The Independent* a story alleging that the army had maimed and killed civilians in northern Uganda. Another photojournalist from another newspaper covering the arrest was apprehended and beaten. Mwenda's case was put on hold indefinitely until the Constitutional Court could rule on the constitutionality of the sedition sections of the Penal Code.

Over the years, police officers have raided the offices of various newspapers and have arrested editors and journalists at publications ranging from *The Monitor,* one of the major independent newspapers, to the *Weekly Observer, The Citizen, The Crusader*, and two Islamic newsletters, *Assalaam* and *The Shariat,* just to name a few. Radio stations have also been raided. Unity FM radio station in Lira was raided by the military during the 2006 elections, and Paul Odonga was arrested for violating the law on no specific charges after he reported that the government was busing in people to a rally for President Museveni. Even the offices of the tabloid *Red Pepper* were set on fire by armed men in July 2008. The paper's editors accused government security forces of the attack since security cameras and the printing press were destroyed but nothing was stolen. They claimed the police were not interested in the security camera footage and did not carry out a serious investigation. They feared they were attacked because of their coverage of military intelligence; indeed, they had been questioned by the Criminal Investigation Department a month earlier about some of their coverage. The minister of information dismissed their allegation and said that because of the nature of their publication, there were many who might have conducted the attack (Committee to Protect Journalists 2008).

During the 2006 election, the Ministry of Information forbade media outlets from running stories on the trial of Besigye, the FDC opposition candidate who was at the time facing what were widely regarded as trumped up charges of terrorism, treason, and rape. Catholic Radio Veritas is constantly threatened with closure for airing interviews with opposition politicians, and other private radio and TV stations are periodically under threat of being closed. For example, NTV was switched off from the Uganda Broadcasting Corporation mast in 2007, allegedly because its equipment did not meet required standards. Radio One moderator Karundi Serumaga was arrested and charged with sedition in 2009 for discussing the causes of the conflict between the Buganda kingdom and the central government. He lost his job on the orders of the Broadcasting Council, which said he was inciting the public. He responded by suing the government for unlawful arrest and loss of employment. Radio Sapientia moderator Geoffrey Ssebagala joined him in suing the government for a similar incident involving his own loss of employment.

Foreign journalists have also been harassed. In 2006, Blake Lambert, a Canadian freelance reporter who had for two years written articles for *The Economist*, the *Christian Science Monitor,* and other major newspapers was not allowed to renew his media accreditation, which is required for a work permit, and was not allowed re-entry into Uganda (Human Rights Watch 2008). Other foreign journalists have faced similar intimidation.

The harassment of media workers takes its toll. While some of the drops in circulation and closures may be tied to competition and natural attrition, there is no doubt that the harassment has had an impact, if only in creating an atmosphere of self-censorship. After 1986, more than thirty magazines and newspapers mushroomed almost overnight. In 1992, the first independent daily after the NRM takeover, *The Monitor,* was launched. By the late 1990s, the number of newspapers had dwindled down to two major outlets: a government paper, *New Vision*, with a circulation of 24,000–30,000, and *The Monitor,* with a circulation of 28,000–35,000 (Onyango-Obbo 1999a and 1999b). By 2009, these were still the newspapers with the highest circulation; however, two other important independent publications, the *Weekly Observer* and *The Independent* magazine had also emerged alongside the Nairobi-based weekly newspaper *The East African*. There are also four local-language newspapers and a handful of smaller papers. Part of the attrition can be attributed to financial considerations and competition; however, some newspapers folded after facing court battles with the state.

Radio outlets, in contrast, have grown to about ninety licensed stations throughout the country, with two stations broadcasting nationally: the government-owned Uganda Broadcasting Corporation and the privately owned Star FM. Most privately owned stations are owned by individuals close to the government or in the government, according to a report by the East African Media Institute.[6] This may explain why the radio stations have had a somewhat easier time than the print media. The major source of information is the radio, with 48 percent of households owning a radio. However, the minister of information has slapped radio stations with prohibitive licensing and registration fees. Private broadcasters are required to air anything the government deems to be in the national interest within short notice. In 2002, the minister banned popular call-in talk shows (*ekimeeza*) aired from bars and restaurants, but the ban has been ignored.

The Ugandan courts have come to the defense of journalists on more than one occasion. In 2004, in a landmark case, the Supreme Court ruled that a legal provision that allowed journalists to be charged with a criminal offense for "publishing a false statement, rumor, or a report which is likely to cause fear or alarm to the public" was unconstitutional. The ruling was the result of a legal challenge when the editors of *The Monitor* newspaper printed a story in 1997 about the late president of Democratic Republic of Congo, Laurent-Désiré Kabila.

Two prominent Ugandan journalists, the aforementioned Andrew Mwenda and Charles Onyango-Obbo, challenged the sedition clauses in the penal code and took their case to the Constitutional Court, arguing that the sedition law under sections 39 and 40 of the penal code violates the constitutional provision for freedom of expression. Already section 50 of the Penal

Code Act, criminalizing the publication of false news, has been ruled unconstitutional ("Uganda's Media Clampdown" 2008).

However, existing and proposed legislation pose constant challenges to the media. The Press and Journalists Statute of 1995 restricts media workers. On November 12, 1999, about a hundred journalists demonstrated and petitioned parliament to demand that the government respect press freedom and repeal this repressive law, which was strangling the press. The statute met fierce opposition from journalists and parliamentarians alike because it gave the Ministry of Information the power to license journalists annually and to appoint members of the Media Council, which, through disciplinary measures, would regulate and enforce journalists' conduct. Similar efforts were underway in other parts of Africa to regulate media workers. Media workers in Angola, Botswana, Chad, Gambia, Kenya, Nigeria, South Africa, and Zambia debated existing or proposed bills regulating the media over the past several years. These bills, which sought to regulate and discipline journalists and media workers and oversee their registration, were widely rejected on the grounds that they restricted the freedom of speech.

Opposition to the media bill in Uganda came from all quarters, including the government's Law Reform Commission and the Uganda Human Rights Commission, on the grounds that it was unconstitutional. Even the deputy editor-in-chief of the government's paper, *New Vision,* argued against the bill, saying, "At this point in our history we need [fewer] laws and more freedom for development" (Wasike 1995). The head of the Uganda Journalists Association argued that the statute contained "draconian provisions which infringe on media freedom" ("UJA Rejects Act" 1998). In a 2004 survey of journalists carried out by the Uganda Media Development Foundation together with the Konrad Adenauer Foundation, 95 percent reported that they felt they needed more press freedom. More than 81 percent said they did not cover some stories because they feared for their personal safety; others feared pressure from law enforcement, security agencies, or government officials, while still others feared prosecution or simply failure to access information. In spite of such complaints about press freedom, in 2005 the government formed its own Media Centre to monitor and vet media licenses, something journalists fiercely opposed.

The government then proposed in 2010 an amendment to the 1995 Ugandan Press and Journalist Act, which if passed, would require newspapers to renew their licenses annually and forbid them from publishing material considered "detrimental to national security, stability and unity" (Mulondo 2010). Journalists worried that it would provide authorities sweeping powers to limit the flow of information and restrict public debate at a key moment leading up to the 2011 elections.

The Anti-Terrorism Act of 2002 is another law that severely restricts the media.[7] Under this law, radio stations in Uganda can be closed down for hosting terrorists on their talk shows. This ruling was used to prevent radio stations from speaking to opposition leader Colonel Kizza Besigye, who apparently was considered a terrorist by the government at the time of the 2006 election. Those convicted of violating the law face up to ten years' imprisonment or death by hanging. Museveni had said this ban was necessary because most stations were focusing on criticizing the government and poisoning people's minds (Muhangi 2002). "The Anti-Terrorism Act clearly was designed with the media in mind; it criminalizes what would appear to be basic functions of the media, putting journalists in a very precarious situation," explains Dr. George Lugalambi, head of the mass communication department at Makerere University.[8]

As of 2008, there were about 2.5 million Internet users and 8.6 million cell phones in Uganda, a country with a population of over 32 million.[9] Usage is growing rapidly, which suggests that this may rapidly become another area of contention regarding rights. Internet restrictions are limited, however; a political gossip Web site, Radio Katwe, was banned in 2006.

Thus, the media in Uganda, which was once regarded as one of the freest in Africa, can no longer be regarded as free. The arbitrariness and unpredictability with which the government restricts media workers limits true freedom of the press and makes for a precarious industry. In spite of the constraints, media workers are at the forefront of the civil society struggles for autonomy from government control and freedom of expression.

Freedom of Association: Political Parties

In many African countries, civil society and political society have been agents of political change. One of the factors preventing further political reform in Uganda and elsewhere has been the weakness of political parties as well as civil society, which faces similar political constraints. In many countries, the opposition parties are too numerous, fractured, and personality driven to pose a credible challenge to the ruling party. Not only are they frequently infiltrated by ruling party operatives, but they must often contend with the co-optation of leading members and the creation of fake opposition parties by the ruling party.

The existing parties in Uganda, for example, while providing important critiques of the NRM, do not generally represent a new cadre of leaders. The leaders of the FDC are former members of the NRM. The UPC, which has been divided, carries the problematic legacy of Obote on its shoulders and has not redefined itself. The DP is similarly divided. Government policies, as seen in Chapter 3, have not allowed sufficient political space for the development of political parties and have actively sought to destabilize them, making the price of participation in political parties too high, given that party leaders have had to live in fear of harassment, intimidation, and death. Some of the parties have been plagued with divisions and leaders have been subject to co-optation by the NRM, making them less attractive to voters. The weakness of parties is not limited to the opposition. The NRM itself appears to be suffering from a lack of internal democracy, which is endemic in semiauthoritarian states. Its own internal democracy has steadily worsened since the NRM first took over Uganda. One founding member of the NRM, James Magode Ikuya, has described his experience at a 2006 NRM congress that launched the NRM as an official party thus:

> Previously, the NRM had been born as a liberation organisation. It had been incisive in its hatred of injustice. It intoned the dreams of our people for dignity and freedom. It articulated the fullest empowerment of the people. It stressed that without this, there could be no guarantee that the basic direction and priorities of the country would be set by them. In addition, it emphasised the paramount need for the cultivation of a visible culture of leadership in genuine service of the population, free from all forms of corruption and abuse of power.
>
> I was struck that the meeting of the esteemed promoters of the NRM was not imbued with [many] of these ideals. Instead the preoccupation seemed to be designing the positioning and placement in the future of the country of professional politics-stars. Their main talk was [about] candidature and funding of them. It appeared that the scene had been specially set for the politicians' paradise to share the carcass amongst those who were craving for public offices.
>
> Since then, there [have] not been any activities of the main organs of the NRM. Only the parliamentary caucus has occasionally met, being made to marshal through some government pet legislative programmes or to vent out the personal bickering of the MPs themselves. There are numerous complaints by party members and officials that even the party's Secretary General cannot be accessed.
>
> The NRM as a whole is glaringly denied political life, its affairs being dispensed in eerie secrecy and mainly by the sheer chivalry and grace of a few people from on high. The effect of this is a depressive curtailment of popular participation and morale in running the country. ("NRM Historical Attacks Party" 2007)

A new chapter may finally be emerging in the tale of Uganda's political parties. The Inter Party Cooperation was formed in 2008, involving the five opposition parties with parliamentary seats (FDC, DP, UPC, Justice Forum of Uganda or JEEMA, and CP). The DP eventually dropped out of the agreement. The remaining four parties sought to come to agreement on the electoral, constitutional, and political reforms that were necessary to level the playing field before the 2011 general elections. They sought a joint electoral platform and joint candidates and pooled resources to achieve their common ends. Their goal was to create conditions for a genuine multiparty system that would allow them to compete independently in the 2016 elections (Oguttu 2009). For the first time there was the possibility of mounting a credible challenge to NRM dominance.

Freedom of Assembly

The record on freedom of assembly has also slowly improved with the introduction of multipartyism, but limits persist. The 1995 constitution allowed for freedom of assembly, but in practice this freedom was limited, since political rallies, demonstrations, NGO assemblies and party conferences were banned. The 2007 Police Act further restricted public assemblies by allowing the inspector general of police to stop a public rally, demonstration, or procession. A 2008 Constitutional Court ruling eventually overturned these restrictions on assembly and allowed police to regulate but not prohibit rallies. Nevertheless, security forces have continued to disperse and arrest various demonstrators on the grounds that they believed the actions might turn violent. Most of those targeted after the Constitutional Court ruling were members of opposition parties.

Freedom of Association: Civil Society

The Museveni regime initially allowed for greater freedom of association, especially compared with previous governments. In 1993, two authors of a report on nongovernmental organizations (NGOs) to the Ministry of Finance and Economic Planning observed, "The NRM government has certainly, whether by design or by default, allowed NGOs a great deal of freedom. . . . The last seven years are seen against the background of the preceding ten, when formation of groups and associations was severely repressed by regimes fearful of subversion and intolerant of opposition" (Kwesiga and Ratter 1993, 18–19).

The number of new NGOs has mushroomed since 1986. Some interest groups, like women's rights groups, have organized vigorously and have been able to influence policy in some cases. Independent organizations have emerged in a wide variety of sectors in Uganda, as is evident in the proliferation of coalitions of NGOs around land, debt, hunger, and poverty. Donor funding gave added impetus to the NGO sector. As long as NGOs veered away from engaging in activities that were deemed too political, they were able to operate. But those engaged in advocacy faced restrictions. Some had their workshops closed down; others experienced difficulties registering or were threatened with closure. While not pervasive, the restrictions were enough to keep them wary of what they said and did publicly.

Some civil society actors were explicitly warned against becoming too political. For example, some religious institutions have criticized the government's use of violence against the opposition. The Uganda Joint Christian Council and many other organizations openly opposed the third-term presidency (Kyamutetera and Mugarura 2003). This stance prompted Museveni to warn the churches not to make political statements but to focus on spiritual affairs. He reminded them that religious leaders were prohibited from being active in politics.

The government attempted to create numerous state-sponsored or state-controlled organizations, including women's councils, youth councils, and the Uganda National Students' Association, in lieu of independent ones, and it heavily influenced others, such as the Uganda Public Employees Union, Uganda Medical Workers Union, and Uganda Civil Servants Union (Mujaju 1997, 49). The government also systematically undermined the strength of the cooperatives and trade unions. In 1986, 80 percent of the labor force was unionized; today, only 20 percent remains unionized. Similarly, cooperative societies, which had about 500,000 members, have virtually disappeared (Sebunya 2003). As described in Chapter 5, parent-teacher associations, which emerged in the thousands in the 1960s and took over the running of the schools under Idi Amin, were banned in 1996, although many resurfaced in the urban areas. Prior to 1996, over 90 percent of the funding for the schools—including money for salaries, furniture, educational materials, and building and equipment maintenance—came from parent-teacher associations.

For years, the government tried to impose heavy-handed legislative restrictions on NGOs. In spite of strong protests from NGOs and donor countries, parliament eventually passed a restrictive Non-Governmental Organisations (NGOs) Registration Act in 2006. NGOs opposed the domination of the NGO board by government officials and security agents; the act's stipulation that NGOs need to register on an annual basis; and the board's powers to deregister an NGO for violating any law. They felt this act gave the board too much control that could be used for political purposes and that it undermined associational autonomy.

As leader of the Development Network of Indigenous Voluntary Organizations (DENIVA), a coalition of NGOs, Jassy Kwesiga has reflected on one of the core concerns of NGO activists: "As for denial of registration on the basis of incompatibility with government policy, plans and public interest, what if the NGOs are expressing the will of the people that may be at odds with government policy and government definition of public interest? History in Uganda and elsewhere is full of many state inspired undemocratic misfortunes in the name of public interest." Rather, he argued, state and society need to respect the "independence, rights and obligations of the other" (Kwesiga 2001).

Many associations worried that this legislation challenged their capacity to function and feared that it would have a crippling effect on ordinary advocacy, which might unnecessarily be perceived as antigovernmental. For example, when the NGO Forum was denied registration, the NGO board said it believed the organization was a political party. The NGO Forum was concerned with poverty and believed the government should have worked with it to come up with the best antipoverty policies. According to one of its leaders at the time, "They say, 'But some of you are using this for a political agenda.' I wish you could define politics, because for me it seems that whatever we do is politics. Our political agenda is to advance the status quo in this country and we cannot stop talking. But they said 'You are being a political party.'"[10]

As a result of the many concerns regarding the NGO Registration Act, the government eventually established a committee to review the act, which was temporarily suspended. The struggle over NGO registration is not unique to Uganda. These types of issues have animated civil society and transformed state-society relations throughout Africa, particularly in semiauthoritarian countries. In the late 1980s and 1990s, NGOs found themselves fighting for the right to autonomy while opposing governmental efforts to monitor and control NGO activities in Tanzania, Botswana, Ghana, Kenya, Malawi, Zambia, Zimbabwe, Uganda, and other countries (Bratton 1989, 577; Gyimah-Boadi 1998, 22; Ndegwa 1996). In the mid-2000s, governmental efforts to regulate NGOs, which had largely stalled in the previous decade, were revived.

Nevertheless, NGOs have continued to mobilize. Since 2000, NGOs have responded to a series of environmental challenges on a scale not seen in the 1990s, from Uganda to Nigeria and Côte d'Ivoire. When the Ugandan government granted a request by the Mehta Group's Sugar Cooperation of Uganda to take over 7,100 hectares of the Mabira Forest Reserve to expand its sugarcane plantation and double sugar production, a broad coalition of NGOs protested the move. They forced the cabinet to halt the proposed giveaway of the forest until a policy was developed to determine the use of such land.

Another area where there has been considerable activism has been in the women's movement. Uganda went from a situation in which women had virtually no visibility in politics to one in which the country had a woman vice president, one-third female representation in parliament, and one-third female representation at the local level. Women were visible in key government appointments. Antirape legislation was passed in 1992. Women's organizations were active in the constitution-writing process and were able to get extensive clauses on women and gender equality into the constitution. The women's movement was able to get an affirmative action policy in place in the university. It also influenced school curricula to include gender concerns in sex education classes, which was important, given the high rates of HIV infection. In 2006, women's organizations were instrumental in the passage of the Disability Act, which was moved as a private-member bill to provide for equal opportunities in education and employment for people with disabilities. The movement around disabilities in Uganda was an offshoot of and has been closely related to the women's movement.

Women's rights activists have also been vocal around a number of other major pieces of legislation. They lobbied for legislative and policy changes regarding issues of inheritance and property rights, land rights, domestic violence, trafficking, disabled women's rights, female genital cutting, and numerous other issues affecting women and other politically marginalized people. An active Gender and Growth Assessment Coalition is at the forefront of a lobbying and advocacy initiative around issues of women's access to land and finance, the reform of labor laws, and commercial justice.

Although some of these issues have brought the women's movement into conflict with Museveni's NRM, one might argue that a high level of interest-group activity by women has been tolerated because women as a group have for a long time been among the staunchest supporters of the NRM. Many women initially endorsed the NRM because of its antisectarian stance, believing that sectarianism would lead to the return of civil conflict. They also were encouraged by the NRM's support of women's advancement politically, economically, educationally, and in other areas. It is widely acknowledged that women voted heavily in support of Museveni in the 1996 presidential elections; however, that support has been waning since then, especially after the government withdrew support of an amendment to the 1998 Land Act that would have provided the right to spousal co-ownership of land. In 2006, the government finally shelved a Domestic Relations Act, which had been in the works for more than two decades. As a result, some women leaders began aligning themselves with opposition parties, disaffected with the Museveni regime. A series of demonstrations by an active Inter Party Cooperation women's group drew media attention, particularly a February 2010 protest of the reappointment of the Electoral Commission, which had overlooked alleged irregularities in the 2006 election. The demonstrators were brutally attacked by police, resulting in thirty-two arrests.

To shore up diminishing support, the Museveni government passed a law in 2006 to establish the Equal Opportunities Commission, which was mandated by the 1995 constitution to implement policies regarding women's rights. The number of maternity leave days was increased from forty-five to sixty ("Struggle for Equal Status" 2007). In 2007, a constitutional court struck down key provisions of the Succession Act, regarding women's right to inherit property. The law was found to be discriminatory and unconstitutional because it did not allow a woman to inherit property of a deceased person, including her husband. In a related ruling, the court also decriminalized adultery because the law, as it stood, discriminated against women. It penalized a married woman for having sex with any man but did not penalize a married man for having sex with an unmarried woman.

In 2009, three pieces of women's rights legislation were advanced with backing from women's rights organizations. The Domestic Violence Bill was passed along with the Anti-Female Genital Mutilation Bill, which primarily affected the Sebei in eastern Uganda, where the practice had been dying out as a result of efforts by women's and health organizations. Women activists were also pressing for the Marriage and Divorce Bill, which banned men from inheriting widows as wives, forced pregnancy, and forced marriages and set the age of marriage at eighteen. It required the courts to divide wealth between a couple in the event of divorce and made bride price nonrefundable. The bill also replaced bride wealth with the giving of nonmandatory gifts. Even cohabiting couples would be required to share the wealth accumulated in the time they stayed together. Spouses or cohabitees could, however, come up with an alternative agreement with respect to the ownership and distribution of property on dissolution of the marriage or cohabitation.

Thus, the experiences of the environmental and women's movements illustrate both the possibilities and the constraints of collective action in a hybrid regime.

Conclusion

A decade after the passage of the 1995 constitution, Uganda adopted a multiparty system. It is only by understanding the broader historical and legislative context that one can explain why, after such enormous effort went into building up a no-party system, the NRM finally relented and opted for a multiparty system. Parliamentarians were forced to make a Faustian bargain, agreeing to lift presidential term limits in exchange for a move toward multipartyism. In other words, the executive office was strengthened in the process and positioned to control the electoral process in the future. The NRM opened up to multipartyism, not because it wished to encourage open competition but because in so doing it could ensure that it would win future elections and maintain its dominant political position with greater legitimacy and credibility. The opening allowed it to operate and develop more freely as the party it had already become. Meanwhile, unfavorable conditions limited the possibilities for growth and development of opposition parties. The UPC and the DP are weaker today than they were in 1994. Both are wracked with internal problems of accountability, opportunism, and infighting. The major opposition party, the FDC, has also suffered from divisions, and its members have been harassed, intimidated, tortured, hounded, or forced to flee the country for fear of their lives. At the same time, the new coalition that has been formed between all but one of the major parties suggests that there may be some new, forward-looking strategies emerging.

To understand how such undemocratic outcomes could emerge from a constitution-making process that was touted as unprecedented in its participatory character, one needs to examine the broader context within which the constitution was drafted, debated, and voted on. It is especially important to look at the relationship between the process and the outcomes because it was the Constituent Assembly elections in 1994 that marked the end of the broad-based coalition that had characterized the ruling NRM and the beginning of the era in which the NRM acted as a de facto single party under an increasingly authoritarian rule. Ultimately, however, the NRM's efforts to entrench itself through the constitution and various pieces of legislation became subordinated to the even more important goal of expanding executive power and staying in power.

The goal of remaining in power superseded concerns for freedom of speech, freedom of association, political freedoms, and even human rights. It became more important than the independence of the legislature and the judiciary. The continuing challenges to the freedoms of association and speech combined with the corruption of the legislature and other state institutions have hurt the development of civil society, political parties, the legislature, and the judiciary. All democratization measures have been controlled by the regime, which has been limiting political space and centralizing power since the mid-1990s, both within the Movement itself and within the country. The system that has resulted has kept one person in power for more than two decades and limited the possibilities for the development of a truly competitive electoral system and loyal opposition. Ironically, in order to shrink the political arena, the leadership had to expand its boundaries in a way that would suppress innocuous civil society advocacy and press freedom.

Notes

1. "A new element was introduced into our parliamentary methods of work, whereby the legislators of a particular persuasion, namely the NRM, were given large sums of money outside their normal remuneration in order to 'facilitate' their voting for some proposals, particularly the removal of presidential term limits." ("Constitution Has Become a Temporary Document!" 2005; "When the Loan Shark Comes Knocking" 2005).

2. Many of the following sections are adapted from Tripp (2010).

3. As we have noted, the historicals are NRM members who were given parliamentary seats in recognition of their role in the guerrilla war that brought Museveni into power.

4. The Coalition Against Torture includes the Public Defenders Association of Uganda, the Human Rights Network, the Uganda Discharged Prisoners Aid Society, the Foundation for Human Rights Initiative, the Refugee Law Project, the African Centre for Treatment and Rehabilitation of Torture Victims, the Human Rights Focus, the Kumi Human Rights Initiative, and the Association of Human Rights Organizations in the Rwenzori Region.

5. Press Freedom Index, http://en.rsf.org/press-freedom-index-2009,1001.html. Accessed April 27, 2010.

6. Committee to Protect Journalists, http://cpj.org/2009/02/attacks-on-the-press-in-2008-uganda.php.

7. Section 11 of the Anti-Terrorism Act of 2002 states, "Any person who . . . willfully arranges or assists in the arrangement of a meeting to be addressed by a person belonging or professing to belong to a terrorist organisation . . . commits an offence."

8. Media Channel, http://www.mediachannel.org/wordpress/2008/07/10/ugandas-media-clampdown-part-of-regressive-regional-trend. Accessed July 9, 2009.

9. Central Intelligence Agency, *World Factbook*, https://www.cia.gov/library/publications/the-world-factbook/geos/ug.htmlhttps://www.cia.gov/library/publications/the-world-factbook/geos/UG.html. Accessed April 27, 2010.

10. Interview with author, June 15, 2001.

5

Participation, Patronage, and Power in Local Politics

The National Resistance Movement (NRM) has used both violence and patronage to establish itself. Because of the democratic impulse within semiauthoritarian regimes, the relationship among the NRM, the government, and the grassroots is established primarily through mechanisms that are noncoercive, which basically have to do with patronage. One way in which the NRM came to assert its dominance was through the central government's relationships with local government, historic kingdoms, and local associations. The objectives were somewhat different in each case, but they are indicative of the various strategies the NRM has used to build its power base by creating vertical relations between the center and the regions. In the process, horizontal relations between societal actors have been suppressed or constrained, as we saw in Chapter 4. The development of political parties and civil society faced limits and the media was harassed.

Relations with local government have been an extremely important part of NRM control of rural areas, which have been a major base of electoral support for Museveni and the NRM. In the 2006 local elections, the NRM claimed about 80 percent of local council (LC) positions, while the Forum for Democratic Change (FDC) won about 10 percent of the seats, in contrast with its much larger gains in the 2006 presidential election of 37 percent ("Local Council Achievements and Failures in 2006" 2007).

This chapter explores the NRM's relations with local government and kingdoms, showing the common imperatives behind the relations. Through the local government, the NRM sought to build a patronage network that would serve it well during elections. A variety of mechanisms were used to expand the network, including (1) control of district-level appointments, (2) the use of central government funds, (3) the use of tender boards responsible for awarding contracts and tax collection rights, and (4) the appointment of staff and district civil servants through district-level commissions.

As a result, most local councillors today are NRM supporters. So prevalent is the use of these councillors as agents during elections and for other purposes that the NRM barely disguises the machine it has created. In 2004, the national political commissar openly urged the district chairs and mayors to campaign for the lifting of presidential term limits (Tangri and Mwenda 2005). The resident district commissioners were especially important during elections, when they reportedly served as political mobilizers for the NRM and prevented non-NRM supporters from campaigning (Green 2005, 217). Even though candidates were to restrict themselves to campaigning as individuals rather than as members of a political party at the local level, this was not the practice. Elliott Green cites a *New Vision* article from August 14, 2004:

> Geoffrey Ekanya (Tororo) and Miria Matembe (Mbarara) said resident district commissioners were barring politicians including anti-Movement MPs from holding meetings. Matembe said RDCs [resident district commissioners] had taken on the role of parroting instead of monitoring or overseeing developments by local governments on behalf of the Government. "If you are not carrying *mashansha* [dry banana leaves, a symbol of the third term for presidency], the RDC hates you," she said. (Green 2005, 217–218)

It was widely believed that LC executives at the village level were "facilitated" prior to the elections to garner votes for the NRM ("NRM Thrives on Rented Support" 2007).

In spite of these efforts to control electoral outcomes at the local level, the NRM machine was not ubiquitous, nor was it the only party that mobilized votes. In Kampala, for example, most of the top leaders of the LCs have belonged to the Democratic Party (DP), including the mayor. However, as the ruling party, the NRM certainly had greater advantages in strengthening its position through the LC system in the rest of the country and in continuing to fuse the NRM and the state.

This chapter also shows how NRM policy toward Buganda reflects the way that the center relates to the regions within Uganda. Knowing that it needed to reach some kind of accord with the kingdom of Buganda, the NRM ended up pursuing an unhappy arrangement in order to avoid granting Buganda the federal status it sought. First, it granted all kingdoms in Uganda cultural but not political power, then it offered them a relationship within the decentralization framework, and finally it attempted to insert the kingdoms into a five-tier local government scheme. All of these compromises were rejected by the kingdom of Buganda, whose support the NRM has needed to stay in power.

Local Government

A key strategy of the NRM for maintaining control and meeting its partisan objectives has been the creation and maintenance of a patronage network within the popular governance structure of LCs. Decentralization, which has had many benefits at the local level, also connected the districts and the center in a way that kept the former beholden to latter and the NRM in particular. The weak commitment to seeing decentralization through is evident in the closing of the Decentralisation Secretariat in 2004 as it was deemed that the process was complete. The secretariat had been formed in 1992 within the Ministry of Local Government and was ended midstream in a process that ultimately had little to do with real distribution of power and resources from the center to the districts. Moreover, ministries themselves have been reluctant to transfer staff and functions to local government, given the low salaries and poor work conditions in local government compared with the public service (Mitchinson 2003, 247). Uganda's administrative districts are shown in Figure 5.1.

Background

Initially the NRM created local Resistance Councils (RCs) throughout the country, patterned along the lines of the village RCs that had been established during the guerrilla war in Luwero to facilitate communication between the NRA and the population. They recruited fighters for the NRA, maintained administrative control, evacuated conflict zones of civilians, and provided food and water to displaced peoples and fighters (Tideman 1994, 26, 29). With the 1995 constitution, the RCs were renamed Local Councils (LCs). To avoid confusion in this chapter, the councils are referred to as LCs even for the years prior to 1995.

The 1987 Resistance Councils and Committees Statute established the initial LC structure as part of a new system of local government. Briefly, Local Council 1 was made up of the entire adult population of the village, which elected nine members to the LC1 committee. Each committee elected two members to form the LC2 parish council, which in turn elected a committee of nine. The pattern repeated itself at the LC3 (subcounty or *gombolola*), LC4 (county), and LC5 (district) levels. The LC4 had generally been inactive, but together with the LC3 it formed the electoral college for the National Resistance Council (NRC) elections. Alongside this structure at the LC5 level at this time was the district administrator, a presidential appointee, and the district executive secretary, an appointee of the minister of local government.

This council system was initially conceived as a forum for popular democratic participation and local governance, giving local communities greater control of their own affairs with relatively little interference from central gov-

Figure 5.1   Map of Uganda's Administrative Districts

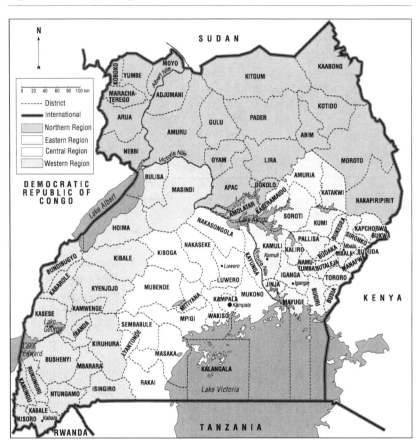

Credit: Eva Swantz

ernment. It marked a break with the past system of local government through centrally appointed district commissioners. The LCs could make and enforce local bylaws, settle civil cases and customary land disputes, and embark on local self-help projects (Burkey 1991, 11). They were seen as an engine for rural development.

Outside commentators often described the council system favorably as a generator of democracy (Furley 2000; Karlström 1999; Tideman 1994; Villadsen 1996). A 2000 World Bank report praised the LCs for giving power to people at the grassroots to choose their own leaders. Uganda's decentralization policies were applauded for going further than most African countries, winning greater donor approval (Langseth 1996, 1, 19).

In the early years after the NRM takeover, the LCs were highly popular and their meetings were well attended. However, this level of involvement tapered off with time. In 1991, Ingvild Burkey reported that LC meetings at the 1 and 2 levels had relatively low turnout. She attributed this to the onerous duties that were demanded of the LCs without commensurate power, authority, and autonomy in decisionmaking (1991, 12). No doubt the limited compensation to councillors also may have dampened enthusiasm for some LC activities. According to Frederick Golooba-Mutebi's 2004 study, by the late 1990s, the participatory element of the LCs had all but disappeared in Rakai and Mukono, and other studies from other parts of the country show similar results (see also Uganda Participatory Poverty Assessment Project 2001). However, while the participatory dimension may have declined, other aspects of LC performance remained and may have improved over time.

A 2005 Afrobarometer survey revealed continuing support for the LC system, with councillors at the LC1 level winning positive ratings for their performance from 92 percent of the respondents, while LC5 leaders received positive ratings from 52 percent of the population. Two-thirds (67 percent) thought that LC leaders were accountable to the community. The district councils were regarded more favorably than they had been five years earlier in the first round of the Afrobarometer survey.

In the 2005 Afrobarometer survey, at least 77 percent saw improvement in the LC5's delivery of primary education services, 69 percent felt the same with respect to primary health care services, 64 percent with respect to the construction and maintenance of feeder roads, 54 percent with respect to water and sanitation efforts, and 46 percent in the area of agricultural services.[1] The Afrobarometer findings parallel the more detailed findings of the 2004 National Service Delivery Survey, which discovered that 61 percent of households throughout the country regarded the performance of village councils as good and 26 percent as fair, whereas only 38 percent thought that subcounty councils performed well, with 23 percent believing that they performed fairly.[2] Even Golooba-Mutebi's 2004 study, which was critical of the local LCs as vehicles of popular participation, found that they met with approval in specific areas like keeping law and order and resolving disputes.

Although the decentralization of power and the institutionalization of local councils became vital measures in enhancing local control and decisionmaking, the extent to which they were also intended to subsume all local participation blurred the lines of accountability and narrowed the fora for popular participation. The focus on the LCs as the main vehicles for popular participation also limited interest group formation and coalition building, but more importantly, it enhanced the political monopoly of the NRM and, in fact, became a key mechanism linking the NRM to the grassroots.

As Mamdani (1988, 1993, 1994) and Ddungu (1989) have pointed out, the focus on the councils delayed the emergence and development of political parties that could coalesce various societal interests. They limited possibilities for making politics issue-oriented by basing electoral contestation on personality rather than platform. This often shifted the focus of elections toward clan, ethnic, and religious identification. Moreover, the LCs limited the freedom of assembly and expression by making residence the main basis for political participation.

The LCs served as organs of the people, the state, and the NRM—all in the same instance. This created a certain ambiguity in their purpose and function. As organs of the people, they were intended to be the key vehicle for popular participation and were expected to hold civil servants and the state accountable to the people. At the same time, the LCs were under the jurisdiction of the Ministry of Local Government, acting as extensions of central government. And finally, prior to multipartyism, they served as the political organ of the NRM, which was supposed to be a substitute for political parties by containing members of all parties and political leanings within the Movement (Burkey 1991, 5; Ddungu 1989; Mamdani 1988).

The LC system received a boost with the launching of the Local Government Decentralisation Programme in October 1992. This decentralization policy was part of a larger program of administrative, political, economic, and juridical reform (James, Francis, and Pereza 2001). Considerable responsibilities were devolved to the district—for example, primary and secondary education, health services, and water services. Urban councils were to be in charge of street lighting, ambulance services, and fire brigade services (Steiner 2006). Authority for security, foreign affairs, the judicial system, fiscal and economic policies, the administration of universities and hospitals, and other national concerns remained with central government. The 1993 Local Government (Resistance Councils) Statute provided for the transfer of power and resources to local governments and attempted to define a structure of LCs as distinct from the NRM resistance council framework. The 1995 constitution elaborated on the roles of various local government positions and included the provision that 30 percent of all local government positions be held by women.

This was further specified in the 1997 Local Government Act, which replaced the district administrator with the LC5 chairman as the chief administrative officer and head of the District Development Committee. The district executive secretary (DES) became responsible to the LC5 rather than to the Ministry of Local Government. The Local Government Act made the LC3 the basic political and administrative unit of local government, while the LC5 was the highest level of local government that was tied to central government. Technical personnel were posted at this level to administer agricultural extension, veterinary services, fisheries, educational provisioning, and health services. The act provided for holding direct elections for the LC3 and LC5 representatives rather than using an electoral college system. It also ensured that women made up one-third of the council and that special councillors representing youth and the disabled were selected through electoral colleges at the LC3 and LC5 levels. The LC1 and LC2 were to decide how to use development funds at the local level, and they were involved in settling minor community-level disputes.

Even though power was devolved, central government maintained control of the purse strings. A president-appointed Local Government Finance Commission was created to vet proposals from the LC1 and LC2 for funding from the local governments, allowing it to privilege the poorer districts. Conditional grants were made to improve infrastructure, including schools, clinics, water supplies, toilets, roads, and production projects. This allowed communities to identify and prioritize their particular needs and address them directly. While the design and implementation project was to be carried out by the district, municipal, or divisional staff, the LC1 and LC2 local councillors and executives formed project management committees to supervise the projects. Local contractors and labor were to be used for the projects, and local communities were required to contribute 10 percent of the costs. However, at the end of the day, the resources were controlled at the center.

The LCs remained an important institution since they became a key mechanism through which the Movement built its patronage machinery. They did this in several ways: through control of political appointments, through budgetary control, and through the allocation of tenders and appointments to the District Service Commission, as detailed below.

Control of Political Appointments

Although the 1997 Local Government Act removed central government from control of the district chairmanship, it nevertheless maintained control of key governance mechanisms. The president directly appoints the RDC, who represents the government and the president in the district and advises the district chairperson. The chief administrative officers are appointed by and report to the LC5; however, the central government can influence these appointments (and has done so), because it controls the funding of district administration. Such political appointments ensure political control is maintained. These are generally not people with experience in administration; their main qualification is their allegiance to the NRM.

Various measures were introduced to strengthen local ties to the center by narrowing channels of authority. For example, two amendments to the Local Government Act were passed in 2001, which stipulated that only the LC1 chairperson would be elected, and he/she would nominate five out of the eight other members, leaving the remaining positions to be selected as before via elections for women, youth, and people with disabilities.

In the case of Kampala, the cabinet approved a bill to take over the city due to mismanagement and corruption. Kampala was to be run by a chief executive officer appointed by the president, while the mayor would be elected by the LC5 councillors of Kampala and would function only as a ceremonial or political head of the district. The mayor would not be directly elected, as had been the case, but would be selected through an electoral college. The plan, which was adopted by parliament, was vigorously opposed by Buganda's administration in Mengo, which saw it as a thinly veiled attempt by the government to implement the regional tier system of government, which the Buganda kingdom rejected in 2006 in favor of its own federal system (see the section on kingdoms to come).

Budgetary Control

A second way the NRM has used the LC system to build its power base and control the structures of patronage is through taxation and funding of local government. The 1997 Local Government Act created a formal structure of revenue collection in which the LC3 at the subcounty level collected revenue and gave 35 percent to the district, keeping the remaining 65 percent. The retained funds in turn were distributed to the LC1 and LC2 levels. The local governments gained revenue from graduated personal taxes, market dues, property taxes, and parking fees and permits, all of which are difficult to collect and yield low returns because of their unpopularity (Green 2005, 222). The tax was widely criticized as retrogressive. Some complained that they were unfairly assessed and overtaxed, while others were critical of the way payment was enforced, namely by apprehending alleged defaulters ("Local Govts Revenues Fall After Tax Confusion" 2004).

During the 2001 presidential campaigns, the graduated tax was cut to USh 3,000 (US$2.40); in 2005, prior to the 2006 presidential elections, the tax was eliminated altogether. Taxes on *boda-boda* (bicycle taxis) and market dues were also scrapped to garner votes, but this seriously undermined the little capacity LCs had to provide services like garbage collection. In 2005 and 2006, for example, local governments had expected to collect USh 80 billion (US$46 million) through such taxes, but central government promised them only USh 35 billion (US$20 million) to compensate for their losses as a result of the elimination of the tax. In the end, central government delivered only USh 25 billion (US$14.4 million) to the districts. By 2008, the situation had not changed, as the promised allocations had risen to only USh 33 billion (US$20 million) (Agaba 2007).[3] The elimination of the graduated personal tax was done as a pure political ploy, without consideration of district budgets and planning. No doubt it had a fruitful political impact on votes, given how unpopular taxes were. But at the same time, it undermined efforts to create a culture whereby citizens paid for the services that they received. Moreover, it made the districts even more reliant on the center. Today, about 90 percent of the local government budget comes from central government, and

27 percent of the overall national budget goes to local government (Steiner 2006). Because of the way tax revenue is collected and allocated in the districts, there is increasingly greater reliance on central administration resources. Nevertheless, these resources are subject to cuts and are not fully disbursed, nor are they evenly disbursed. Moreover, most of these resources remain at the district level, with little of the revenue collected there trickling down to the other levels of local administration.

Because of the politicized nature of the funding provided to the districts, very little is spent on infrastructure, sewage and water systems, fire prevention, and other such long-term objectives. Moreover, there has been little effort to educate administrators on their duties and responsibilities; as a result, a large number are not fully aware of their mandate. Many are poorly educated and do not have the requisite skills to perform their duties. In short, the commitment to developing local administration is extremely weak.

Another, perhaps more dramatic consequence of the dependence on the center for funding was that it created incentives for communities and ethnic groups to press for their own districts in order to access resources (Mwenda 2007b). Thus, a country that had thirty-three districts in 1990 had increased its number of districts to ninety-seven by 2009, creating new jobs and opportunities for patronage.

Tenders

A third mechanism of control and influence has been the tender boards, which are responsible for awarding contracts and tax collection rights. Levels of corruption became so high that measures ostensibly had to be taken to enhance transparency and accountability in service procurement in local governments ("Contract Committees to Replace Tender Board" 2005). In 2005, the cabinet approved an amendment to the Local Government Act that would replace tender boards with local government contract committees appointed by the chief administrative officers rather than by the LCs, thus bringing them more directly under central control and creating yet another realignment of channels of patronage to flow from the center to the localities.

The use of tenders for political patronage was one key reason people sought public office. Tenders are to be allocated on the basis of a system that accounts for price, experience, record of tax payments, and other such criteria. In reality, a politician's recommendation suffices, and tenders often go to family members, friends, or proxy companies (Steiner 2006).

Several construction companies were blacklisted in 2005 after having won millions of shillings in tenders from the Jinja Municipal Council to supply substandard quality poles and for doing shoddy work on schools in town. In previous years, pharmaceutical companies, construction companies, and taxi park managers were implicated in similar forms of corruption, along with their LC patrons. District councillors would grab contracts or give them to their associates to build schools, roads, and bridges, with the consequence that the work was not completed or was shoddily executed. This explains, in part, why district elections are so bitterly contested and why district governments have been considered among the most corrupt institutions in Uganda ("Councillors Shouldn't Eat Where They Worketh" 2002; "Local Council Achievements and Failures in 2006" 2007).

Popular views of corruption confirm these claims: 79 percent of the population surveyed in a 2003 National Integrity Survey commissioned by the inspector general of Uganda believed that tender boards were the most corrupt institution in Uganda.[4] Only traffic police were found to be more corrupt, with 83 percent of those surveyed regarding them as the least honest. By comparison, 78 percent found the electoral commission to be most corrupt, 67 percent the regular police (excluding traffic police), 54 percent the courts, 47 percent the district council, 34 percent local administration, 34 percent the LC3, and 27 percent the LC1. Bribery rates, however, were seen as being considerably lower in most areas compared with a 1998 version of the survey.

District Service Commissions

Finally, a fourth mechanism of control is the appointment of staff and district civil servants through the District Service Commission (DSC). The DSC itself is appointed by the district council with input from the DES. DES involvement and pressure make it difficult for the DSC to question the use of unconditional grants by various local politicians for personal purposes and take other independent measures (James, Francis, and Pereza 2001).

Thus, one finds that real decentralization has been limited, especially with respect to district capacity to tax and provide services to local residents. Districts have been undermined by political ploys, eliminating key sources of tax revenue. They have also been limited by efforts to redirect patronage from the center to the locales in order to keep the ties of obligation in vertical configurations with the center and with the NRM. The districts thus become important suppliers of votes at election time.

Federalism and the Status of Buganda

One of the less successful efforts to shape the central government's ties to the districts can be seen in the NRM's relations with Buganda. A major conflict erupted over federalism and the governance of Buganda after Museveni took over. It dragged on for three decades; by 2009, relations between Mengo and Museveni's government had reached an all-time low, as became clear when

King Ronald Mutebi was prevented from visiting a district within the Buganda kingdom, sparking riots in Kampala that left over thirty dead. The handling of the riots by government forces has seriously undermined Museveni's electoral base among the Baganda, a base that he needs to win presidential elections. Museveni's difficulties in reconciling with Buganda have their origins in developments that predated his government.

On September 17, 1967, President Milton Obote abolished the three kingdoms of Buganda, Ankole, and Bunyoro as well as the Busoga chieftaincy. With Museveni's takeover in 1986 and especially during the debates over the 1995 constitution, Buganda royalists sought to reestablish Buganda's pre-1967 autonomous status, in which all districts in the kingdom paid taxes to the government in Mengo rather than the central government. The royalists proposed that the kabaka would administer Buganda, while serving primarily as a titular head. Some wanted the name Republic of Uganda changed to Sovereign State of Uganda. The Constituent Assembly (CA) that debated the 1995 constitution resolved this in part by naming Uganda both a sovereign state and a republic.

The Buganda parliament, Lukiiko, promoted the creation of fourteen federal states in Uganda in order to gain greater acceptance for a federal structure. Within the CA, however, the Baganda representatives had mixed feelings about federalism and, although many supported the recognition of Baganda culture, they were not ready to give up Uganda's republican identity. Many also feared that federalism was the first step toward secession by Buganda. They were wary of the Lukiiko's authority and of attempts to undermine their legitimacy as elected representatives of districts within Buganda.

Prior to the Constituent Assembly, the Uganda People's Congress (UPC) and DP both endorsed Buganda's demands for federalism. This was a dramatic change from their earlier positions, given that the UPC-led government under Obote had abolished Buganda's special status when it replaced the 1962 constitution. The NRM sought to preempt the CA debate on the subject by passing the Traditional Rulers Statute in 1993, which allowed for the restoration of traditional rulers as cultural leaders (Mukholi 1995, 33). In addition, fearing an alliance among the opposition parties and the Buganda leadership in Mengo, the NRM met with the latter and agreed that Buganda would form a regional government under the new constitution.

In the end, Buganda gambled and lost its bid for federalism. After it agreed to support NRM positions on anti-multiparty aspects of the constitution in exchange for federalism, the NRM reneged on its end of the perceived bargain. The majority of the CA delegates took the view that federalism would undermine the unity of the country. They agreed to recognize Buganda as a distinct entity, but instead of federalism they opted for decentralization and devolution of power from the center to the district level—in other words, the policy that was already in place prior to the convening of the CA. The CA rejected the NRM's agreement on federalism and other promises made to

Mengo prior to its deliberations. Opportunism by Mengo and the multiparty caucus ended up hurting both as each tried to use the other (Barya 2000, 42).

The Regional Tier Arrangement

In 2009, the government passed the Regional Government Bill, which resulted in the creation of forty-eight regional governments with forty-eight regional chairpersons, but more important, it undermined the status of the kingdoms and traditional rulers. Parliament had already in principle approved a regional tier system in 2005 to coalesce the country's districts.

The regional tier system was met with opposition in Buganda and Busoga. Having been granted symbolic cultural recognition in the 1995 constitution, the kingdoms continued to press for greater political power and a more public role. Ongoing pressure for a federal system from Buganda resulted in negotiations over a government proposal for regional parliaments. These discussions between the government and Mengo were part of the constitutional review process that took place in 2004 and 2005. The Mengo team was led by then katikkiro (prime minister) Joseph Ssemogerere, and the government team was headed by Vice President Gilbert Bukenya, Prime Minister Apolo Nsibambi, and Amama Mbabazi.

Buganda had strong objections to key aspects of the regional tier arrangement. In particular, Mengo objected to the requirement that its katikkiro be elected and that Kampala, which is situated within Buganda, be excluded from the kingdom.[5] However, the national government remained firm in its efforts to institute a regional tier system and would not entertain a federal arrangement of any kind.

In developing this regional tier system, the NRM government sought to appease the Baganda monarchists and pinned its hopes on an arrangement that was intended to meet most of their objectives, without according the Baganda special status. The intent was to strike a balance between acknowledging Buganda's prominence and not offending other kingdoms, chiefdoms, or regions of Uganda. With waning political backing nationwide and elections coming up, Museveni was eager to shore up his support among the kingdoms, especially Buganda. He sought to make some accommodations without conceding to the *federo* status that Buganda desired.

This bid for Buganda's approval, however, failed as key Baganda royalists rejected the regional tier arrangement, as did Busoga. The Lukiiko unanimously rejected the arrangement a few days prior to the 2006 presidential elections, demanding *federo* instead. The timing of the rejection was indicative of the uneasy relationship between Mengo and the NRM and of the inability of the NRM to come to a satisfactory compromise with Buganda. The fallout from the arrangement resulted in the ouster of the katikkiro at the end of 2005; his replacement was Dan Muliika, who vehemently opposed the regional tier system. The regional tier arrangement, which was to go into effect July 1, 2006, was put on hold until 2009, when a regional tier bill was introduced.

The regional tier system was an effort to appeal to ethnic institutions by acknowledging entities like Buganda and Busoga through an administrative arrangement. Even if there had been political support for the regional tiers in the kingdoms, there were major constraints on implementing it. Central government barely had the resources to pay for the LC system and district administration. Moreover, the government had continually increased the number of districts, which as of 2009 totaled ninety-seven, and it had seriously underfunded them, as we have explained. A regional tier system would require considerable additional expenditures that many believe the country did not have.

Buganda was not the only kingdom that opposed the regional tier arrangement. Busoga had adopted its own document, the Busoga People's Charter, in 2004 that outlined its understanding of their regional status. The Busoga People's Forum and the Busoga Parliamentary Group lobbied for federal status to bring together the districts of Jinja, Kamuli, Iganga, Mayuge, Bugiri, and Jinja Municipality to "cooperate in areas of infrastructure, energy and water development, promotion of health, education, tourism, trade, communication, physical planning development, planning employment, mobilisation, and cultural development" ("Busoga Gets Its 'Federo' First" 2002). The deputy speaker of the House, Rebecca Kadaga, and former Vice President Speciosa Kazibwe spearheaded this initiative. The entity was approved by the National Assembly and by the relevant district councils. Thus, in 2004, Busoga, with 2,586,000 people, became the only recognized geographical administrative unit larger than a district in Uganda. It would not collect taxes and was to serve as a nonpolitical, cultural leader of the kingdom (the Obwa Kyabazinga). The move was not universally supported; Samia peasants from Bugiri and other non-Basoga ethnic groups objected to the entity and petitioned parliament to stop its implementation.

At the same time, the Busoga kingdom rejected the combination of political and cultural functions in the proposed regional tier arrangement. It argued that this would kill the Busoga People's Charter. Many monarchists felt that the cultural and political roles needed to be separated in this context, as they were wary of finding themselves trapped in an arrangement in which they would be totally at the mercy of central government. They felt the regional tier arrangement would result in demands on them that they would be unable to meet because of the way in which central government had constructed the resource base ("Busoga Rejects Mengo Federo Deal" 2005).

The Land Bill Amendment

Other issues also divided central government and the kingdoms. From 2007 to 2009, one of the most contentious issues between the government and Buganda was the proposed National Land Policy and the controversial Land Amendment Bill, which was passed in 2009. They were aimed at modernizing land rights and making the administration of land more efficient in the interests of promoting development. The land law prevents forceful evictions of tenants without a court order under the penalty of up to seven years in prison.

The current land policy is perceived by the Baganda as well as many northerners and easterners to be a land grab by westerners. The Buganda leadership accused Museveni of aligning himself with foreign investors to steal their land and feared that if government-backed investors settled on their land, they would be powerless to evict them. The discovery of oil in western Uganda along the Lake Albert Basin in 2006 made the land issues all the more contentious, even though reserves had not been discovered in Buganda territory.

Many feel the president has asserted too much control in decisions regarding land. In one cited dispute, after land had been allocated to Ugandan hotelier Sudhir Ruparelia, it was withdrawn, and President Museveni gave the land instead to the Kenyan government. In another instance, when the Madhvani Group sought in 2009 to purchase 40,000 hectares of land in northern Uganda in order to build a sugar plantation, President Museveni backed the request but was immediately accused of land grabbing by northern politicians. The case went to court and the Madhvanis started looking for a new plot in a neighboring country.

The government argues that the land amendment protects tenants from unlawful evictions; however, many Baganda leaders feel that the government is using the legislation to allow outsiders to illegally settle on their land. A common slogan in Buganda is "Ettaka Ligenda," which translates into a claim that the government is hiding behind its amendments to grab land from the Baganda. Population pressures have given rise to increased tensions between landlords and squatter tenants who have no legal title but have lived for generations on the land. Prime land cannot be developed by landowners or tenants as a result of this situation. The government wishes to convert *mailo* and freehold land into leased land. But presently the land cannot be developed because *mailo* landowners and tenants are in a deadlock over ownership.

Mailo tenure was introduced with the 1900 Buganda Agreement between the king of Buganda and the Protectorate Government in which land was divided into square miles (hence the name *mailo*). Official *mailo* land became public land in 1967 for which titles were issued and land was held in perpetuity. However, absentee landlords often controlled the land that was occupied by squatters, leading to conflicts. Freehold systems, found primarily in the eastern and western part of the country, are similar to the *mailo* system with ownership in perpetuity and the issuance of titles.

It is feared that the conversion of *mailo* and freehold land to leased land would deprive landowners of their titles without clear guidelines for compensation. Opponents argue that although the amendments contain many important reforms, their objectives are being subverted by those who want to remove power from the district land tribunals and transfer decisionmaking power to the minister of lands.

Conclusion

A persistent theme emerges from the central government's dealings with districts, local councils, kingdoms, and local associations: its repeated efforts to create vertical linkages of dependency and patronage. These vertical linkages were to replace the harder-to-control horizontal societal and political linkages discussed in Chapter 4. The LC system was initially to serve as a political machine for a Movement system that was to replace political parties; and the regional tier system was to preempt any political role the kingdoms might aspire to.

The creation of an NRM machine within the LC system, the flawed regional tier system, and the difficulties the NRM has experienced in building alliances with the kingdoms all provide clues to the priorities of the NRM for local development and decentralization. There has been much more interest in creating a loyal electoral base and keeping locales dependent on the center for resources than in creating and allowing governance capacity at the local level. The haphazard way, for example, in which Busoga was allowed to develop its own regional system without reference to the ongoing plans to create regional tiers suggests that political motivations to garner votes superseded governance considerations every step of the way. The cavalier way in which the already small tax base of districts was undermined by an election year promise without consultation with the districts and parliament suggests a lack of commitment to decentralization. All of these features of governance in Uganda are indicative of the imperatives of semiauthoritarian states to concentrate power in the center and limit potential bases of opposition or fragmentation of power in the hinterland, in civil society, and within parties and competing centers of power, such as the kingdoms.

Notes

1. Afrobarometer, http://www.afrobarometer.org. Accessed July 17, 2008.

2. The 2004 survey of 17,608 households in all districts of Uganda was carried out by the Uganda Bureau of Statistics, http://www.ubos.org/onlinefiles/uploads/ubos/survey%20documentation/nsds2004/survey0/overview.html. Accessed July 17, 2008.

3. The exchange rate changed by 2008, which accounts for the difference between the aforementioned USh 35 billion = US$20 million.

4. The survey was carried out by K2-Consult Uganda Limited.

5. Buganda's attorney general, Apollo Makubuya, explained why Mengo objected to the bill: "Buganda's concerns are based on the hierarchy and reporting structures of districts with and between the regional government and the central government; the provisions on the appointment of the katikkiro; the management and control of land; the president's power to take over a regional government where there is a failure to recognise regional diversity; [and] the demarcation of Mengo Municipality and Kampala without consultations, as well as the role of the regional governments over primary education and agriculture" (Namutebi 2009b).

6

The Carrot and the Stick

In semiauthoritarian states, power generally rests with the security forces, which are used to deal with dissent and threats to power. Because power is regarded in a zero-sum fashion, those who seek electoral office are seen not as competitors but as forces readying to vanquish their opponents. A shared history of retribution creates a basis for fear and repression. Such opponents are to be either co-opted through patronage or crushed by security forces. Extralegal security forces are especially convenient for silencing and intimidating one's opponents, since they are not legally accountable to the public for their actions; no one can really say who controls them.

Herein lies yet another paradox of power: past violence and excessive corruption themselves become reasons to stay in power. Those who have suppressed opponents and have "eaten too much," as corruption is commonly referred to, cannot leave office and must protect themselves from prosecution or other forms of retribution. They do so by continuing to use violence and patronage in order to remain in power. They fear that once they are out of power, their opponents may take revenge for their past misdeeds.

Unlike power in authoritarian and semiauthoritarian states, power in democracies comes from the ballot box; former leaders have little to fear in terms of retribution from their successors. This may even be the case in semidemocracies. But for those who obtained or sustained power by force, the loss thereof may mean exile, imprisonment, or even death. This is why, for a brief moment in the first round of the 2008 Zimbabwean elections, when it appeared that the opposition leader, Morgan Tsivangirai, was about to win (that is, before the results were annulled), military generals started trying to cut deals with him to ensure that they would not face prosecution. The military does not have the same immunity President Mugabe has from prosecution in Zimbabwe, and for this reason they have been keen that he remain in power. While

127

Uganda's situation is not nearly as dire as that of Zimbabwe, there are parallels in some of the dynamics that keep the leadership of both countries fiercely holding onto power at all costs.

This chapter explores the connections between patronage and (in)security. It first looks at the "carrot": how corruption feeds patronage and clientelistic networks to build and maintain political loyalty. The chapter then looks at the "stick," or the remilitarization of Uganda under Museveni and the perverse forms of so-called security that emerged, which have more to do with suppressing internal dissent and oppositional political parties than with protecting Uganda from external attacks. It focuses on the particular role played by paramilitary and extralegal forces, which carry out much of the intimidation and harassment of political opponents. The chapter also examines the centrality of the security forces in terms of expenditures and looks at the militarization of society. The chapter concludes by analyzing the relationship between patronage and security forces in the case of scams involving ghost soldiers.

Understanding Clientelistic Networks

State-based clientelism has been one of the main obstacles to democratization, especially when it has favored certain groups over others, permeated the military, and become the main source of power (along with the use of violence). Clientelism is defined, according to René Lemarchand and Keith Legg, as "a more or less personalized relationship between actors (i.e., patrons and clients), or sets of actors, commanding unequal wealth, status or influence, based on conditional loyalties and involving mutually beneficial transactions" (Lemarchand and Legg 1972, 151–152). In neopatrimonial states like Uganda, the boundaries between the public and private are porous, resulting in the relatively easy diversion of state resources for clientelistic purposes.

The expectation of many donors, academics, and policy analysts is that countries like Uganda will adopt rational-legal bureaucracies and merit-based administrative systems, even though, historically, these kinds of systems did not evolve until there was a fairly developed capitalist system, capitalist class, and civil society. Levels of government corruption in postindustrial democracies far exceed levels of state-based corruption in African countries, in part because the resources are so much greater in economically developed countries (Szeftel 1998). Nevertheless, the issue of corruption and patronage has drawn considerable attention in Africa for a variety of reasons. Patrimonialism in least developed countries is focused on the state rather than on a wider range of institutions, as it is in more developed countries where the business sector features more prominently in profit or rent seeking. The reliance on kinship, ethnicity, or clan in Africa interferes more visibly with administrative systems and can become especially problematic when a dominant ethnic matrix becomes a matrix of political power with clear winners and losers. Moreover, in developed countries, a culture of public administration honed over decades if not centuries has resulted in greater efficiencies and fewer opportunities for abuse than there are in developing countries (Theobald 1999, 493). Poverty makes petty abuse more pervasive. Moreover, corruption often comes at the expense of foreign aid agencies and multilateral donors, whose noisy constituencies demand accountability. And finally, in developing countries, corruption noticeably undermines already underresourced agencies, further exacerbating problems of administration and governance.

I have often wondered why one rarely sees former generals and politicians quietly living out their days, raking in profits from businesses they started with money they accumulated and diverted while in power. There are far easier, less risky, and more lucrative ways to make money in Uganda than through state-related corruption. Yet politicians and army generals remain absent from the ranks of the wealthiest people in Uganda. The most striking feature of the one hundred wealthiest individuals in Uganda is the fact that they made their wealth through a wide variety of businesses in all sectors and not through their connections to the state (see Table 6.1). The majority of these individuals can be found owning and selling land, owning and renting buildings and shopping centers, owning hotels and resorts, and manufacturing a wide number of products. One finds them also in construction and transportation, retail and wholesale of a wide variety of products, entertainment (bars, discos, clubs), private education, and the media (radio, television, newspapers, magazines). Half of these individuals are based in Kampala; the rest are evenly dispersed throughout the country, with a surprising number running businesses in parts of the north and east. Only a handful of the wealthiest individuals are politicians, but even these exceptions made their wealth and bought their property before going into politics. Perhaps those in government or the military who have ill-gotten wealth feel pressure to hide it and therefore do not appear on such lists of investors. One might nevertheless expect that the resources they "diverted" from the state might be invested in legitimate businesses in order to hide their illicit origins. However, this does not appear to be the case.

Thus, the location of prosperity today contrasts starkly with that of the mid-1960s, when one found the most prosperous and influential Ugandans in top government positions. Even in rural towns like Mbale, the elite could then be found in the state or parastatal domains, such as district governments, parliament, or the leadership ranks of the Bugisu Cooperative Union.[1]

Although it appears that there is a business class that is slowly emerging, with interests independent of those in power, it is also important to note that they are still prone to cutting deals and obtaining favors from those in power. Indeed, they must; the state patronage machine relies on these sorts of arrangements. One may even say that the business class benefits too much from the political system and the way it is presently configured to mount a serious challenge to the

Table 6.1   The Super Rich in Uganda

Abid Alam	Owned and sold Gold Trust Bank; has manufacturing interests in steel rolling in Uganda and Kenya
Muhammed Alibhai	Owns Tight Security
Hassan Basajjabalaba	Works in education, hides and skins, and hotels
Patrick Bitature	Owns Simba Telecom and has an interest in National Insurance Corporation; also owns airtime dealerships in Kenya, Tanzania, and Nigeria as well as a hotel run by the South African–based Protea Group
Karim Hirji	Owns the Grand Imperial, the Botanical Hotel, and the Imperial Resort Hotel
Bob Kabonero	Runs gambling outfits
Elly Karuhanga	Works as a corporate lawyer for Kampala Associated Advocates; is a former MP for Nyabushozi
Bulayimu Muwanga Kibirige	Imports and sells motorcycles; owns Hotel Africana
Godfrey Kirumira	Serves as chairman of Express FC, a football club, and owns hotels and commercial properties
Mohan Kiwanuka	Owns Oscar Industries, the leading manufacturer and supplier of a wide range of paper and packaging products; deals in real estate
Sikander Lalani	Owns Roofings Limited, which exports to southern Sudan, Democratic Republic of Congo, and Rwanda; is constructing a steel rolling plant in Namanve
Charles Mbire	Has interests in MTN, a mobile company, and the UK-based Aggreko, an air-conditioning company
Isabirye Mugoya	Involved in construction and real estate
Amos Nzeeyi	Owns a Pepsi franchise, real estate, the Hot Loaf bakery chain, and a hotel in Kabale
Joseph Roy	Owns Das Air Cargo, Royal Daisy Airline, and Daisy House, as well as ranches and commercial property
Sudhir Ruparelia	Owns Crane Bank, Goldstar Insurance, and a large amount of real estate as well as Kabira Country Club, Speke Hotel, and Speke Resort Munyonyo; also owns Kabira International School and Kampala Parents School, as well as Sanyu FM Rosebud Flower Farm, and more
Somani	Owns Rwenzori Water, a bottling company, as well as Metropole House and Cineplex
Aga Sekalala	Owns Ugachick, a poultry breeder

status quo. In that sense, the business class is weak; it has not been able to artic-ulate its own demands for stronger governance, and it has no incentive to do so at this time. Thus, the business class contributes to propping up a clientelistic system that eventually must undermine its own long-term interests.

Not only does corruption constrain the business environment for local investors, it also affects a country's image among foreign investors. According to Transparency International, Uganda ranked 88 in its 2001 global corruption perceptions index but had slid down to a rank of 130 by 2009.[2] Regionally, Uganda fell from fourteen to twenty-seven in this same six-year period. Such statistics ultimately have an impact on Uganda's attractiveness to foreign investors and reflect some of the serious constraints on a poor country struggling with governance problems.

To go back to my original question about why politicians and military leaders are so rarely found among the wealthiest individuals in a country like Uganda, one has to understand the motivations of those in power. Their acquired resources are not intended primarily for capitalist enterprise or even for self-aggrandizement. The resources are most likely acquired to feed various patronage networks, which is why they can dissipate so quickly. Politicians and military leaders also need liquid assets for payoffs and purchases that are quickly and easily available, which is why acquiring resources through investment is less likely.

Instituting and Subverting Anticorruption Measures

Most treat state-based clientelism and corruption in Uganda and in Africa more generally as problems of morality, culture, and political will; as consequences of a pervasive economy based on kinship; or as a problem requiring fine-tuning institutional incentives and constraints—that is, a technical problem. Although these are contributing factors, what these accounts may miss are the political purposes that patronage serves. If one identifies clientelism only as a technical problem, then one becomes inattentive to the ways in which the technical solutions themselves are subverted or overridden by political considerations.

Everyone in Uganda agrees that corruption must be fought. President Museveni himself declared 1996 the year of fighting poverty and corruption. The government revitalized the Office of the Auditor General, the Public Accounts Committee, and the government ombudsman; it created new institutions to address the problem, including the Inspector General of Government, a National Fraud Squad, and a Ministry of Ethics and Integrity. The government introduced various laws to strengthen governance and accountability, such as the Leadership Code of Conduct (Flanary and Watt 1999). Nevertheless, corruption seems to have increased exponentially since these policies and offices were initiated. A string of reports to the president by commissions of inquiry headed by justices like Julia Sebutinde, David Porter, and James Ogoola have implicated top government officials with little if any response. For example, the recommendations of Justice Sebutinde's commission into alleged financial mismanagement of Uganda's police force, the privatization of Constitution Square, and the closure of city banks were ignored. Government and military leaders are named in scandal after scandal with virtually no attempt at prosecution except in a handful of cases. Sometimes individuals are removed from their positions and redeployed elsewhere or even rewarded with promotions, scholarships, and more training. In the late 1990s, President Museveni pardoned his half brother General Salim Saleh, who had confessed to accepting a bribe of US$800,000 in the purchase of defective army helicopters.

The reason that these revelations are even possible has to do with the contradictory nature of semiauthoritarian states; they would not be as likely to be exposed in an authoritarian state. But the incapacity of the state to respond has to do with the delicate political bargains that must be made in order to maintain the status quo. Who rises and falls has little to do with justice and far more to do with power at the end of the day. Ultimately, the political imperative is what needs to be accounted for in explaining corruption and patronage.

On occasion, when there is sufficient international pressure, one individual may end up taking the fall for a scam, although the individual in question may not be the most culpable but rather the most politically convenient. For instance, it appears that the late Dr. Suleiman Kiggundu was forced to take the blame for scams implicating government officials. Kiggundu, who was governor of the Bank of Uganda from 1986 to 1990, believed he had become the scapegoat in a scam in 1999. He alleged that those involved in the scam included President Museveni; other Bank of Uganda officials; the late Governor Charles Kikonyongo; Finance Minister Jehoash Mayanja-Nkangi; Attorney General Bert Katureebe; Museveni's half brother, Major General Salim Saleh; Museveni's son, Lieutenant Kainerugaba Muhoozi; and the Privatisation Unit. The scam involved a dubious sale of shares of the now defunct Uganda Commercial Bank (UCB).

Donors—in particular the World Bank, which had just invested USh 70 billion (US$40 million) in the UCB—were increasingly concerned about rumors of corrupt dealings involving the bank. Kiggundu had been managing director of Greenland Bank, which had made USh 36 billion (US$21 million) in bad loans. He was accused of selling 49 percent of shares of the UCB to a Malaysian company, Westmont, which then illicitly sold 49 percent of its shares in UCB to Greenland Bank. Kiggundu claimed that the purchase was overseen by Saleh and Kainerugaba Muhoozi with Museveni's approval. Saleh diverted attention from the illegal sale by throwing what Kiggundu described as a "perfect red herring": he admitted that he had used funds from Greenland Investments Limited to buy the UCB. This took the heat off the government, and Saleh's resignation as presidential adviser appeased the donors in time for their consultative meeting ("Confession on Commercial Bank" 2001). Attorney General Bert Katureebe supported Kiggundu's account, but no legal action was taken against anyone except Kiggundu, who ended up having his assets confiscated and landed in jail for six months. Later he served as chairman of the Forum for Democratic Change but died in 2008 of cancer. Kiggundu's account is just one. And even if his allegations were to be proven false, in all the various corruption scandals described in this book and elsewhere—including the ghost soldier scam, the looting of resources in Democratic Republic of Congo, the loss of US$4 million from an immunization fund for the Ministry of Health, the mismanagement of the police force, the junk army helicopter scam, and so on—the same top military officials and presidential associates are generally implicated.[3]

As we have seen above, for many leaders, acquiring wealth through state-related corruption is not an end in itself but rather a means of acquiring resources and privileges that can be used to stay in power and purchase loyalty. Patronage in the semiauthoritarian context is especially toxic in the ways it interfaces with security forces to create a catch-22 that makes democratization difficult. To understand the nature of the relationship between power, patronage, and the state's monopoly on violence, one has to understand the centrality of security forces within society and how they evolved. The next section takes us back to trace the evolution of Uganda's armed forces and provides a history of the paramilitary and extralegal forces in Uganda to show how they have been used to crush political opponents.

The British and Postindependence Legacies of Military and Security Forces

The British had originally used the Baganda to disarm the fighting forces of the other kingdoms, replacing them with the Uganda Army. The army eventually served Obote and Amin until Amin's ouster in 1979, when it was replaced by the Uganda National Liberation Army (UNLA). The UNLA was in turn replaced by the National Resistance Army (NRA) of Yoweri Museveni, which took over in 1986 and was renamed the Uganda People's Defence Forces (UPDF) in 1995 with the enactment of the new constitution (Brett 1994b, 134).

From 1894 to 1945, the King's African Rifles reflected a wide spectrum of Ugandan society. However, after World War II, the colonial state was cognizant that many of the leaders of the anticolonial struggle were former servicemen. Fearing that an independence movement might emerge in the south of the country, where the country's elite were based, it concentrated its recruitment for the army in the north in Acholi, Lango, and West Nile and in the east in Teso. Military service eventually became a major livelihood for thousands in northern Uganda (Kayunga 2000, 112).

The highest rank soldiers could aspire to was that of sergeant. In 1964, the army mutinied, demanding better pay, improved working conditions, and the Africanization of the ranks of officers. Although revolters were suppressed, they succeeded insofar as junior officers were promoted and a group of northerners with limited education gained in influence, including Shaban Opolot, who served as army commander, and Idi Amin, his deputy (Brett 1994b, 135).

Opolot and Amin colluded with the Buganda leadership to remove Obote; in response, Obote removed Opolot and promoted Amin to the position of army commander. To preempt a military takeover, Obote repealed the constitution in 1966 and attacked the palace of the kabaka—who at the time was a nonexecutive president—forcing him to flee the country. As described in Chapter 2, Obote, who had been prime minister up until 1967, took over the presidency, introduced a new constitution, and abolished all kingdoms. As a result, Uganda became a unitary state, with increased control in the hands of a highly politicized army. The army expanded from 1,200 soldiers in 1962 to 9,000 in 1971; in 1966, it enjoyed a defense expenditure of 10.2 percent of the budget, more than two-and-a-half times that of its neighbor Tanzania to the south. The main criteria for leadership in the army was not military skill but rather political allegiance to the president, and ethnicity became the most salient factor in recruitment and promotion.

Obote, who was keen to improve ties with Khartoum, suspected Amin of providing unauthorized support to a rebellion of Anya Nya in southern Sudan. In turn, Amin believed Obote thought Amin was behind the murder of the second in command of Uganda's army, Brigadier Okoya, and his wife, and was about to take action against Amin. Amin feared losing his position in the army and possibly meeting an even worse fate. He also was concerned about losing Israeli support for Anya Nya should Uganda improve ties with Sudan. He therefore preempted action on the part of Obote by overthrowing him while he was traveling outside the country in 1971 (Woodward 1978).

According to David Gwyn (1977), a technical adviser to the Ugandan military for twenty years, the Ugandan army at the time of Amin was an agglomeration of groups. The largest were the Acholi, numbering around 2,000 or 3,000. The army also consisted of Iteso; West Nilers (a mixture of Madi, Kakwa, Lugbara, Kuku, and Madi Okollo); some from the western region, who tended to be better educated; and finally some Langi, including some top officers. Amin himself was Kakwa. Following Amin's takeover, the Luo-speaking Acholi and Langi were pitted against the West Nilers from Amin's home area with disastrous and violent consequences (Brett 1994b, 135).

As we can see, then, one of the features of postindependence politics in Uganda has been the central role played by the armed forces and other so-called security forces. The centrality of the army, even under civilian rule, has meant military control of the state and its resources. Political and ethnic contestation has expressed itself through military contestation in cycles of retribution. It has, as Frank Van Acker puts it, "created a sizeable and almost unemployable 'lumpen militariat' class, which solidified violence as a means of interaction in society" (Van Acker 2004, 338). Although Museveni may have put his uniform aside with the introduction of civilian rule, the civilian parliament has no vote when it comes to Uganda's military ventures abroad, nor do civilians have any say in the activities of the large number of paramilitary armies and extralegal militia that have emerged. Yet these same forces, which are said to be security forces, have become one of the biggest sources of insecurity for Ugandan citizens.

The use of extralegal security forces has a long history in Uganda. Their presence and role in suppressing domestic dissent has expanded as growing numbers of people have become disillusioned with the Museveni regime and have sought to express that discontent by campaigning for opposition politicians, protesting the lifting of presidential term limits, publishing dissenting views in the media, exposing corruption of the authorities through the media and legislature, and engaging in protest actions. Increasing numbers of critics of the regime have found themselves tortured in so-called safe houses, arrested without charges, or even charged with sedition and treason for relatively benign activities. In other words, security forces have often become the greatest source of insecurity, especially for those who criticize the government. However, the repression is unpredictable and inconsistent, allowing for the perception that political openness is the norm, while perpetuating a climate of uncertainty for those who wish to express their views openly. Indeed, repression seems to have subsided somewhat since the 2001 elections, especially after the opening to multipartyism.

In spite of the Ugandan government's attempt to portray itself as a source of peace in the region, its actions in the northern part of Uganda and Democratic Republic of Congo as well as against its own domestic critics suggest otherwise. The overriding imperative of creating new militia appears to be not enhancing security but rather suppressing opposition to the government.

Agencies of Insecurity

One of the legacies of colonialism was the creation of police and paramilitary forces more loyal to those in power than to the citizenry. The British had trained and used the paramilitary Special Force (SF) to suppress dissenters. After independence, the SF remained, and an additional secret paramilitary, the General Service Unit, was formed and headed by Obote's cousin, Akena Adoko. The General Service Unit recruited primarily from the Soroti and Kumi districts from among the youth wingers and party stalwarts of the Uganda People's Congress (UPC). In addition, in 1967, Obote established the Military Police under the army commander, Major General Idi Amin. The top SF leaders fled with Obote when he was overthrown by Amin in 1971 (Amaza 1998, 119). The General Service Unit was then replaced with the notorious State Research Bureau; the SF was also disbanded and the Public Safety Unit was created in its place. However, when Obote returned to power in 1980, the SF was revived to replace the Public Safety Unit and the State Research Bureau was eliminated (Omoding 2007). Regional paramilitary groups formed by Idi Amin, such as the Iteso Home Guard—created to protect Teso from Karimojong cattle rustlers—were retained as militia by Obote because of their perceived effectiveness.

Under Museveni, these types of paramilitary units proliferated and played an increasing role in the activities of the regime, especially after the passage of the Anti-Terrorism Act of 2002. Some of these forces involved small armies, while others were smaller units working in collaboration with legal security entities. Thus, the more prestigious Presidential Guard Brigade (PGB) was created to supplement the UPDF; the Chieftaincy of Military Intelligence (CMI) took over many Internal Security Organisation (ISO) functions, and the Violent Crime Crack Unit (VCCU) supplemented the police. A host of other paramilitary and extralegal forces were formed, including the Kalangala Action Plan (KAP), the Civic Defence Team, the Joint Anti Terrorism Task-force, and the Black Mamba squad.

The extralegal nature of these groups allows them to engage in activities that fall outside of what is legally and constitutionally permissible. Reports by the Human Rights Watch, Amnesty International, the African Centre for Treatment and Rehabilitation of Torture Victims (ACTV), the Foundation of Human Rights Initiative, and the Uganda Human Rights Commission have documented the extreme methods of torture used by these various units. These methods range from tying victims' hands and feet behind them (*kandoya*) to suspending them from ceilings and tearing off their nails, as well as subjecting them to waterboarding, severe beatings, burning with metal or molten plastic, electrocution, genital mutilation, death threats, mock executions, and confrontations with red ants, snakes, and crocodiles, and other such horrific methods.

With time, these agencies became more sophisticated in their use of torture. Doctors at the ACTV have seen increasing numbers of patients who are subjected to so-called invisible torture, which leaves behind no physical evidence but is every bit as damaging—for example, hitting joints so as to cause internal bleeding that requires amputation, smacking ears hard enough to burst eardrums, and other forms of psychological torture ("Torture Changes Face in Uganda" 2007).

Security Agencies

The Presidential Guard Brigade

The Israeli-trained Presidential Protection Unit (PPU), with between 2,000 and 3,000 soldiers, was expanded in February 2003 into the new, considerably larger PGB, which includes the PGB Command Headquarters, the Fourth Battalion, the PPU, and the PGB Tank Battalion. The PGB was used in the offensive against the Lord's Resistance Army (LRA) in early 2003. The PGB serves as Museveni's private army or praetorian guard. It is made up of 12,000 soldiers, with roughly 9,000 more soldiers than a typical brigade. The PGB is well equipped with artillery, tanks, and armored units in addition to anti-aircraft guns, armored personnel carriers, and mine-protected vehicles. The soldiers' wages are considerably higher than those of soldiers in the regular forces, and their job comes with the promise of promotion in the army and other security agencies. They are not assigned to the more dangerous frontline positions and enjoy better training, food, clothing, and benefits, leading to reported resentment within the armed forces (Barkan 2005).[4]

The PGB, as well as the Black Mambas and Museveni's closest security detail, are thought to be dominated by Museveni's own Bahima group and Basiita clan to cultivate loyalty.[5] Museveni's father was of Basiita descent, and his mother was from the Beene-Rukaari branch of the Bashambo, who were the traditional rulers of most of Ntungamo, where he was born (Museveni 1997, 1; "President Museveni Donates Vehicle to Toro Clan" 2005). Historically, the PPU and the PGB have been overseen by Museveni's most trusted associates—first by Colonel Leopold Kyanda, followed by Museveni's son, Muhoozi Kainerugaba, and then by Museveni's brother, Lieutenant General Salim Saleh.

The PGB has come under criticism by the Democratic Party (DP) and other opposition leaders. In 2006, the DP sent a memo to President Museveni insisting that the PGB be incorporated into the national army to better reflect the "regional diversity of our country" and that the PGB be "compensated like the rest of the UPDF." The memo continued, "We are mindful of the grave consequences this country and especially some particular communities have suffered as a result of regimes maintaining sectarian and ethnic armies" ("DP Gives Museveni Memo" 2006). A year later, in 2007, an estimated five hundred soldiers sought to leave the PGB. Most of those who left were not westerners, lending credence to the rumors that the PGB was plagued by ethnic tensions.

The Internal Security Organisation and the External Security Organisation

The ISO and regional District Internal Security Organisations are responsible for internal security, while the External Security Organisation (ESO) is responsible for external security. They are legal entities; however, they do not have powers of detention. Nevertheless, the network of numerous powerful security agencies that act as de facto extralegal agencies works closely with legal entities like the ISO and ESO to detain and interrogate suspects.

The Chieftaincy of Military Intelligence

Another legal entity, the CMI, was headed first by Colonel Henry Tumukunde and then by one of Museveni's close associates and advisers, Brigadier Noble Mayombo, until his death of acute pancreatitis in 2007. According to Human Rights Watch, the CMI's so-called safe houses and offices were used for torture, and CMI personnel frequently participated with other ad hoc security agencies, like the Joint Anti Terrorism Taskforce and the extralegal VCCU, in interrogating people (Human Rights Watch 2004; Mwenda 2007a). The VCCU started as a military unit code-named Operation Wembley, but it was later put under the control of the police. Like the ISO and ESO, the CMI does not have legal powers of detention, yet it frequently detains and interrogates individuals. Previously known as Military Intelligence, the unit attracted little attention until it came under Tumukunde and Mayombo's control and became associated with safe houses and torture.

In addition to the CMI, there are Chief Intelligence Officers. The main purpose of these officers is to gather intelligence, ensure the maximum safety of the First Family, and prevent the growing number of leaks about Museveni's family to the press ("NRM Boss Fears for His Life" 2006).

The Kalangala Action Plan

The KAP is headed by Major Roland Kakooza Mutale, who has been a close associate of Museveni's since the bush war, beginning in 1983. The KAP is widely regarded as a paramilitary group, although the NRM claims it is a nongovernmental organization (Nganda and Oluka 2004). In order to garner greater legitimacy for the organization, the National Resistance Movement (NRM) recruited members of parliament to join the KAP as a litmus test of their loyalty to the NRM. Close to 180 (out of 333) MPs signed up to be a part of the KAP's parliamentary wing, led by Sitenda Sebalu (from Kyadondo East). The KAP was allegedly responsible for arbitrarily arresting and detaining people without legal authority and harassing and beating up Museveni's political opponents in the 2001 and 2006 elections, including supporters of Kizza Besigye (Human Rights Watch 2004, 40). The KAP apparently is a special operations unit of the UPDF but does not have formal status as a security agency. A similar organization operates in Gulu Municipality known as Labeca (or Labeja), and it carries out similar harassment and violence against the population.

State-Sponsored Thugs

There are groups of thugs that have appeared on different occasions to brutalize and intimidate the public. The Black Mambas appeared in broad daylight, in the presence of the media and foreign diplomats, when opposition leader Kizza Besigye was arraigned in court prior to the 2006 elections. They had come with the intention of rearresting him. He and his associates, who had also been arrested for treason, escaped being apprehended by this group. A Kiboko Squad, also known as a Stick Brigade, clobbered environmental demonstrators protesting the sale of the Mabira Forest on the streets of Kampala during a demonstration. Among those beaten by this squad in the demonstration were MPs Beatrice Atim Anywar (Kitgum) and Hussein Kyanjo (Makindye West).

Citizen Militias

In addition to these extramilitary units, there were militias of ordinary citizens who served a somewhat different function. In 2001, the Ugandan government formed militia forces to protect IDP (internally displaced person) camps and civilians in towns in the north and east from attacks by the LRA. The militias, which involved at least 25,000 people, were created within a span of six months. They were known as the Rhino (Amuka) Brigade in the Lango subregion, the Arrow Boys in the Teso and Acholi subregions, the Elephant Brigade in the Gulu district, Pader Mig Stream in the Pader district, and the Frontier Guard in Kitgum. These types of militias had antecedents in the earlier governments of Obote and Amin.

The UPDF was supposed to actively engage and pursue the LRA; however, there was a widespread perception in the regions in which the militias operated that they were being orchestrated to engage the LRA directly, allowing the UPDF to avoid combat. A Tufts University study of the north and east found that the militias had improved security in Teso and Acholi (but not in Lango), and they found that the militias were quicker than the UPDF in responding to and repulsing LRA attacks. However, the study also found that the militias were not compensated sufficiently, and so they also looted and stole food and goods from communities, often from the most vulnerable populations in the IDP camps. These militias included underaged, orphaned youth who were seeking a livelihood and protection against abduction. Others were seeking revenge against the LRA or cattle rustlers, and still others were themselves bandits, able to infiltrate the militias due to poor screening. While in some areas security had improved, in other cases the militias were reported to have participated in the abuse and rape of IDPs ("In Search of Security" 2005).

In Moroto in 1992, local community forces recruited their own armed warriors to create vigilante groups to protect their cattle and property from being raided. They were supported by NGOs and churches until Museveni put them under the UPDF, which paid them a nominal monthly fee. Security improved substantially and road thuggery and raiding decreased, while looted property and cattle were sometimes recovered by the vigilantes and returned to their owners. They were not corrupted and had their roots in the communities. In

2001, Local Defence Units were created in Karamoja and neighboring districts to replace the more informal defense groups. Like the other aforementioned militias, they ended up being treated as extensions of the armed forces. They were shipped to barracks in the north and were often used as a reserve force of the regular army, but they received little pay. Often they ended up deserting with their guns and thus became new sources of insecurity (Mkutu 2007).

Defense Spending and the Size of the Armed Forces

Another manifestation of the preoccupation with security can be seen in the military budget. In spite of continued pressure by donors to reduce the military and its share of the national budget, the defense budget has expanded over the years. First, the NRA was hastily expanded after the Museveni takeover. At the end of the war, the army had numbered 20,000 (Watson 1988). Several thousand of the soldiers in the original NRA who were of Rwandan descent defected to the Rwandan Patriotic Front. By 1991, the NRA had been built up to a force of 80,000 soldiers. Museveni felt he needed to keep a large force because of continued insurgencies in the north and northeast as well as in the border regions. Between 1988 and 2007, the military budget grew from US$69.2 million to US$237 million (in 2005 dollars).[6]

When the NRA took over Kampala in January of 1986, it was primarily a force of westerners and southerners. This balance changed with the merging of armies, resulting in a feeling among some soldiers from Museveni's own Banyankole and Bahima subgroup that they had been sidelined (Watson 1991).[7] Museveni incorporated 40,000 former rebels along with soldiers loyal to Okello, Obote, and Amin into the army under a 1987 amnesty arrangement. He included in the NRA the UNLA, the Federal Democratic Movement (FEDEMU), the Uganda National Rescue Front (UNRF), and the Uganda National Army (UNA). The hope was that incorporating these armies would minimize the possibility for armed opposition to the regime. However, it also created its own set of problems, since some of these forces, like the former FEDEMU troops, allegedly engaged in repression of the population, exacerbating tensions between the people and NRA in places like Namokora and Kitgum (Amaza 1998, 150; Mudoola 1991, 239).

New ranks were introduced in the army to help shed its guerrilla identity, giving it a structure that was more in line with other armies around the world. Museveni also saw the army as a source of development through its National Enterprise Corporation, which was to carry out agricultural, scientific, technological, and industrial activities as well as generate income for the military.

Military expenditures reached a high of US$197 million in 2005 (SIPRI 2008), roughly the equivalent of expenditures on health in Uganda (Global Integrity 2006). The increase in military spending together with that of public administration more generally was the main reason for the expansion of government spending, resulting in fiscal deficits amounting to 13 percent of the gross domestic product in 2004 and 2005 (Tangri and Mwenda 2005).

As for the police, the Museveni government dishonorably discharged about 75 percent of the national force when it took over, giving rise to fears that Museveni was targeting cuts at northerners and easterners, who predominated in the force (Omara-Otunnu 1987, 178). Local militias that had been set up to protect against Karimojong raids were also disbanded, which led to increased cattle raiding in Iteso and nearby areas (Jones 2009).

The number of UPDF soldiers today is roughly estimated to be between 50,000 and 70,000, depending on how the various militias, paramilitary forces, and ghost soldiers are counted.[8] The government itself claims to have demobilized 60,000 of its soldiers since 1986, resulting in an army of about 40,000. Museveni states that the soldiers were retired because they needed to reallocate funds from personnel to equipment (Museveni 1997, 176). However, this does not account for the increased expenditures on paramilitary organizations, which have, in fact, expanded.

International donors were said to have pressured Uganda to put a ceiling on defense spending after 1996 and to undertake military reform. There is no evidence that there was a decline in military spending after 1996, although it has received the same proportion of the national budget. Nevertheless, the amount spent on agricultural development, for example, has been a small fraction of the defense expenditures. Between 1986 and 2007, for example, the government has spent twenty-six-and-a-half times more (USh 3,733.78 billion or US$1,867 billion) on defense than on agriculture (USh 141.28 billion or US$70 billion), which is a mainstay of the country's economy (Nyakairu 2007). As a result of both a World Bank Logistics and Accounting Reform Programme and a Uganda and Defence Efficiency Study by the UK, a comprehensive defense review was conducted in 2004, resulting in extensive reform of the UPDF. This included the passage of a defense-related bill aimed at improving civilian-soldier relations and the addressing of issues of recruitment, promotion, reserve force status, and command structure. US International Military Education and Training programs provided training in human rights, officer professionalism, and civil-military relations. Moreover, the Uganda Human Rights Commission carried out UPDF training programs to educate officers on internationally recognized human rights standards.

The Militarization of Society

In addition to creating a plethora of security agencies, the NRM infiltrated societal organizations and activities in a variety of ways. For years, communities have been organized to carry out state-funded political and military training (*mchakamchaka*) every morning. While marching in formation with wooden guns, citizens were also given political education and taught the virtues of the NRM and the ills of sectarian party politics. This was part of the NRM effort to "demystify the gun," so that arms would not be seen as the prerogative of a particular social force but rather as an instrument of political liberation (Mudoola 1991, 241). In 2008, the NRM announced it was reviving *mchakamchaka*, which had been voluntary, and would make it compulsory in accordance with Article 17 of the constitution, which requires every Ugandan citizen to "defend Uganda and to render national service when necessary" (Golooba-Mutebi 2008).

The military was well represented in parliament. The constitution ensures that ten representatives of the UPDF (of whom two must be women) hold parliamentary seats. An additional thirteen seats in the National Assembly are allocated to the original National Resistance Council members, most of whom were war veterans (that is, the aforementioned historicals).

Military personnel were frequently placed in key ministerial positions, named district administrators, and even given positions reserved for civil servants. In 2005, for example, the late Brigadier Nobel Mayombo, a close associate of Museveni, was appointed permanent secretary in the Ministry of Defence. The appointment was widely regarded as evidence of the militarization of the civil service (Nganda 2005a). The idea behind these appointments was to integrate the military into society and to seamlessly blend military institutions with administrative ones in order to create an image that the military was part of society rather than dominating it (Mudoola 1991, 243). Another way of reading this is that the military extended itself beyond the limits established by civilian rule to control society more directly.

Some of the ways in which society has been militarized are less conspicuous, but no less pernicious. For example, NRM-affiliated members of parliament and ministers have been known to wear military fatigues, undergo military training, and take military courses at the National Leadership Institute in Kyankwanzi. The media has also at times been infiltrated by spies and the military, according to a former reporter of *The Monitor* and Forum for Democratic Change (FDC) opposition spokesperson Wafula Oguttu ("FDC Raps Kyankwanzi Movt MPs Retreat" 2007). A military officer was arrested for taking photos of opposition leader Kizza Besigye's house, claiming to work for *Bukedde*, a Luganda daily newspaper.

Around the time of the 2006 elections, military personnel were promoted to key positions in the police and media. President Museveni appointed Noble Mayombo as board chairman of the government-owned newspaper *New Vision*. Relative to most government-owned newspapers in other African countries, the paper had been fairly balanced. It did not surprise observers that soon thereafter the editor-in-chief of twenty years, William Pike, was forced to resign.

These efforts to militarize society have often been met with resistance. Amid bitter protests by civil society organizations in 2006, parliament passed an NGO registration act that gave an NGO oversight board wide regulatory powers. The NGO board is dominated by government officials, including security officers. The act was soon thereafter suspended due to protests from NGOs. Nevertheless, the concerns remain. NGOs need to renew licenses every year and are concerned about the provision in the bill that gave powers to the board to deregister an NGO for contravening "any law." The act permits "nonpolitical and nonpartisan" advocacy. However, the Ugandan government will often construe ordinary advocacy activity by NGOs as antigovernmental and political. In the past, it has refused to renew licenses on these grounds for organizations like the Uganda Women's Network, the Uganda National NGO Forum, the Uganda Human Rights and Documentation Centre, and the National Organisation for Civic Education and Elections Monitoring (Kakande 2006). NGOs also resisted the 1989 NGO Registration Statute on similar grounds as well as the placement of NGO activities under the Ministry of Internal Affairs, which suggested that the supervision of NGOs was a security concern rather than a developmental one.

Corruption and Patronage in the Military

One of the main ways in which military loyalty is maintained in semiauthoritarian regimes is through patronage, which takes many forms. In Uganda, it has ranged from kickbacks and overbilling on sales of military supplies and equipment to allowing soldiers to plunder and loot property and wealth in occupied areas, such as Democratic Republic of Congo in the late 1990s. The discovery of tens of thousands of ghost soldiers on the military payroll was one of many such scams, which provides some insight into how patronage in the military works and how difficult it is to call to account individuals who are part of the network of patronage—unless there are other compelling reasons to get them out of the way.

In 2007, a new plan to reform the accounting system was put in place after ghost soldiers were found on the payroll. Museveni had asked a three-person High Command committee to investigate the ghost soldier phenomenon in the army in 2003. It included Defence Minister Amama Mbabazi, General David Tinyefuza, and General Caleb Akandwanaho (whose nom de guerre is Salim Saleh), and the late Brigadier Noble Mayombo ("Uganda Ghost Soldiers Discovered on Army Payroll" 2007; Kiggundu 2008). As a result of their report, dozens of army officers were prosecuted. One of them included the former army commander, Major General James Kazini, who was found guilty in 2008 for the loss of USh 61 million (US$35.5 million) as a result of the creation of ghost soldiers.

In the course of the investigation, Salim Saleh produced a minority report claiming that the problem went back to 1987 with the conflict in the north against Alice Lakwena and that it was exacerbated during Uganda's incursions into the Congo in 1997, during which time soldiers often were not paid until they returned. He attributed the problem to poor record keeping, the increase in NRA soldiers fighting in the Congo, and the loss of soldiers to AIDS without commensurate adjustments in bookkeeping (Mubangizi 2007). Former Minister of State for the Reconstruction of the North Betty Bigombe has argued that the weakness of the UPDF as a result of the ghost soldiers may prove to be one of the reasons that the army failed to extinguish the northern insurgency for two decades. This charge was corroborated by the committee, which had questioned Noble Mayombo, then chief of Military Intelligence, about the fact that more than half the UPDF's Fourth Division operating in the north were ghost soldiers. Mayombo admitted that during Operation Iron Fist in March 2001—which was to once and for all stop the rebel LRA—the Fourth Division was a ghost division and the army had had to deploy an additional 4,000 troops to support the operation.

The most revealing explanations, however, have come from rank-and-file soldiers themselves.[9] Sergeant Gitta Musoke, whose story has been covered by both *The Monitor* and *Weekly Observer,* said he joined the NRA in 1983 when he was abducted as a child soldier at the age of fourteen under the threat of death. He fought with the NRA in the guerrilla war and helped capture Kampala. Then he was deployed to the north and helped capture Koboko, Lira, and Gulu. He was part of the effort to defeat Alice Lakwena's forces, chasing them all the way to their demise in Jinja. He then fought Joseph Kony until 1993, after which he was deployed to Rwanda. In 1994, his war-weary unit asked Museveni to be redeployed. He was retrained as an auditor for the army, and took his job, as he had his previous duties, very seriously. He was so diligent that he started reporting the ghost soldiers he found on the payroll to his superiors. This landed him in a military jail cell and got him redeployed to Democratic Republic of Congo. He continued to report the discrepancies to higher-ups, resulting in more imprisonment and torture. Being the resourceful person he was, he persisted in trying to convey his message to higher authorities within the military, including the president himself.

Musoke's story is a riveting and horrifying account of someone trying to do the right thing in the midst of widespread corruption, patronage, and theft. Given the way he was treated all the way to the top ranks of the military, it is clear those responsible had no interest in hearing from this whistleblower. It is not difficult to draw the conclusion that many of the top military brass had a lot to hide and little interest in pursuing an accusation that might implicate their own wrongdoing (Mubangizi 2007).

The late Major General James Kazini, who was the former chief of land forces of the UPDF and a nephew of the president, eventually took the fall for the ghost soldier scandal. But for a long time Kazini suffered no consequences for his blunders. He had served as full colonel to the UPDF Fourth Division based in Gulu fighting the LRA. Then he was in charge of Operation Safe Haven against the Allied Democratic Forces rebels in western Uganda and Democratic Republic of Congo from 1998 to 2002. While in Democratic Republic of Congo, his forces clashed with Rwandan troops in Kisangani in 1999 and 2000, allegedly resulting in the deaths of seven hundred soldiers in the first clash alone (Kiggundu 2009). There were no repercussions for these incidents. Kazini was also involved in the 2002 Operation Iron Fist to flush out the LRA from their southern Sudanese positions, which not only failed but energized the LRA to carry out even more brutal attacks on the population in northern Uganda. In fact, Kazini was promoted to major general in 2001 at the same time that the UPDF was alleged to have been plundering the Congo for diamonds, gold, and timber and was investigated by the Porter Commission as a result of UN allegations regarding exploitation of resources. Andrew Mwenda has speculated that Kazini was promoted to major general because, unlike his predecessor Jeje Odongo, he was willing to engage in corrupt practices to help pay off the personal debts of other top military personnel.

However, Kazini's fortunes changed in 2003 when he was suspended as army commander and sent to Nigeria to a war college. At this time donors were clamoring to see signs of action against corruption and were making noises about withholding key external funding from government projects. Uganda has been unable to gain entry to the elite club of African countries that are benefiting from the multibillion-dollar US Millennium Challenge Account because of the perception that the government lacks the will to fight corruption.[10]

In 2008 the General Court Martial charged Kazini with maintaining ghost soldiers and insubordination. The High Command investigation produced evidence that he had abused his office and caused financial loss for the army by creating ghost soldiers, through forgery, and by transacting false documents. He had allegedly maintained 24,000 fictitious names on the army payroll, costing the armed forces USh 62 million (US$37.4 million) (Kiggundu 2009). Kazini was sentenced to three years in jail for these crimes in March 2009 but was released on bail, allegedly due to pressure from his colleagues in the top ranks of the military, which appeared to be split over his fate. He was, however, also charged with not carrying out the orders of the commander in chief, specifically of not transferring UPDF soldiers. He was believed to have built up a semiautonomous army unit, the 409 Brigade in West Nile, and some may have thought he was plotting to stage a coup (Sserwanga 2009). These charges might have resulted in the death penalty or life imprisonment. The Constitutional Court halted all cases against Kazini before the General Court Martial as of July 2009 but reversed its decision later that year. He was about to be sentenced when he was killed in 2009 in what appeared to be a lovers' quarrel.

Even after he died, the question remained, why was he charged and convicted as late as 2008 when there had been ample evidence of wrongdoing from the Porter Commission earlier on? The press also asked why he was singled out among many others involved in these practices. While it is impossible to know the exact reasons, some felt he had been stirring up dissent within the army, especially among frustrated officers who had no possibility for promotion (Onyango-Obbo 2001; "What Does the Imprisonment of Former Army Chief Maj Gen James Kazini Mean?" 2008). Andrew Mwenda suggests that Kazini was singled out because he had claimed that the ghost soldier scheme was sanctioned by the president to pay off Congolese rebels (2009). Regardless of the real reasons, the ghost soldier scam reveals the extent to which war had become business for those who profited from the UPDF's engagements in the north and in neighboring Democratic Republic of Congo. It provides important clues about what has kept the UPDF embroiled in war in so many parts of the country for so long. It is also a crucial piece of the puzzle necessary to explain the conflict in northern Uganda that has taken such a toll on the lives of millions of people.

Conclusion

This chapter has explored the crucial links between patronage, violence, and power. It has shown how central the military is to controlling society in a semiauthoritarian state. It has also provided evidence of how military and paramilitary forces are used to quell the opposition, and, finally, it has offered some clues of how patronage is used within the military via the case of the ghost soldier scandal. All these pieces of the story help us better understand our final paradox, namely that power is exercised in semiauthoritarian states through both patronage and repression. Both are necessary to co-opt and crush one's political opponents. They become the very reason that power is pursued and that leaders cling to power in semiauthoritarian and authoritarian regimes long after their welcome has been worn out. They cannot relinquish power because they have engaged in corrupt and violent actions to suppress their political opponents, and to leave is to invite retribution of the same kind upon themselves.

Notes

1. Personal correspondence with Crawford Young, January 2009.
2. Transparency International, http://www.transparency.org/policy_research/surveys _indices/cpi/2009/cpi_2009_table.
3. The former minister of health, Brigadier Jim Muhwezi, and other associates faced criminal charges of abuse of office, causing financial loss, embezzlement, theft, obtaining funds by false pretenses, and other charges relating to the mismanagement

and disappearance of US$4 million from funds of the Global Fund for HIV/AIDS, Tuberculosis, and Malaria (Mpagi 2007b).

4. Also see AfDevInfo, http://www.afdevinfo.com/htmlreports/org/org_53968.html. Accessed April 28, 2010.

5. Basiita (plural) refers to the Siita people; Musiita is the singular form.

6. SIPRI, http://milexdata.sipri.org/result.php4. Accessed July 7, 2009.

7. *Africa Confidential* puts the strength of the NRA in 1986 at 5,000 ("Uganda: A Man in No Hurry" 1990).

8. Also see http://www.iss.co.za/Af/profiles/Uganda/SecInfo.html. Accessed November 9, 2007.

9. See, for example, the account of Lance Corporal Godfrey Masaba ("Who Maimed, Killed Civilians in Northern Uganda?" 2008).

10. Also see *Uganda Observer,* http://www.ugandaobserver.com/new/news/news 200804034.php. Accessed May 5, 2008.

7

Peace and Insecurity

At the heart of the armed conflicts, there are issues of ethnicity, marginalization, abject poverty, national disunity, revenge, oppressive policies, and problematic governance. The LRA insurgency led by Joseph Kony is a direct manifestation of this. . . . The way out of chronic cycles of violence needs all stakeholders to stop blaming and accusing each other. We should be involved in finding the solution that is acceptable to all. This has been very difficult because of the militaristic approach to ending the northern Uganda conflict.
—George Omona, Acholi Leaders' Retreat, Paraa, June 23–26, 2005

A major factor impeding democratization has been the prevalence of conflict in Africa. African countries with limited political and civil liberties have tended to be more conflict prone. In the 1990s, many semiauthoritarian states—ten sub-Saharan states to be exact (43 percent)—experienced conflict, coups, and unrest *after* they liberalized. In that same decade, eleven authoritarian states in sub-Saharan Africa were beset by conflict, compared with only two democratic countries (18 percent of democratic countries in Africa) (see Table 7.1). In the semiauthoritarian states, the roots of conflict generally existed prior to political liberalization, and it is very likely that these states would have experienced the same conflicts with or without liberalization. What one can say with greater certainty is that countries that are democratic are less conflict prone.

Not only is conflict associated with the lack of democracy, it is also inextricably linked to poverty in Africa. Of the twenty-one African countries that experienced conflict after political reform, twenty were the poorest countries on the continent (using the Przeworski and Limongi [1997] scale).[1] It is perhaps stating the obvious to point out that Africa's poverty has had an impact on the frequency of conflict in the region.

At the same time, the steady end to a significant number of conflicts in Africa has been one of the most important changes on the African political landscape since the mid-1980s. Sometimes low-grade conflict has continued in the aftermath of a negotiated peace agreement. But overall there has been a decline in conflict: a decline in conflicts starting, an increase in conflicts ending, a drop

Table 7.1   African Countries Experiencing Conflict Following Political Liberalization

	Authoritarian Countries	Semiauthoritarian Countries	Democratic Countries	Total
No conflict	2 (15%)	13 (56%)	9 (82%)	24
Conflict	11 (85%)	10 (43%)	2 (18%)	23
Total	13 (100%)	23 (100%)	11 (100%)	47

Source: 2005 dataset created by the Centre for the Study of Civil War at the International Peace Research Institute, Oslo, and the Department of Peace and Conflict Research, Uppsala University. Freedom House, http://www.freedomhouse.org. Accessed June 19, 2009. International Peace Research Institute, http://www.prio.no/page/CSCW_research_detail/Programme_detail _CSCW/9649/45925.html.

in intensity of conflict, and a decline in long-standing conflicts, notwithstanding the continuing violence in the Democratic Republic of Congo, Sudan, and Somalia.

Uganda has been in a vortex of conflict in a region that has seen some of the worst conflicts in the late twentieth and early twenty-first centuries. The conflict in Democratic Republic of Congo (DRC) has involved a large number of its neighbors since 1998, including Uganda, whose leaders and generals have been implicated by the UN for plundering the country for their own personal ends. It is no accident that most of the countries involved in the extraction of wealth that has fueled the conflict, especially in the eastern part of the country, are authoritarian or semiauthoritarian. The causes of insecurity are directly tied to the ways in which power is configured and patronage distributed as well as to the survival methods of such regimes. Uganda's internal and external conflicts are reflections of the ways in which power is maintained in the country.

Nevertheless, since the 1990s at least thirteen conflicts have come to an end in sub-Saharan Africa and others have diminished in intensity. Factors mitigating against conflict more generally in Africa have come into play in Uganda as well, including greater international attention, regional mediation efforts to end the conflict, and a more active civil society. The Lord's Resistance Army (LRA) that had plagued northern and northeastern Uganda for over twenty years is still active, albeit diminished, having shifted operations into the DRC, southern Sudan, and Central African Republic. It has yet to be subdued.

Even though the National Resistance Movement (NRM) claimed to have brought peace to Uganda in 1986, this peace was not enjoyed equally throughout the country. After its 1986 takeover of Kampala, the Uganda National Army (UNA) had little rest, battling dozens of armies and militias on almost all of its borders. Within two years of the NRM takeover, the government was fighting twenty-seven different rebel groups (Bond and Vincent 2002, 27). The war that had begun in Luwero in the early 1980s continued in the north and northeast, turning at least one-third of the country into a war zone for almost the entire period the NRM has been in power.

Not surprisingly, when a 2005 Afrobarometer survey asked northerners about the main problem the government should address, their answers differed significantly from other regions, highlighting civil war, food shortages and famine, and political instability.[2] The continued expansion of the army—more than 20 percent of the national revenue went to the defense budget from 2002 to 2004—had not made large parts of the country more secure. By 2007 and 2008, about 10 percent of the budget was going into defense, which was almost four times the amount allocated for health (Ministry of Finance, Planning, and Economic Development 2009b).[3]

The most troubled region has been the north, where, after Museveni's takeover, the spirit-medium Alice Lakwena mounted her Holy Spirit Movement (HSM) until it was suppressed in 1987. After her defeat, Joseph Kony, who portrayed himself as another spirit-medium, launched the LRA to fight Museveni's National Resistance Army (NRA), embroiling the north in over two decades of fighting that targeted local residents, including Kony's own Acholi ethnic group. The national army was also implicated in some of the attacks on northerners and was often perceived as an additional source of insecurity by internally displaced persons (IDPs) living in camps. Uganda's military ventures have not been restricted to suppressing internal opposition; most notably they have involved entanglements in DRC.

While the decline in conflict in many parts of Africa, including Uganda, provides a context for the chapter, the focus is primarily on what it has meant for Uganda to be embroiled in so many conflicts after 1986 and the regional dimensions of these conflicts. The chapter simultaneously shows how integral conflict and insecurity are to semiauthoritarian rule. The lack of societal, legislative, and other constraints on the executive enable military adventures abroad. The plunder of resources from Democratic Republic of Congo and the false deployment of ghost soldiers in the north were seen by many as ways in which the military was rewarded for maintaining loyalty to the government.

The Origins of Conflict Under the NRM

The fighting groups that had helped oust Milton Obote's second government (1980–1985) and his Uganda National Liberation Army (UNLA) included an alliance of Museveni's NRA, the Uganda National Rescue Front (UNRF), the UNA, the Uganda Freedom Army/Movement (UFA/UFM), and the Federal Democratic Movement (FEDEMU). Once Tito Okello and Bazilio Okello's forces within the UNLA had overthrown Obote, they deserted the NRA. Tito

Okello opened the prison doors and released many thugs and criminals who had been recruited by the UFM and FEDEMU, which gave them uniforms and guns. They fought the NRA until the fall of Kampala in January 1986 (Mutibwa 1992, 170). Though a peace agreement between Okello and Museveni had been signed on December 17, 1985, the NRA, which felt the agreement was a trap, continued fighting. When the NRA took over Kampala, the UFM and FEDEMU returned to the NRA fold along with the former UNA and UNRF.

After former president Milton Obote was overthrown, he fled to Dar es Salaam and later to Lusaka; General Tito Okello was ensconced in eastern Sudan and Idi Amin was self-exiled in Saudi Arabia. There were reports as of March 1986 that Khartoum supported Okello's UNLA, which was attacking the Sudanese government's enemy, the Sudanese People's Liberation Army (SPLA) in southern Sudan. But Museveni's woes were only just beginning. According to Museveni, 10,000 UNLA troops had regrouped in Sudan and northern Uganda, forming the Uganda People's Democratic Army (UPDA) also known as Cilil. Having looted money and cars in southern Uganda, they lived well in southern Sudan until they ran out of money. Then they had to farm in Sudanese gardens to eat, while their leaders fled to the United States, Europe, and Kenya.[4] Amama Mbabazi, the former defense minister, says that they were disarmed by Sudan on August 19, 1986, but were immediately rearmed, and on August 22, 1986, the fighters, led by Bazilio Okello, mounted an attack on the Ugandan government's military units at Bibia, seeking to take over Gulu, Kitgum, Lira, and eventually Kampala ("Is Museveni Using Kony War to Stay in Power?" 2004).

The UPDA was repelled by the NRA and dispersed into Gulu and Kotido; at their height, their number may have reached as many as 50,000 (Amaza 1998; Museveni 1997, 177). They continued to conduct guerrilla warfare, harassing and intimidating citizens, burning houses, robbing cattle, and killing elders, chiefs, and local council (LC) officials who worked with the NRM administration, although they were regularly overpowered by the NRA, according to NRA commanders (Amaza 1998, 121). Their activities hardly endeared them to the local population; soon they retreated and elements began to regroup within the context of the HSM.

Conflict in the East

Insecurity ensued and spread throughout northern and eastern Uganda (see Table 7.2). During their brief stint in power, the Okellos had recruited hundreds of people from Karamoja into the army; when they were ousted a year later, the Karimojong retreated to Karamoja with their arms. They joined forces with the rebel militia of Colonel Ojuku. Together they mounted cattle

Table 7.2 Major Rebel Groups That Fought Government Troops (NRA-UPDF) After 1986

Name of Group	Years Active	Leaders	Bases of Operation
Former Uganda National Army (UNA)	1980–1986	Former military personnel serving under Idi Amin	West Nile, northwest Arua
Uganda National Rescue Front (UNRF)	1980–1998	Brigadier Moses Ali	West Nile
National Federal Army (NFA)	Mid-1980s		Northeast Arua
National Army for the Liberation of Uganda (NALU)	Late 1980–early 1990s	Amon Bazira, Jafari Salimu	Eastern Rwenzori mountains, eastern Congo in Kivu, carried out attacks in Kasese
Holy Spirit Movement (HSM)	1986–1987	Alice Lakwena	Gulu
Uganda People's Army (UPA)	1986–1992	Peter Otai, Hitler Eregu	Teso
Lord's Resistance Army (LRA)	1989 to present	Joseph Kony	Northern Uganda, southern Sudan (Garamba National Forest), Democratic Republic of Congo
Uganda National Democratic Army (UNDA)	1994–1995	Herbert Itongwa	Buganda
Ninth of October Movement (NOM), joined UPA	1994–1996		East Bukeddi, Mbale, Tororo (Kenya)
West Nile Bank Front (WNBF)	1995–1997	Juma Oris	Northwestern Koboko, northwestern Arua
Allied Democratic Forces	1996–2001	Taban Amin, Jamil Mukulu	Bundibugyo, Kasese, Kabarole
Uganda National Rescue Front II (UNRF II)	1998–2002	Colonel Ali Bamuze, Brigadier Nasur Ezaga	West Nile

Note: Other rebel groups include Action Restore Peace (ARP), the Allied Democratic Movement (ADM), the National Democratic Front (NDF), the Uganda Federal Democratic Front (UFDF), the Uganda People's Democratic Army (UPDA), the Uganda National Federal Army/Movement (UNFA/M), the Uganda National Liberation Front (UNLF), the Uganda Salvation Army (USA), and the Uganda Muslim Liberation Army (UMLA). Force Obote Back Again (FOBA) was allegedly a creation of the NRA, according to UPC.

raids on neighboring Kitgum, Lira, Apac, Soroti, Kumi, and Kapchorwa (Amaza 1998, 118–119). The Karimojong had acquired a large number of guns in 1978 and 1979 during the campaign to oust Amin and now employed these same guns for cattle raiding, stealing almost all the cattle from Teso, Acholi, and Lango (Mirzeler and Young 2000; Museveni 1997, 179). In 2001, three thousand head of cattle remained in Gulu, only a fraction of the previous amount. This looting of cattle was profoundly disturbing to the northerners who saw it as part of a deliberate strategy to subdue the north (Finnström 2008, 72).

Many of the rebel groups were based in Kenya; overtaken early in 1987, some shifted into cattle rustling. The rebellion was fragmented, which added to people's sense of insecurity and impoverishment. Rather than fighting the government, the rebels ended up often exacting revenge on local residents for small grievances and exacerbating local disputes. Local leaders, in particular village council chairmen and parish chiefs, were targeted (Jones 2009). Some of the unrest in the east was fueled by the NRA, which carried out atrocities in places like Soroti ("Straining at the Edges" 1990).

In Mbale and Tororo in 1987, former UPC elements led by ministers under Obote, David Anyoti, Masette Kuuya, and Wilson Kwenga formed a group called Force Obote Back Again (FOBA), later renamed the Ninth of October Movement or NOM (Amaza 1998, 120). FOBA became part of the Uganda People's Army (UPA), led by former Obote minister Peter Otai in Teso. In a particularly gruesome incident in Mukura, Teso, in 1989, several hundred people (accounts range from sixty-nine to three hundred) were suffocated and killed in a train wagon during the battle between the NRA and UPA (Obore 2006). The UPA was eventually suppressed in 1992.

As a byproduct of these internal conflicts, Museveni faced strained relations with Kenya. The disputes were partly over commercial losses that Kenya incurred when Uganda shifted to using railways rather than Kenyan trucking companies. But a major aggravation of the tensions was Uganda's suspicion that Kenya was harboring Ugandan rebels, while Kenya blamed Uganda for fomenting dissent in Kenya. Because some NRA forces had been trained in Libya during the bush war, the Kenyan government accused the NRM government of helping Kenyans travel to Libya for training to oppose the Moi government. In retaliation, it allegedly allowed Ugandan NOM rebels to establish bases in Kenya from which to launch attacks. It also provided asylum or safe passage to UPA rebel leaders like Peter Otai and Colonel Omaria, in spite of objections from the Ugandan government. The Kenyan border with Uganda provided ample opportunities for cattle rustling by the Karimojong and Turkana. Cattle-rustling networks throughout Uganda, Kenya, Sudan, Somalia, and even Ethiopia helped fuel small arms sales in the region. These arguments resulted in the intermittent closing of the border between Uganda and Kenya (Watson 1988). While never going to war, they came to the brink in 1987.

Conflict in Rwenzori

In the eastern Rwenzori Mountains, the National Army for the Liberation of Uganda (NALU) was formed under the leadership of Amon Bazira, who had served in the Obote administration as a deputy minister. Drawing on the older, secessionist Rwenzururu movement of the Bakonzo and Baamba peoples, the NALU was based in eastern Congo in Kivu, and carried out attacks on government officials in Kasese. Zaire suspected that Uganda was harboring rebels associated with a movement calling itself Parti de Libération Congolais, which aimed to overthrow the Mobutu government in Zaire. As a result, it allowed the NALU to operate on its soil, and it is also rumored to have provided the NALU with logistics and personnel (Amaza 1998, 139).

Conflict in West Nile

In the West Nile region, UNRF and former UNA elements resisted the NRA takeover but were not welcomed home and retreated into Sudan and DRC. These remnants of Idi Amin's UNA came to be regarded during Amin's time as a West Nile institution, since so many of the high-ranking officers came from this region. The UNRF and former UNA attacked the United National Liberation Front government in 1980 (which had ousted Idi Amin with the help of Tanzanian forces). The UNRF and UNA then battled the Obote government until 1985, when they joined the Okello-Lutwa government that took over. There had been a short-lived alliance between the UNRF and NRA brokered in Libya, which allegedly backed both organizations in their fight against the Obote government. When the NRA took over Uganda in 1986, it fell into disarray, especially with the arrests of key leaders. However, they resumed fighting against the Museveni government in the mid-1990s, operating from bases in DRC and Sudan (Refugee Law Project 2004, 5).

UNRF II was formed in Sudan in 1998 with a force of about three thousand soldiers, who attacked Uganda from bases in southern Sudan. Internal divisions within the UNRF led to the formation of UNRF II, which aimed to create conditions that would allow the splinter group to return to West Nile. It felt that the NRA had not lived up to its end of the agreement with the UNRF. Moreover, the West Nile region had not been developed and was perceived as being marginalized. Ex-UNRF fighters faced growing insecurity, harassment, and arrests without trial.

In 1995, Juma Oris, a former army officer and minister in the Amin government as well as a former UNA member, led another contingent from Arua and Moyo to collaborate with the Sudanese government in the hopes of regaining power. His West Nile Bank Front (WNBF) offered money to recruit fighters, but the money was rarely forthcoming. Abduction became a primary way of recruiting fighters; the WNBF became increasingly brutal and, not surprisingly, lost what popularity it had. It is suspected that the brutal tactics of the WNBF were learned from the LRA, also based in Sudan. The West Nile population believed that UNRF II had also adopted these tactics and thus it, too, lost whatever popular support it might have had as the local population increasingly became targets of abductions and violence (Refugee Law Project 2004, 5–16). The WNBF was eventually obliterated by the Uganda People's Defence Forces (UPDF), as was its successor organization, the Allied Democratic Forces (ADF), under the command of Idi Amin's son, Major General Taban Amin.

Most of the conflict involving the UNRF and WNBF was based in the West Nile region, particularly Arua, Moyo, and Yumbe, creating enormous instability in the region until 2002, when the government of Uganda signed a peace agreement with UNRF II, bringing the conflict to an end.

Allied Democratic Forces

Yet another source of instability in Uganda came from the ADF, which launched an insurgency in 1996 to overthrow the government. The ADF was a Khartoum-supported rebel group backed by the Sudanese Islamic leader Hasan al-Turabi operating in the Rwenzori Mountains and the Bwindi Forest with bases in Kasese and eastern DRC. The ADF was comprised of an odd mixture of ex-soldiers of the Mobutu regime, the NALU, as well as some ex-members of Rwanda's militias (Forces Armées Rwandaises, or FAR, and Interahamwe) who were implicated in the 1994 genocide in Rwanda and had fled to the DRC. They also included Muslim fundamentalists known as Salaaf Tabliqs, originally from Iganga. The ADF recruited primarily from the Busia, Masaka, Mpigi, Kampala, and Ntungamo districts.[5]

The Tabliq Youth Movement had emerged in Uganda in the early 1980s to carry out reform within the Muslim community. The Tabliqs objected to government interference in their affairs and started agitating to prevent the government-supported Ugandan Muslim Supreme Council leader from assuming office. The Tabliq movement then split, and the more radical of the two movements, led by Jamil Mukulu, went underground and started receiving military training, supported by Sudan. The movement resurfaced as the ADF in 1996 (Kayunga 1993, 116).

One of its leaders, Taban Amin, was Idi Amin's son and was also close to Laurent-Désiré Kabila. He commanded a rebel group backed by Kabila in 1998 in Kindu. For years, the ADF sponsored almost daily killings of five to fifty citizens in the west and northwest, even reaching Kampala, where it killed dozens in random grenade attacks in 1998. It abducted children and was involved in hit-and-run operations. By May 2007, it appeared that the ADF command in eastern Congo had been destroyed and the last remnants of the army were surrendering. At the height of the ADF's activities, many Muslim leaders claimed they felt unjustly targeted for roundups and detentions by the government in its efforts to suppress the ADF. In areas of rebel conflict, government soldiers allegedly tortured ADF suspects who had been charged with treason.

Conflict in the North:
Alice Lakwena and the Holy Spirit Movement

Yet another group, Alice (Auma) Lakwena's HSM and her army, the Holy Spirit Mobile Forces, was formed in 1986 out of splinter groups of the UPDA. Even her father, Severino Lukoya, had his own army. She was a Protestant who converted to Catholicism, then claimed to have been possessed by the spirits of an Italian military engineer, Lakwena; a North American called Dr. Wrong Element, who spoke with a loud voice and was quarrelsome and impolite; Ching Poh from China; Franko from Zaire; some Muslims; Nyaker from Acholi; and others (Behrend 1999).

She recruited soldiers, sometimes forcibly, killing hundreds who refused to join the HSM (Watson 1988). Some of her soldiers were armed only with sticks and rocks, singing hymns as hundreds of troops died in battle. They believed that a magic lotion of shea butter would prevent them from being penetrated by bullets, which would boomerang back to the army.

Museveni never saw Alice Lakwena's war as politically motivated. He believed her movement was made up of gangster groups of ex-soldiers who were fighting because they feared prosecution (Novicki and Dennis 1988). However, others, like Amaza (1998, 127), have argued that her cause resonated with the population, giving her considerable popular support in the region. She played on fears of retribution and called on Acholis to rise up against the NRA to prevent them from annihilating the Acholi as a people. Her status as a medium further enhanced the appeal of her message and her goals of overthrowing the NRM government. In 1987, as she prepared to mount an offensive against Jinja (eighty kilometers from Kampala), she was finally stopped, thanks in part to the participation of an active Resistance Council (RC) system in Busoga (Mudoola 1991, 235). Lakwena was forced to flee to Kenya, where she maintained refugee status until her death in 2007.

Conflict in the North: The Beginnings of the LRA

After Museveni's takeover in 1986, various armies were integrated into the NRA. One battalion of former FEDEMU soldiers was sent to the north, unleashing atrocities that were perceived as retribution for what the UNLA had done in the south in Luwero. Other NRA units similarly terrorized the population. While battling the UPDA and HSM, the NRA engaged in extra-judicial killings of civilians, brutalized them, and decimated their livestock in what was experienced by northerners as extreme punishment, humiliation, and retribution. Hundreds of thousands of people were displaced. NRA Generals Samson Mande and David Tinyefuza, who were involved in these activities, have openly admitted to such atrocities. In fact, all these forces—the NRA, HSM, and UPDA—engaged in looting, killing, and arson in 1986 and 1987, resulting in enormous devastation and the loss of schools, dispensaries, homes, and granaries from Gulu to Kitgum, Lira, and Apac. Not surprisingly, people in these regions became enraged at the NRA.

At the same time, disaffected soldiers of the UNLA feared the kind of retribution carried out when Amin ousted Obote, especially because they had carried out extensive killings, looting, and brutalities in the predominantly Baganda Luwero region during Obote's Operation Bonanza. Lacking discipline and having no marketable skills, they remained unemployed in the north. They had become virtual strangers in their own communities. They fled to Sudan because they thought Museveni would never forgive them for what they did in Luwero and that their best recourse would be to fight him and get back to power. They benefited from easy access to small arms at a time when AK-47s were selling for US$12 in markets along the border with Sudan. They lured child soldiers with false promises and started recruiting for their army. The systematic use of child soldiers was being practiced by many armies, including the NRA; it was not all that unusual at this time. Some of these former UNLA soldiers joined forces with ex-UPDA soldiers.

A 1987 amnesty and various presidential pardons provided the necessary carrot for many defecting fighters, who crossed over to the side of the government and the NRA. Over 2,500 fighters in UNRF II, a splinter group of the WNBF, for example, took advantage of the amnesty (Dolan 2005, 54). By the end of 1988, the UPDA had disintegrated and key commanders had surrendered to the government ("Dusting Off the Jewel" 1988).

In Kampala, Andrew Kayiira, the former head of UFA/UFM, had been made energy minister under Museveni but was then implicated in a coup attempt and arrested. The charges were ultimately dropped; however, he was killed soon thereafter under circumstances that to this day are being debated. Allegedly he was killed after announcing that he would investigate the killing of hundreds of UFA soldiers that had been absorbed by the NRA. The outcome of a Scotland Yard investigation into the causes of his death mysteriously disappeared. In 2007, a widespread debate erupted over the cause of his death, feeding into Baganda frustrations over the way their hopes for *federo* were dashed.

On October 9, 1988, Museveni announced the end of the war in the northern and eastern provinces of Uganda. Whatever peace he experienced, it was elusive, as conflict continued in the north and northeast. On March 29, 1989, it was reported that a secret military cooperation agreement was signed between Uganda and the Colonel John Garang's SPLA, the aforementioned rebel force operating in southern Sudan against the Khartoum government. The agreement committed Uganda to providing equipment and training for the SPLA as well as passports for travel abroad. Uganda also provided SPLA with free passage through Uganda in conducting its operations. The Sudanese government itself had allegedly armed the UPDA and, later, the LRA, led by Joseph Kony in northern Uganda. In 1990, the UPDA signed the Addis Ababa Accord, and some rebels were integrated into the NRA, while others joined the LRA. By 1991, the LRA was the only rebel movement in the north. Thus a proxy war was fomented. Uganda and Sudan broke off diplomatic ties in 1995 after relations between the countries had deteriorated as a result of the accusations by Uganda that Sudan had backed the LRA and Sudan's counteraccusations that Uganda had supported the SPLA.

Conflict Between the Ugandan Army and the LRA

Nowhere has the Museveni government failed its own people as much as in the north and northeast from 1986 to present. The lack of serious effort to resolve the crisis in the north despite ample opportunities—not to mention the active sabotage of some of the peace talks—left the northerners feeling that they were being punished for the actions of previous governments, armies, and armed groups.

Most of the international community similarly failed Uganda in this part of the country until Jan Egelund, the UN's undersecretary for humanitarian affairs, brought attention to the issue in 2003, calling it "the biggest neglected humanitarian emergency in the world" and a "moral outrage" ("Northern Uganda 'World's Biggest Neglected Crisis'" 2004). As former minister for reconstruction of the north, Betty Bigombe explained to me: "The international community only wanted to focus on success stories; nobody wanted to talk about the problems in the north. Until recently, the perception was that the economy in Uganda was picking up, tourism was increasing, [and] HIV/AIDS was down."[6] The World Bank was reluctant to get involved in a region embroiled in war, yet the lack of development was adding fuel to the conflict.

Caught in a proxy war between Uganda and Sudan, northerners felt ignored by the rest of the country, the government, donors, and the international community. They were not treated as full citizens of Uganda and had been left to languish. Many Acholi political leaders and many in the Acholi diaspora, rightly or wrongly, felt that the continuation of the war between government troops and the LRA was part of an effort to punish the Acholi for the brutalities inflicted by northern soldiers during the Luwero war and to eliminate them as a people. The government itself has claimed that the LRA rebellion was supported by the

Acholi leaders themselves and was a consequence of the leaders' failure to work with the government to suppress the rebellion (Amaza 1998, 133). Stereotypes and distortions regarding the Acholi as a people ran rampant. For example, in one of his speeches, President Museveni described the Acholi as grasshoppers in a bottle who would eat each other before they made their way through the neck (Finnström 2008, 106).

By 2005, the conflict in the northern part of Uganda had become the longest standing conflict in Africa, given its origins in the 1986 hostilities. Many representatives of the Ugandan government, the international news media, and nongovernmental organizations (NGOs) as well as some academics argued that the rebels, under the direction of a deranged leader, Joseph Kony, had no clear political agenda and were simply seeking to take over and run the country according to the Ten Commandments. In contrast, Sverker Finnström (2008) has argued that the LRA had political objectives that were expressed in radio interviews, manifestos, and fliers. However disingenuous the LRA may have seemed given its own part in creating the very problems it claimed to abhor, it had demanded the dismantling of the massive IDP camps of 1.5 million people, the placement of the Acholi on an equal footing with the rest of the nation, an end to the killing of the Acholi, reparations for lost cattle, the holding of free elections, multipartyism, and peaceful negotiations as a way to end the conflict.

LRA soldiers believed they were messengers of God sent to fight evil and oust the NRM for its sale of Acholi land and the privatization of its industries. Their goal was to literally create a new Acholi people and a new society, to be known as Acholi Manyen (Dolan 2005, 79). The violence seemed irrational, but its symbolism was not lost on the people in the north. For example, the ears of those who listened to government propaganda were cut off, as were the lips of those who spoke to government officials. The goal of the LRA was to traumatize the population as a whole and bring the activities of normal life to a halt. They attempted to justify their violence by saying it was moral because God had decreed it.

The LRA was not supported by the local population because of its heinous military tactics, such as abducting children (as well as adults) and forcing them to kill, rape, and torture family members or to observe such acts. Chris Dolan (2005) argues that what little support there may have been early on for the LRA dissipated after 1990 when their tactics became more brutal.

However, outside of the north, the misperception was common that because northerners had voted against the NRM, they must support the LRA. The UPDF similarly treated the population with suspicion, because it believed there were LRA supporters in the midst of the IDP camps. During interviews I carried out in three IDP camps near Gulu in 2005 (Pabbo, Unyama, and Palenga), people expressed nothing but antipathy for the LRA. They might on rare occasions have helped the LRA when forced to do so or in cases involving an injured relative who was with the LRA. Some orphans and other vulnerable people may have joined the LRA in order to obtain food. Others remained with them because returning to their communities would be too difficult given the atrocities they had committed. But there was no widespread popular support among the local population for what could only be perceived as a tragedy. Some support came from the diaspora in Europe and the United States—that is, from individuals who were out of touch with the situation on the ground and whose hatred for Museveni drove them to support any force resisting his government.

By 1996, 2 million northerners were IDPs, and 1.5 million of them were residing in 242 IDP camps in eighteen districts. They had been moving into the camps since the mid-1990s, sometimes willingly and sometimes by force, to escape LRA attacks and abductions. Tens of thousands of children and adults were abducted, and thousands of children were forced to walk to urban areas at night for safety.

Joseph Kony had led the LRA in carrying out systematic violence against people in northern Uganda since 1989. Some of the worst violence—which involved the cutting of ears, lips, and genitalia—occurred between 1991 and 1996 and then reemerged in 2005 (Dolan 2005, 79). The worst atrocities involved large-scale massacres, which began in April 1995 with the murder of two hundred people in Atyak, after which Uganda broke ties with Sudan. This mass murder was followed by many others; 150 Sudanese refugees were massacred in July 1996; four hundred people were clubbed or hacked to death in Lamwo County in January 1997; ninety people, mostly children, were killed in Mucwini, Kitgum; 120 were massacred in Amyuel in October 2002; three hundred were burned in their huts in Barlonyo, Lira, in February 2004; and there were still more. In most cases the UPDF arrived on the scene long after the LRA had departed (Rodríguez Soto 2009). The LRA abducted tens of thousands of people, who were used as soldiers, sex slaves, and porters. The majority escaped, while thousands died in captivity. Sometimes they would be used as porters for a day and then released. Between 1986 and 2001, as many as one-third of those abducted were children (about 10,000). About 78 percent of all abductees were returned within a year of abduction and another 16 percent in the following year (UNICEF 2001, cited in Dolan 2005, 75). In this same period, about 21 percent of the abductees were women from Kitgum and about 17 percent women from Gulu, with about 2,250 women remaining in captivity. Most became "wives" to the LRA soldiers.

IDP Camps

Nowhere is the security fallacy of the Museveni government more clear than in the IDP camps in northern Uganda. The situation in northern Uganda became a severe humanitarian crisis as famine and illness ravaged the internally displaced population. The government abdicated virtually all responsibility to the people in the northern and northeastern third of the country. The population interpreted their internment in IDP camps and the lack of food, services, and development initiatives as punishment and indication of their status as second-rate citizens. Oxfam Australia was the only NGO based in northern Uganda in the late 1980s. The Red Cross came and went with blankets and supplies. The World Food Programme came in 1994, and World Vision and the Norwegian Refugee Council followed, providing humanitarian support. Small amounts of international funding trickled in from the Danish International Development Agency (DANIDA), the British government, and USAID for escaped abductees and for the development activities administered through the UN Disaster Management Team, UNICEF, and UN Office for the Coordination of Humanitarian Affairs (UNOCHA) (Dolan 2005, 56).

Ironically, this modest assistance made it even easier for the government to do virtually nothing in this part of the country. My interviews with about fifty women in camps showed that women were growing food, farming other people's gardens, and carrying out business in order to provide for their families under extremely precarious circumstances. The World Food Programme's donations covered about 8 percent of their food needs, in contrast to its claims that it was providing 75–80 percent of their food needs. People I interviewed in 2005 went to sleep hungry one or two nights each week.

Although there was considerable donor and international NGO support for former abductees and children who commuted to the urban centers at night to escape the LRA, there was virtually no assistance for children and adults in the IDP camps. This is because the stories of the abductees and the night commuters evoked greater international sympathy and donations. But the plight of those in the camps was every bit as dire. It raised troubling questions about the role of the international community in supporting IDPs. It also raised questions about the utility of providing only humanitarian food aid when far more substantial income-generating and development assistance was required to allow for real subsistence above starvation levels. The IDPs were pawns in a conflict that the state did not appear interested in resolving. Indeed, some military leaders may have been actively drawing it out, given that war had become a business for some (see the discussion of ghost soldiers in Chapter 6).

In the camps, the population faced massive human rights violations at the hands of their protectors, the Ugandan army. Many IDPs told me the soldiers would beat people if they talked at night in their huts or if they were late from the fields, coming in after the 4 p.m. curfew. They stole food from people's meager plots of land in areas surrounding the camp. Even with supposed UPDF protection in the camps, the IDPs were vulnerable to rebel attacks and kidnappings. Some UPDF soldiers took advantage of the hunger and poverty in camps, impregnating girls lured by food, money, and promises of marriage. Some IDPs became infected by HIV/AIDs in this manner.

Human rights activists in the north, meanwhile, drew attention to torture by the UPDF soldiers. Every month, fifty cases on average were being documented by groups like Human Rights Focus in Gulu. When I visited the camps surrounding Gulu in 2005, there were eighteen cases of torture pending in Gulu courts. In one case, a woman from Awach camp, after sleeping in the field she had been cultivating, went back home in the morning to be discovered by a soldier who put feces on her head and paraded her in public as a warning to others. In another case, a woman had gone home to pick passionfruit for her children. She saw a small bag in the thicket and became scared. The mother told her children to go back to the camp and tell the soldiers that their mother had found a bag of money owned by the rebels. The soldiers beat her. At the end of the day, an old man in the camp said the money was his and admitted he had hidden the bag in the bush for fear of looting.

Along with rates of congestion in the camps, the mortality rates for children were above emergency levels, according to UNICEF studies. Malnutrition was rampant, and the health conditions were dire for the population at large.

People were reduced to a level of hopelessness and helplessness rarely seen in other parts of Uganda. Whereas in central Uganda, women's organizations typically adopt names that signify the strength that comes from togetherness, empowerment, and progress, the women I interviewed in Gulu IPD camps had groups with names like Poverty Does Not Leave Us, The Poor Do Not Sleep, Poverty Is Not a Relative, Where Should I Go? Fighting Follows Us, We Have No Hope, We Have No Strength, and Digging Sand Is Hard. Noticeably, many men had stopped seeking strategies to cope and had resorted to alcohol, which had additional implications for violence against women.

Proxy War

Another dimension of this war was its proxy nature. Sudan accused the NRM government of supporting SPLM/SPLA forces in Arua, Koboko, Midigo, and Oraba in West Nile and Gulu. The Ugandan government denied these accusations and, in turn, accused the Sudanese government of harboring UPDA soldiers, who launched attacks into Ugandan territory in 1988 and 1989. Later on they claimed that it was impossible for the LRA to operate without support from the Sudanese government, considering that a Sudanese plane had bombed Moyo in November 1989 (Dolan 2005, 45). The Sudanese capacity to support Ugandan rebels was curtailed when the SPLA captured the Eastern Equatoria region in 1989, making it difficult for the UPDA to purchase ammunition, which it had done on the open market in the border town of Nimule.

However, after 1991, rebels reestablished contact with and began obtaining supplies from the Sudanese government.

Divisions within the SPLA facilitated the rise of the LRA and its backing by Khartoum. In addition to the main faction led by Colonel John Garang, another faction (of what came to be five factions) was led by Dr. Riek Machar (of SPLA-Nasir, renamed SPLM/A-United), who reunited with Garang in 1995 after earlier establishing connections with Khartoum in order to obtain support to fight Garang's group. This led to further fractionalization within the southern Sudanese armies and loss of territory to Khartoum (Johnson 2003).

In 1994, according to the Swiss Small Arms Survey (GIIS 2007), Machar—who later became vice president in the government of southern Sudan and mediator in the Juba peace process—formed another group, the Southern Sudan Independence Movement/Army, which was in alliance with pro-Khartoum Equatorial Defence Forces. William Nyuon Bany, who was then commander of Machar's forces, established ties between the LRA and Khartoum. He was said to be in alliance with Sudanese government troops and provided sanctuary and training facilities to the LRA in the area bordering the Kitgum district. From 1994 onward, the Sudanese government provided the LRA with military training, soldiers, and weapons. According to a Sudanese Acholi close to Kony, Dr. Lenzio Angole Onek, "Khartoum armed Kony with everything an army needs to fight a ground war. He had his major base in Jabelein and two offices in Juba [plus] one in the major military garrison. Kony once told me that he also visited Egypt and Libya and had some of his forces trained in some Asian countries" (Nyakairu 2008). The NRA claimed killing and capturing several Sudanese in Uganda in 1992. Further evidence of Sudanese influence was seen in the LRA's adopting such Muslim practices as not eating pork and treating Friday as a day of rest, even though the army had identified itself as Christian.

To assuage Sudanese fears that the SPLA was not based in Uganda, Uganda allowed the Sudanese Monitoring Team to enter Arua, Moyo, and Gulu in 1989. Uganda later accused the team of recruiting spies and making contacts with Kony's forces. In turn, Uganda was alleged to have signed a military cooperation agreement with the SPLA in 1989 providing equipment and training as well as free passage through Ugandan territory (Amaza 1998, 137). Thus the conflict took on the dimension of a proxy war between the two countries, with neither openly admitting its role in backing rebel soldiers.

Government Strategy

Throughout the conflict, Museveni adopted contradictory strategies of simultaneously fighting the LRA, attempting to negotiate with it, and offering its fighters amnesty, none of which was successful. Of course, offers to negotiate were consistently undermined by military action and by efforts, as Chris Dolan (2005) explains, to humiliate the LRA in the process of talks. In 2004, the former minister of defense, Amama Mbabazi, argued that the government was more than ready to negotiate truces with rebel groups, having signed sixteen such agreements with different groups in the past. As he explained, "The hallmark of the [NRM] and the Movement administration has been the resolution of political questions by political means rather than by force. . . . It is, therefore, hard to believe that the president would maintain a war, which has drained huge resources from development and has seriously tarnished Uganda's image, scaring away tourists and investors" ("Is Museveni Using Kony War to Stay in Power?" 2004).

Major General David Tinyefuza, who was minister of state for defense, was in command of operations against the LRA between 1991 and 1994. Based in Lira, he adopted such heavy-handed tactics as cordoning off Gulu, Kitgum, Lira, and Apac; cracking down brutally on rebels and alleged sympathizers; and arresting politicians. A media blackout was enforced during this campaign, known as Operation North (1991–1992). This only served to heighten popular discontent with the UPDF, and local residents formed self-defense local militias called Arrow Groups to fight the rebels. They did so with the encouragement of Betty Bigombe, who had been appointed as minister of state for the pacification of the north in 1988. As the fighting escalated, so did the brutality of LRA tactics. Soldiers in the local militias were slaughtered by the thousands, and Bigombe urged Museveni to adopt a new strategy that involved a peace process.

The government initiated peace talks with the LRA in 1993. Kony met with Bigombe on November 25, 1993, at Pagik, Amuru, and asked for a comprehensive peace agreement involving the Acholi community as a whole as well as members of the political wing of the LRA. He sought six months to arrange for the settlement (Atkinson forthcoming). As Dolan explains, the way the peace talks were conducted "contributed to a wider attempt by the government to humiliate and discount the rebels . . . which only served to entrench them in an oppositional mode and created the space for further militarism on the part of the government" (2005, 97). Finally, on February 6, 1994, Museveni issued an ultimatum that the LRA surrender within seven days or face increased hostilities. This basically ended the peace process and instead led to an escalation in violence (Dolan 2005, 46).

In 1994, Tinyefuza was replaced by Brigadier Seif Ali. The heightening of conflict was followed by the creation of protected villages and IDP camps in 1996 and the roundup of residents for identification in a series of exercises called *panda gari* (which literally means "climb into the truck"; under Obote II, the practice was common and often meant those arrested were never seen again). The diaspora group called Kacokke Madit, the Acholi Religious Leaders Peace Initiative, and traditional leaders all called for peace talks, while the eleven-member Acholi Parliamentary Group called for a national investigation into the situation in the north (Dolan 2005, 46). These efforts to find a peaceful resolution to the conflict clashed with the government's insistence on a military solution.

In 1997, the UPDF became more focused on its involvement in DRC and in 1999 became engaged in clashes with Rwanda; as a result, LRA violence subsided. People began to move back to their homes from the camps. In December 1999, Sudan and Uganda signed an accord in which each country agreed to stop supporting rebel activity within the other country's borders; however, the agreement did not include any mention of the LRA. According to Chris Dolan (2005), the fact that the LRA was not included in the signing of the peace agreement on December 8, 1999, between the government of Sudan and the government of Uganda (with the mediation of the Carter Center) contributed to its persistent sense that the Ugandan government considered them too unimportant to take seriously.

The Amnesty Act was passed in 2000 to offer amnesty to anyone who had engaged in war against the government of Uganda from 1986 onward. Only 40 percent of the militia members who turned themselves in belonged to the LRA; the majority were with the WNBF and UNRF II. Since the amnesty went into effect, 23,000 have availed themselves of the program (US Department of State 2008). Of the 2,600 LRA fighters in Gulu who initially took advantage of the amnesty, only a handful received resettlement packets, and half were conscripted by force or pressure into the UPDF (Dolan 2005).

At times, Museveni encouraged civil society to pursue talks with the LRA. Owiny Dollo, minister of state for the north, was given funds by Belgium to strengthen the traditional authorities and their efforts to pursue peace reconciliation (Dolan 2005, 97). In 2002, a presidential peace team of army officers, northern MPs, and government ministers was formed, but it floundered as the conflict escalated in 2003.

Other policies the NRM adopted, however, contradicted its own strategy of encouraging peace talks. Efforts at negotiation were sometimes disrupted by UPDF soldiers. For example, when the Acholi Religious Leaders Peace Initiative, Father Tarcisio Pazzaglia, and traditional chief Joseph Oywak met with some LRA officers on April 26, 2001, at a Bedo Piny pi Kuc ("sitdown for peace"), the UPDF stormed the meetings. To make matters worse, after this incident, the government banned contact between the Acholi initiative and the LRA.

Various offers by elders, local government officials, and relatives of Kony to mediate between the government and the LRA were ignored, as was a 2004 offer by the Concerned Parents Association to make contact with the LRA to engage in peace talks (Dolan 2005, 99). Instead, an antiterrorism law was passed in Uganda in 2002 contradicting the amnesty law and making it more difficult for civil society to make contact with the LRA.

In 2002, Uganda signed another agreement with Sudan to allow the UPDF to make incursions into Sudan to rescue abducted children and capture or kill LRA commanders. The United States trained 6,000 soldiers on the border. Meanwhile, the UPDF directed its efforts against Kony in a three-week campaign called Operation Iron Fist, attacking Kony's bases in southern Sudan. By all accounts this operation failed, resulting in high rates of civilian casualties. During this campaign, the UPDF recruited its own minors and former LRA child fighters into local defense units with the ironic aim of rescuing children from rebel control (Finnström 2008, 91). A few months after the 2002 agreement, the LRA was back in northern Uganda as a result of Operation Iron Fist. Thus violence escalated, spreading in 2003 into eastern Uganda as far as Soroti, Katakwi, and Lira. Abductions increased, as did night commuting and violence. The government once again sponsored local militias to contain the conflict, including the Rhino Boys in Lango and the Frontier Guards in Kitgum, while others in Teso formed their own groups, called Amuka. They carried much of the burden of fighting in this period although they were underresourced, untrained, and had little backing from the UPDF.

As a result of heightened attacks by Joseph Kony and with no end to the conflict in sight, about thirty-four Lango, Acholi, and Teso members of parliament walked out of the National Assembly on November 20, 2003, and refused to return until peace was restored to their areas. They said their many proposals for a peaceful solution had been ignored. They, along with almost all the peace and human rights groups operating in northern Uganda, insisted that peace talks be seen as the means to end the conflict and criticized the use of force.

A further setback occurred in 2004, when the International Criminal Court (ICC) came to Uganda to investigate the possibility of indicting top LRA leaders. It was eager to justify its existence in the face of increasing international criticism, and in 2005 it issued warrants against Kony and four of his associates, accusing them of murder, torture, mutilation, abduction, sexual violence, and forced recruitment of children. The Museveni government was initially eager to cooperate with the ICC. Human rights organizations in northern Uganda protested, feeling that the indictments, coming in the midst of a war, would serve as a further disincentive to negotiate a settlement. Yet the ICC refused to back down. Human rights activists I spoke with in Gulu in 2005 felt that the ICC had already made up its mind when it came to Uganda and had not listened sufficiently to their concerns and those of other peace activists in the north. Civil society organizations also argued that the ICC indictments violated and undercut the 2000 Amnesty Act. Since the indictments were issued in the middle of a war with the encouragement of the Ugandan government, many northern leaders felt that the indictments were one-sided. Northerners felt they had now suffered not only at the hands of the LRA but also the UPDF and government (Branch 2007).

At the end of 2006, the LRA entered into negotiations with the Government of Southern Sudan (GoSS), which was eager to see the LRA leave southern Sudan because it posed a security risk to the new government, which had been established as an autonomous entity in January 2005 after a comprehensive peace agreement was signed between the Khartoum government and the SPLM/SPLA. The LRA and the GoSS produced a formal peace accord in February 2006, which included provisions that the GoSS would mediate peace talks between the LRA and the government of Uganda and that the LRA would cease hostilities in southern Sudan. A third provision stated that the GoSS could force the LRA to leave southern Sudan if it did not comply with the first two provisions (Atkinson forthcoming).

Although Museveni had categorically ruled out peace talks in May 2006 after his defense minister consulted with Khartoum, he reversed his position upon being officially told about the LRA-GoSS agreement and backed down from supporting the ICC indictments. The ICC insisted that the arrests be made, and its position was supported by the United States and the European Union, throwing a wrench into the peace process.

Talks began on July 14, 2006, and continued even as the UPDF kept up its military attacks on the LRA and killed the third-ranked LRA commander. The conflict began to wind down in August 2006 as a ceasefire was negotiated between the LRA and government negotiators in Juba, followed by talks to sign a comprehensive peace agreement. These talks began after LRA's backers in Khartoum ostensibly withdrew support from the LRA as a consequence of the peace settlement in southern Sudan.

The Juba talks surrounding the peace agreement were led by chief mediator and vice president of southern Sudan Dr. Riek Machar, with former Mozambique president Joachim Chissano as facilitator. The Ugandan government's chief negotiator was Dr. Ruhakana Rugunda, while the chairmanship of the LRA delegation alternated between Martin Ojul, David Nyekoratch Matsanga, and Dr. James Obita. The agreement was never signed because of concerns the LRA had for the personal fate of its leaders, especially with the ICC indictments hanging over their heads. The Ugandan government even tried to get the ICC to remove the indictments later on, claiming that it would try the accused in Uganda, but the ICC still refused to back down. Were the ICC cases to have been tried in Uganda, the LRA leaders would have faced the death penalty. Uganda's Ministry of Justice has since said they will be subject to a local traditional justice trial.

As predicted by civil society organizations in the north, the ICC indictments left no incentive for the LRA to sign the peace accord, so international diplomats waited in vain for Kony to show up at the much-heralded signing ceremony in Juba in April 2008. In August 2008, the LRA fled from Uganda to Garamba National Park at the border of DRC and Sudan, where they continued to carry out mass murders, rapes, looting, and the displacement of thousands of people. According to reports in September 2008, the LRA had set up six new bases in northern Congo and was funding its activities from diamond mines it was running in Central African Republic ("Ugandan Radio Says Rebels Running Diamond Mines in Central Africa" 2008). On December 14, 2008, the governments of Uganda, southern Sudan, and DRC launched a joint military operation, Operation Lightning Thunder, against the LRA in Garamba National Park. With 150 rebels killed, five LRA commanders captured, and three hundred abductees rescued, the offensive was claimed to be a success by all three governments, although it did not accomplish its goals of dismantling the rebel's command, killing or capturing Kony, or getting the LRA to sign a peace agreement ("Ninety Days of War in Garamba Forest" 2009). The LRA was reported to have scattered and its top commanders killed, captured, or taken ill. In mid-March 2009, Ugandan military officials withdrew four thousand troops from chasing the LRA in northeastern DRC.

Following the offensive, the LRA went on a massive killing spree in the Congo and as of June 2010 was still attacking populations in southern Sudan and DRC, killing and abducting thousands while displacing hundreds of thousands of people.

Why Has Peace Been So Elusive in the North?

Many questions remain regarding the reasons behind the strategy the government has adopted with respect to northern Uganda. Why did the conflict go on so long? Why did the government pursue a no-win strategy regarding northern Uganda, at times simultaneously working for peace while waging war? Why did it not make every effort to explore the peace option when it could? Until the most recent round of negotiations, it has systematically aborted or undermined peace initiatives and humiliated the LRA in the course of deliberations.

Jan Egeland, the former UN undersecretary general for humanitarian affairs, describes a November 2006 meeting during which Museveni berated him for going into the bush to meet with Joseph Kony and other LRA leaders. "Those talks were not to our benefit," Museveni argued, according to Egeland. "Let me be categorical—there will only be a military solution to this problem" (Egeland 2008, 211).

Why did the government not have the military capacity to end the conflict? Defence Minister Amama Mbabazi has argued that

> one of the greatest constraints is the chronic underfunding of defence. Contrary to public perception, the UPDF has a limited budget. In fact, military expenditure in Uganda went down from 3% of GDP in 1990 to 2% in 2001, according to figures of UNDP. This is lower than most countries in the region. Sudan spent 3% on defence in 2001, Rwanda 3.9%, Ethiopia 6.2% and Eritrea 27.5%! In absolute figures, Uganda this year has a defence

budget of $160m, for an army of approximately 50,000 troops. That is roughly a quarter of the $608m which the UN mission in [the] Congo is spending this year for only 10,000 troops. ("Is Museveni Using Kony War to Stay in Power?" 2004)

But even if one believes that the defense budget was this low, it is difficult to comprehend how the UPDF's twenty thousand troops in the north were unable to overpower the LRA, which even at its height may only have reached as many as five thousand troops over the course of twenty years (Dolan 2005). What is even more difficult to understand is why the government sabotaged the only effective military response there was. Acholi civilians formed militias at least twice to coordinate military efforts with the UPDF, but each time the Ugandan government undermined their military capacity and evacuated UPDF regulars from the region, abandoning the Acholi militias to brutal rebel retaliation. Eventually, the civilian Acholi population, especially in Gulu, refused to participate in further mobilization, which appeared to lead only to their own decimation. Yet popular mobilization had led to the defeat of Alice Lakwena in Iganga in 1987 and had stopped the incursion of the LRA into Teso in 2003; in short, it could have worked.

The government itself blamed the continuation of the conflict on Sudan, saying that after it destroyed the LRA in 1992, the Sudanese government allowed the LRA to establish bases in southern Sudan, thus perpetuating the conflict. Although that was certainly one factor, it was not the only one. Another factor that may have contributed to prolonging the war was economic: the war became more profitable than peace for the army commanders. When one considers the lack of serious commitment to peace talks until the final round in Juba, one can only conclude that the ghost soldier scam and the opportunity to pocket funds allocated for the war against the LRA were more profitable than peace (see the more comprehensive discussion of ghost soldiers in Chapter 6). During the investigation into the ghost soldier problem, Brigadier Mayombo revealed that the Fourth Division's commanders had even sold arms to the LRA (Atuhaire 2008a). In addition, there were rumors that UPDF officers had engaged in land grabbing, especially after the LRA shifted their base to DRC. As a result, President Museveni came out openly in August 2008 and warned generals against land grabbing, vowing to conduct an investigation of the extent of the practice. He made these statements as a result of pressure from Acholi elders after reports had surfaced indicating that there were conflicts over land involving UPDF officers in northern Uganda ("Ugandan Leader Warns Army Officers Against Land Grabbing" 2008).

The continuance of the war allowed the government to justify its adoption of unacceptable methods of repression under the guise of increasing security in the face of a heightened terrorism threat. It could more easily silence political dissent in this environment of counterterrorism. Museveni tried to reinvent Uganda, especially in the wake of September 11, 2001, as the key US ally in the region and thus became the recipient of a significant amount of US military aid and diplomatic support for a so-called war on terror against the LRA.

As the war persisted, it created a crisis environment that allowed the government to increase funding of the military and divert foreign aid to the UPDF, which became especially important with the incursions into DRC, despite donor demands for a decrease. Donors, however, were complicit through their inaction. As they remained relatively quiet, the IDP camps grew from 800,000 in 2002 to over 1.5 million after Operation Iron Fist.

Another explanation for the lack of serious attention to the LRA war is that Museveni himself minimized the scope of the conflict. He commonly referred to the LRA as "a nuisance" composed of "bandits." It was not a war to him, just the activity of a handful of terrorists. His attitude contributed to the feeling of humiliation on the part of the LRA that it was not a formidable force (Dolan 2005, 97). However, if he truly believed LRA troops were simply bandits and that the conflict was not of consequence, why was so little attention given to developing the region? Why was it left to languish for more than two decades?

Low morale within the military due, in part, to the prevalence of HIV/AIDS among troops and to their inability to send reinforcements to the north when needed, has also been cited to account for the failure of the UPDF to confront its major adversary. Museveni continually promised that the conflict was almost over, but it is unclear on what basis those projections were made. Sometimes he claimed he had poor information from his advisers, but he was not entirely unfamiliar with the situation the UPDF faced, having stayed with troops in the north for extended periods of time.

Peace advocates, church leaders, NGOs, human rights activists, women's rights activists, and others in the north argued all along that more effort should go into peace talks with the rebels and into addressing the problems underlying the conflict rather than into military strategy, which generally ended up killing more innocent people than rebels and resulted in greater retribution on the part of the LRA. In fact, it was only when the international community began to seriously press the Ugandan government to go to the negotiating table that Museveni relented and initiated the Juba talks.

Even if the LRA finally dissipates due to lack of resources or is captured, the problems that gave rise to it will not have disappeared; the northern population is still impoverished relative to the rest of the country. The region is three decades behind in development and faces a host of challenges as its people move home from the IDP camps. By the end of 2009, of the 1.8 million who had been internally displaced to camps, only 190,000 remained (Ojwee 2009). Whether the government fully delivers on its promises of assistance to the region will further clarify its position regarding the north.

Uganda's Incursions into DRC

Uganda's conflicts under Museveni were not contained within the country's borders, and its internal and external conflicts were closely connected. Uganda's battles on the homefront with the ADF became a pretext for interventions in neighboring DRC. Moreover, the international exposure of the plunder of resources by key military leaders in DRC (described below), may have resulted in a shift in patronage strategies, including the expansion of the ghost soldier scam that is believed to have prolonged the conflict in northern Uganda.

Although accounts vary, Uganda's intervention into Democratic Republic of Congo was probably motivated by the pursuit of influence in the region and of resources from Democratic Republic of Congo to benefit top military personnel. Uganda's involvement in the Congo was also part of a broader contest with Rwanda for control in the region. Uganda's direct engagement began when it forged a coalition with Rwanda to help oust Zaire's President Mobutu Sese Seko in 1997 through the Alliance des Forces Démocratiques pour la Libération du Congo-Zaïre (AFDL), led by Laurent-Désiré Kabila, who took over as president.

Rwanda's involvement in the Congo had begun earlier. Rwanda sought to crush extremist militias and soldiers who had participated in the 1994 genocide in Rwanda. In 1996, the Rwandan government, led by the Rwandan Patriotic Front (RPF), sent Rwandan Patriotic Army (RPA) troops into the Congo, claiming that they needed to preempt attacks on Rwanda by Hutu combatants and remnants of the defeated FAR.[7] They also went to support the Banyamulenge Congolese of the Tutsi ethnic group, whom they felt would face threats from some of the Hutu who had fled Rwanda. Over a million Hutu refugees poured into Congo from Rwanda following the 1994 genocide, fearing RPA retribution against the Hutu, because among the many innocent refugees who fled were *genocidaire* who had committed atrocities. Together with the AFDL, the RPA attacked the refugee camps of unarmed civilians. They forced hundreds of thousands to return to Rwanda, while two hundred thousand refugees fled westward into the forests. There are no reliable figures, but it is thought that at least three hundred thousand Rwandese civilians were killed or died in their efforts to escape the RPA. Meanwhile, several thousand ex-FAR and Hutu militia members regrouped and continued fighting the Rwandan government in the Congo.

Ugandan and Rwandese troops, together with the AFDL, marched into the capital, Kinshasa, and captured it in May 1997, bringing into power an ascendance of Banyarwanda and Banyamulenge forces. AFDL leader Laurent-Désiré Kabila announced his presidency after President Mobutu died in Morocco in September that same year. Rwandan military personnel and advisers remained in Kinshasa, but relations quickly deteriorated among the three countries. About fourteen months later, Kabila dismissed Rwandese members of his government and asked Rwanda and Uganda to leave the country, claiming that they had overstayed their welcome and fearing that their ambitions were to claim DRC for themselves. It appeared Rwanda was attempting to oust Kabila but was thwarted when Zimbabwe, Namibia, and Angola came to his assistance (Clark 2001, 280).

Uganda withdrew to eastern Congo, where in 1998 it claimed to be pursuing ADF rebels who were using the area as a staging ground for attacks in Uganda. Uganda accused Kabila of complicity in these attacks. Uganda and Rwanda both claimed that their involvement in DRC had to do with its desire to stop the massacres against the Banyamulenge people in eastern Congo.

DRC was, in effect, partitioned into four sections, each under the control of different rebel troops, with the west under government control. Uganda backed the Movement for the Liberation of the Congo (Mouvement pour la Libération du Congo), led by Jean-Pierre Bemba, which controlled much of Equateur Province in the north and parts of the North Kivu and Orientale provinces in eastern Congo. Uganda also backed the Rassemblement Conglais pour la Démocratie–Kisangani (RCD-K), which was later renamed the Rassemblement Conglais pour la Démocratie Mouvement pour la Libération or RCD-ML (Tull 2003). Rwanda threw its backing behind the Rally for Congolese Democracy–Goma (Rassemblement Congolais pour la Démocratie–Goma, or RCD-Goma). In spite of its lack of popular support, the RCD-Goma came to control one-third of DRC, including most of North and South Kivu and parts of Maniema, Orientale, Katanga, and Kasai Orientale Provinces. For a while the Rwandan, Ugandan, and Burundian armies joined forces in their occupation of the northeastern Congo, while Congolese troops sought the support of Hutu militia to oppose the Tutsis.

The RCD-Goma's presence in Kivu was resisted by the Mai Mai. The Mai Mai constituted yet another heterogeneous and loosely coalesced, armed militia in eastern Congo, allied at various times with Hutu groups or with the Congolese government. It consisted of local Congolese who said they were protecting their own communities and claimed an identity of resisting foreign occupation, especially that of the Tutsi Banyarawanda. Many, in fact, ended up killing, raping, and stealing from local villagers.

A ceasefire between the warring parties (DRC, Angola, Namibia, Zimbabwe, Rwanda, and Uganda, as well as some rebel groups, excluding the Rwandan-backed Rally for Congolese Democracy) was signed in July 1999 in Lusaka. The UN peacekeeping force, the UN Observation Mission in the Congo, moved in to supervise the ceasefire and demobilize combatants. The ink had not even dried on the Lusaka ceasefire agreement between the parties involved in the Congo conflict when fighting resumed. Rwanda launched a major offensive on the capital but was beaten back before reaching Kinshasa. Ugandan and Rwandan troops did not begin to move out of Congo until after the assassination of Laurent-Désiré Kabila and the installation of his son, Joseph Kabila, as president in January 2001.

It should be mentioned that, in 1999, fighting broke out between Rwandan and Ugandan armed forces inside the Congo, resulting in more than two hundred deaths and damaging relations between these erstwhile allies. The fighting was, in part, a consequence of conflicts over control of the diamond market (UN Security Council Panel of Experts 2002, 17). But it had an added dimension relating to the close relationship Rwanda's leadership had had with Museveni in the early 1980s, when the NRA was fighting to take over Uganda. Many exiled Tutsis joined Museveni's guerrilla movement then. Paul Kagame, the president of Rwanda, had grown up in Uganda; he joined the NRA in 1979 and fought alongside Museveni for years as one of the NRA historicals. With the NRM takeover in 1986, Kagame became head of the NRA's military intelligence unit, and another founder of the RPF, Fred Rwigema, became deputy minister of defense. Rwigema was killed on the second day of the RPF invasion of Rwanda in 1990. The RPF was based in Uganda for many years and launched a second invasion into Rwanda from Uganda in 1994 when genocide broke out in Rwanda. Relations between Uganda and Rwanda, however, soured as the armies of both countries competed for resources and control in DRC.

The conflict eventually subsided in much of the eastern part of the Congo—though not in North Kivu, South Kivu, and Ituri, where it took horrific proportions, especially for women, who faced brutal rapes on a massive scale. In 2001 there were an estimated 620,000 IDPs in North Kivu, making up 16 percent of the population; and four out of five rural residents had been forcibly displaced since 1998. Armed conflict spread through the eastern region as young men joined militias because they had no other source of livelihood. Child soldiers were drawn into the conflict. In one instance, seven hundred youth from Bunia, DRC—many of whom were between the ages of fourteen and sixteen—were discovered at a UPDF training camp in Tchakwanzi, Uganda (UN Security Council Panel of Experts 2002). Some militias were not paid, but they were armed and allowed to engage in looting, rape, and other forms of destruction.

In April 2001, a UN Security Council panel of experts accused Rwanda, Uganda, and Zimbabwe of systematically and illegally exploiting diamonds, cobalt, gold, coltan (a rare ore used in cell phones and laptops), and other lucrative resources in DRC.[8] It also accused Uganda of using security concerns as a pretext for continued control of parts of the Congo to amass wealth.

The situation was further complicated by fighting between the neighboring and related Hema and Lendu communities in the district of Ituri in Orientale Province. Ituri holds the largest gold reserves in the world. Foreign and local groups have been embroiled in a conflict over access to them, as well as to diamonds, oil, and coltan. Uganda, Rwanda, and DRC waged a proxy war, using local warlords. The conflict between the Hema and Lendu had erupted in 1998, when much of Orientale Province was occupied by the UPDF and the Ugandan backed RCD-K. Groups with long-standing land disputes had historically fought with bows and arrows, but after 1998 the fighting erupted into full-blown war exacerbated by the easy availability of small arms, which heightened the destructiveness of the fighting. The UPDF trained both Hema and Lendu soldiers who had set up their own militias. James Kazini, commander of the UPDF, created the new province, Ituri, out of the eastern part of Orientale Province, naming a Hema to be the new governor. The Lendu feared that Uganda and RCD-K were backing the Hema against them.

According to the UN Security Council expert report (UN Security Council Panel of Experts 2002), the conflict between the Hema and Lendu clans was the result of attempts by powerful Hema businesspeople and politicians, particularly of the Gegere subclan, to increase the benefits they obtained from the commercial activities of Ugandan-owned companies operating in the region. The disputes became a pretext for the Hema to import arms and train militias in order to consolidate their economic base in the region, which was tied, in particular, to the transport business. Fighting subsided temporarily between 1999 and 2001 when a neutral provincial head was appointed. Uganda then replaced the governor with the aforementioned Hema appointee and conflict resumed. The RCD-K eventually split into two based on Hema and Lendu allegiances and fighting continued in Ituri, killing tens of thousands more.

Uganda's military ventures in DRC came under increasing domestic and international criticism. Many opinion leaders in Uganda publicly demanded to know why incursions into neighboring countries such as DRC were necessary when Uganda's borders could be protected from within. The incursion had never been approved by the cabinet or parliament. A newspaper poll showed that 80 percent of Ugandans opposed the country's military involvement in the Congo (Tumusiime 1999). Women peace activists and Jamii ya Kupatanisha (Fellowship of Reconciliation) held demonstrations in May 2000 at the Constitutional Square, demanding that Uganda withdraw from Congo (Ariko 2000).

An inter-Congolese dialogue between the various Congolese rebel forces and the government was initiated in October 2001 and resumed in Sun City, South Africa, between February and April of 2002. With respect to foreign armies in DRC, the Pretoria Agreement signed in July 2002 between the governments of Rwanda and DRC provided for the withdrawal of Rwandan troops and the dismantling of the ex-FAR and Interahamwe forces. Similarly, in September 2002, the governments of DRC and Uganda signed the Luanda Agreement on the withdrawal of the latter's troops from the former's territory.

In December 2002, the Global and All Inclusive Peace Agreement was signed.[9] The RCD-Goma did not sign the agreement, resulting in an impasse between DRC and Rwanda. At the final inter-Congolese dialogue in Sun City, South Africa, April 2, 2003, the RCD-Goma finally did sign a peace agreement, which provided for the establishment of a two-year transitional government and constitution that would allow DRC its first democratic elections in forty years. It established a new army as a conglomeration of the various rebel movements. Elections were held in July 2006 and Joseph Kabila—the son of Laurent Kabila, who had been assassinated in 2001—won the elections with 45 percent of the votes and his party, the People's Party for Reconstruction and Democracy, claimed the largest number of parliamentary seats. Yet there is still considerable instability in the eastern part of the country even though Rwanda pulled its troops out of DRC and Uganda pulled out most of its seven thousand troops by May 2003.

Although Uganda's presence in DRC diminished as major sources of patronage in the army were cut off, it appears that northern Uganda became a new source of patronage with the ghost soldier scam (see Chapter 6) and new rumors of land grabbing by army officers.

The UN Security Council Panel of Experts (2002) implicated Uganda in an elite network based in DRC aimed at controlling the region's natural resources, cross-border trade, and tax revenues. In particular, the network was involved in the trade of coltan, diamonds, timber, and gold. It had established itself in financial centers like Bunia, Beni, and Butembo, where it used the rebel administration as a front for business and revenue generation through the collection of commercial license fees, import and export duties, and taxes on particular products. Unlike the Rwandese network, the Ugandan one was decentralized and loosely hierarchical, consisting of high-ranking UPDF officers, private businesspeople, rebel leaders, and administrators in the region. According to the UN Security Council expert panel, it was also linked to international business.

The UN report named UPDF Lieutenant General Salim Saleh and Major General James Kazini as key figures in the network. It also named other close associates of Museveni, including the late chief of military intelligence, UPDF Colonel Nobel Mayombo, as well as Colonel Kahinda Otafiire, and Colonel Peter Karim. Other well-known private entrepreneurs included the NRM parliamentarian for Lira, Sam Engola. They engaged in military intimidation and manipulated money supply and the banking sector using counterfeit currency and other means. The UPDF and the rebel militias working with them served as the enforcement arm of the network to ensure its commercial monopoly through threats and the use of force. Even as the Ugandan troops pulled out, the UPDF trained local paramilitary forces to facilitate the commercial activities of its officers upon their withdrawal.

The UN Security Council Panel of Experts reported that after the official withdrawal of troops, transfers of funds were made from the Ugandan Office of the Presidency to armed groups in Ituri, and arms and military supplies were being provided to these groups in a coordinated and institutionalized way.[10]

Meanwhile, Uganda established a commission headed by Justice David Porter to investigate the UN panel of experts' allegations that top military personnel had pillaged wealth from DRC during the conflict. However, it lacked funds to carry out a thorough investigation and was blocked by General James Kazini from going to Ituri to speak with witnesses. Justice Porter mentioned to the UN Security Council expert panel that his efforts to conduct the study had met with a "conspiracy of silence" within the UPDF. The UN panel met on several occasions with the Porter Commission and shared key pieces of evidence with them. However, even in the face of witnesses and incontrovertible evidence, the UN panel found that its "many efforts to establish a constructive relationship with the Commission have mostly been met with attempts to dismiss [the panel's] credibility" (UN Security Council Panel of Experts 2002, 25). MP Winnie Byanyima commented in a press conference that "the Porter Commission is a joke. I absolutely have no faith in it." She accused the government of trying to influence the outcome by paying Porter a USh 26 million (US$17,870) honorarium, compared with the USh 3–4 million (US$2,419) honorarium granted the head of the Constitutional Review Commission, Prof. Ssempebwa ("Porter Commission a Joke" 2002).

The report, which came out in November 2002, exonerated the Ugandan government and army of any official involvement in exploiting resources in DRC. However, it did single out the late General Kazini for disciplinary action and recommended criminal investigation into the activities of Salim Saleh, Museveni's brother, for violating the Ugandan Companies Act. No judicial action was taken in relation to these charges.

As a footnote to the story of Uganda's engagement in DRC, even though the latter had not yet reestablished diplomatic ties with Uganda, Joseph Kabila actually invited Rwanda and Uganda back into the country to engage in joint operations to pursue the LRA in 2008. About 1,300 Ugandan troops as well as forces from DRC and Sudan pursued the LRA in the Orientale Province and in North Kivu Province, while Rwanda's 3,500 soldiers pursued the mainly Hutu Democratic Forces for the Liberation of Rwanda, which are said to have carried out genocide in Rwanda and were at the source of ongoing conflict in the east. Rwanda apprehended Laurent Nkunda, head of the Congolese Tutsi–dominated National Congress for the Defence of the People, which was said to have been backed by Rwanda.

Conclusion

This brief study of the various rebel movements that have persisted since the NRM took over shows just how volatile the country has been during its frequent claims at this time of having brought peace to Uganda. Moreover, in spite of the NRM's efforts to build up its many security forces, it has become less secure for large segments of the population. The government's treatment of the north from the outset contradicted many of its goals of being broad based and antisectarian. The lack of developmental attention to the northern and northeastern districts has contributed to the feeling of alienation and second-class status on the part of those who live in these regions.

At the end of the day, then, the claims that NRM brought peace to Uganda ring hollow in that one-third of the country has yet to enjoy peace or benefit from the development that accompanies peace. The dual nature of semi-authoritarianism has played out in a perverse way when it comes to war and peace in Uganda: while the northern third of the country has experienced almost continuous conflict since 1986, the southern part of the country has experienced mostly peace, virtually oblivious to the horrors of conflict not so far away. The northerners were sidelined and treated as second-class citizens because they refused to give the NRM their political support. At the same time, there was no incentive to do so, given that they had been basically ignored and deprived of a slice of the proverbial "national development cake."

Underlying the conflicts in DRC and the delay in resolving the conflict with the LRA is the use of conflict itself as a source of enrichment and patronage. In both DRC and the north, the existence of conflict and chaos has created opportunities for pursuing resources that fuel a system that perpetuates patronage. Moreover, the ways in which military leaders have profited from the conflict via patronage in the form of revenue obtained from the sale of resources extracted from the eastern Congo and from the creation of ghost soldiers further illustrates why it is so difficult for leaders to exit gracefully or allow electoral losses—a key scenario under authoritarian and semiauthoritarian rule.

Notes

1. There is a simple bivariate correlation between the absence of conflict and GDP per capita in Africa from 1960 to 2008 (Pearson's $r = .153$, $p < .01$, $N = 288$) and an expected negative correlation between high-intensity conflict (high rate of deaths) and GDP per capita ($r = -.120$, $p < .01$, $N = 288$). Based on Freedom House data, http://www.freedomhouse.org/ratings. Accessed March 2008. Source of data: Human Development Reports 2007/2008, http://hdr.undp.org/statistics/. Accessed March 2008.

2. Afrobarometer, http://www.afrobarometer.org. Accessed July 1, 2009.

3. The projected budget for 2009–2010 indicated defense expenditures of 8 percent of the overall budget.

4. Interview with Betty Bigombe, April 2, 2008.

5. Institute for Security Studies, http://www.iss.co.za/Af/profiles/Uganda/SecInfo.html. Accessed July 1, 2009.

6. Interview with Betty Bigombe, April 2, 2008.

7. Sometimes the Hutu exiles are referred to as Interahamwe, implying that they were all involved in the 1994 genocide in Rwanda. Some were involved, but the majority were not.

8. UN Security Council press release, http://www.un.org/News/Press/docs/2002/sc7547.doc.htm. Accessed July 10, 2009.

9. The signatories to the 2002 agreement included the government of DRC, the Congolese Rally for Democracy (RCD), the Movement for the Liberation of the Congo (MLC), the political opposition, civil society, the RCD-ML, the Congolese Rally for Democracy–National, and the Mai Mai.

10. Human Rights Watch, http://www.hrw.org/reports/2005/drc0505/12.htm#_ftn ref433. Accessed July 10, 2009.

8

Legitimating Repression and Corruption

This book has focused on several key contradictions of semiauthoritarian rule. Our final paradox relates to economic growth and economic bases of democratization. Historically, substantial economic growth has created conditions for political liberalization and democratization. In Uganda, however, economic gains have helped legitimize some of the more undemocratic tendencies of the Museveni regime at least in the short term. Moreover, donor support, often provided with the intention of strengthening political liberalization, at times unintentionally encouraged some of Museveni's most repressive and regressive tendencies by providing an external stamp of approval for some of the more problematic aspects of the Ugandan regime. Massive donor support for universal primary education, for example, weakened lines of accountability between the electorate and those in office and slowed the development of synergies between taxpayers and policymakers. In this chapter it becomes evident that the heavy donor focus on economic development unwittingly helped legitimate undemocratic practices, corruption, and clientelism, which, in turn, undermined governance and the capacity of the state to foster growth.

This chapter first examines the strengths and weaknesses of Uganda's economy since Museveni's takeover and then explores the ways in which Uganda's economic success has predisposed donors favorably to the regime and helped legitimate many of its undemocratic aspects.

Economic Growth

Low levels of economic growth generally create structural conditions that make democratization less likely (Lipset 1959; Rueschemeyer, Stephens, and Stephens 1992; Inglehart, Norris, and Welzel 2002). Moreover, although several poor countries in Africa have democratized, the odds are against their being able to sustain democratization (Przeworski, Limongi, and Papaterra 1997). In the long term, economic development is accompanied by the strengthening of the state, the tax base, civil society, an educated workforce, and other factors that make democracy more likely and sustainable. Adam Przeworski, Neto Limongi, and Fernando Papaterra (1997) have found that a country with a per capita income of less than US$1,500 may democratize, but it is not likely to remain democratic beyond eight years. Countries with a per capita income of between US$1,500 and US$3,000 survive as democracies on average eighteen years, while a per capita income of more than US$6,000 indicates they will be highly resilient. These findings are confirmed in the African context (see Table 8.1).

Regardless of regime type, most nations in Africa have less than US$1,500 GDP per capita. Countries with more than US$3,000 GDP per capita are more likely to be democracies. Although lack of economic growth makes countries more vulnerable to reversal, the fact that poverty does not always impede democratization means that one cannot adopt a strictly deterministic approach. However, with a GDP per capita rate of US$303 (as of 2007), Uganda is a long way from being in the category of countries that, should it democratize, might be predicted to remain democratic. Moreover, the fact that Uganda has made substantial economic gains since Museveni took over has helped legitimize the regime and some of its semiauthoritarian tendencies, pointing to some of the serious challenges semiauthoritarian regimes face in contemplating their prospects for further political liberalization.

Before the 2008 financial crisis, Africa was experiencing the fastest economic growth rates it had seen since independence. Although Africa's economies are among the most fragile in the world, since 1999, real average GDP growth rates had remained at more than 5.7 percent, and no African country had succumbed to negative GDP growth rates. Africa was experiencing increases in exports, foreign reserves, remittances, and foreign direct investment, and its debt had decreased. China and India were emerging as important

Table 8.1 Relationship of GDP per Capita to Democratization in Africa

GDP per Capita	Not Free	Partially Free	Free	Total
Less than $1,500	9	20	6	35
$1,500–3,000	2	0	1	3
$3,000–6,000	0	1	4	5
More than $6,000	1	1	0	2
Missing data	2	1	0	3
Total	14	23	11	48

Source: Freedom House, http://www.freedomhouse.org; United Nations Statistics Division, http://unstats.un.org/unsd/databases.htm. Accessed July 11, 2008.
Notes: N = 48. Currency in US$.

new trading partners. In 2004, inflation in Africa fell below double digits to its lowest rate in a quarter of a century, and these rates have been maintained.

These developments have been the result of overall continued improvement in monetary and fiscal policies, somewhat better access to markets in the global north, and increased foreign aid and debt relief, as well as higher commodity prices. There has also been increased spending on pro-poor measures: major allocations of money from governments and other multilateral and bilateral donors have gone toward education, health, and other social services, including AIDS programs; there have also been improvements in infrastructure and a larger role for microfinancial institutions. The decrease in major civil conflicts has also allowed for recovery in many countries.

Although the overall trends are clear, there are many factors that temper this picture. The ripple effects of the financial crisis in the West—including dropping remittances, lower exports, and high food and energy prices—were putting many of the gains made through economic reform and growth strategies in peril. The benefits of the earlier growth have not been uniformly felt across the continent, nor have they been enjoyed by the poorest members of society. Very few countries have maintained the 7 percent growth rates necessary to reduce poverty. Job creation remains the number one concern in opinion polls across Africa. This is an especially pressing issue given the youthfulness of the continent, with 62 percent of the population under the age of twenty-four. The tax base is still limited, which has implications for state building. Africa still lacks the necessary commodity diversification, making it vulnerable to changes in international markets and climatic changes. Competitiveness is hampered by weaknesses in infrastructure, governance structures, skills, and the technology base.

Nevertheless, the overall improvement in economic growth ought to bode well for democratization and political liberalization in the long run. Uganda exemplifies many of these economic trends in Africa today. Since the mid-1990s, poverty levels have dropped markedly in Uganda. Uganda's annual growth rate, more than 5 percent between 1995 and 2007, was one of the highest in Africa. In 2009, the GDP growth rate stood at 6 percent, and in spite of the global financial crisis it continued to grow. It could be attributed to a strong export sector supported by coffee, flowers, and fish; increased foreign direct investment in key sectors; growing fixed private investment driven by construction; large concessional inflows from donors; and a macroeconomic environment that held stable until the 2008 global crisis (Ministry of Finance, Planning, and Economic Development 2009a). At the same time, donor transfers have multiplied more than eightfold in the decade following the National Resistance Movement (NRM) takeover, reaching US$819.5 million annually by 2000, where they have roughly remained since. The majority of foreign transfers between 1997 and 2008 were private ones that increased dramatically after 1995, reflecting a growing confidence in Uganda's economy.

Unlike previous Ugandan governments, Museveni's administration has promoted business and is less apt to interfere with the private ownership of property. In 1993, Uganda devalued its shilling, resulting in the stabilization of its currency. It liberalized trade, lifted producer prices on export crops, and liberalized investment laws to facilitate the export of profits and encourage foreign investment; in 1988, it opened up capital markets. Export growth has grown to 8 percent per year, with exports going primarily to Kenya, Belgium, the Netherlands, France, and Germany. However, the country remains overly dependent on one export, coffee, which accounts for 21 percent of all exports (Ministry of Finance, Planning, and Economic Development 2009a). Dependence on primary products, especially agricultural crops, means the country is especially vulnerable to unstable market prices and weather conditions. Nevertheless, strict monetary discipline and the opening of market forces resulted overall in significant drops in inflation throughout the 1990s (although 2007–2008 inflation rates went up to 7.3 percent as a result of hikes in food prices, oil prices, and the cost of electricity).

Debt has been cut significantly. In 2000, Uganda qualified for enhanced Heavily Indebted Poor Countries (HIPC) debt relief worth US$1.3 billion and Paris Club debt relief worth US$145 million. These amounts combined with the original HIPC debt relief added up to about US$2 billion. In 2005, Uganda's debt was cut from US$4 billion to US$1.4 billion. As we have mentioned, Uganda has increased spending on pro-poor measures, setting aside major allocations of funds from the 1996 World Bank and IMF-sponsored HIPC toward education, health, and other social services, including AIDS action plans, rural road maintenance, and improvements in microfinance institutions. Since 2003, the US government has been fighting AIDS in Uganda through the President's Emergency Plan For AIDS Relief (PEPFAR). In spite of drops in poverty levels, however, 85 percent of the population is nevertheless living on less than US$1 a day.

The 2008–2009 financial crisis created its own setbacks, as remittances by Ugandans abroad—which had risen to US$800 million by 2007—slowed down, the Ugandan shilling fell in value, the trade deficit widened with the decline in the volume and value of exports, and the Uganda Securities Exchange Index fell ("Museveni—From Grand Reformer to Simply Surviving" 2009). However, the Ministry of Finance regarded these setbacks as a "blip" and expected growth to continue into 2010 at a 6.3 percent level (Nakkazi 2009).

The discovery of significantly large oil reserves in 2006 led to speculation that Uganda would become a major producer of oil in Africa. There are reports that there may be as many as 2 billion barrels of extractable deposits in Uganda. The leading exploration company, Tullow Oil, has found enough oil on the border with Democratic Republic of Congo to yield more than a hundred thousand barrels of oil a day for between fifteen and thirty years. The amount of oil is worth US$2 billion a year, which is two-thirds of the country's budget (Kavuma 2009). Although this opens up enormous developmental possibilities, many fear that the oil revenue will expand clientelism and corruption unless processes to ensure transparency are enforced.

In sum, the general patterns of economic growth Uganda has enjoyed since 1986, even with the setbacks experienced as a result of the 2008–2009 global financial crisis, have (1) provided resources to fuel a political patronage machine; (2) helped the Museveni government garner legitimacy among key sectors of the citizenry, especially those who fear that the alternative to his rule is a return to a past of uncertainty and civil war; and (3) earned donor support, which has in turn validated some of the more repressive elements of the Museveni regime. Nevertheless, the growing gap between the rich and the poor in Uganda may also serve to mitigate some of the political benefits of economic growth.

Contradictory Donor Agendas

Relations with the West and donor pressures are often said to be factors in pushing countries toward democratization. Although they may have helped prevent the reemergence of the kinds of dictatorships seen in the past in Africa, the Ugandan case reveals some of the limits of donor support, which at best has involved mixed messages. Uganda is a country where donors have not been especially aggressive in demanding political reforms compared with other countries where conditions such as the adoption of multipartyism and other steps toward democratization had to be met. Museveni has shown little visible concern with donor pressure since donors have almost always been forthcoming with funds at the end of the day—even when he meddled in Democratic Republic of Congo, prolonged the war in the north, and made heavy-handed efforts to silence his opposition. At times, donors have unwittingly emboldened even the most undemocratic tendencies of the Museveni government. Massive donor support for Uganda often weakened lines of accountability between the electorate and the elected and slowed down the evolution of a connection between taxpayers and policymakers, as we saw in the case of the universal primary education policies in Chapter 5.

William Muhumuza (2009) argues that the inconsistency in donor pressure in Uganda has to do with the fact that Uganda has performed so well on the economic front that donors are eager to highlight their star performer and provide models for other postconflict countries. Because they have committed substantial amounts of funds to Uganda, they do not want to be seen as supporting a failure. Furthermore, donors have at times been seduced by the government's claims that it is democratizing, decentralizing, downsizing the military, dealing with the conflict in the north, and adopting other such policies, which on the surface seem plausible. The donors' willingness to believe that the government is serious about a program like universal primary education has made them unwilling to carefully examine the way it was introduced or the fact that it was driven first and foremost by political imperatives. It made them, with some important exceptions, gloss over the patronage and corruption shaping many policies that seemed like a step in the right direction. Muhumuza adds that another reason for the oversights has to do with the fact that, compared to other war-torn regions of central Africa, Uganda appears to be a relatively peaceful country. Donors need to believe in this oasis of relative regional stability for strategic reasons (Muhumuza 2009).

Although this book has focused on the internal factors that have given the NRM leadership a monopoly of power in Uganda, it is important to recognize the role of donors as well. Inconsistency in donor policy on Uganda has unintentionally bolstered the creation of a Movement patronage system, encouraged undemocratic and exclusionist tendencies, expanded executive power, and strengthened the weapons of insecurity, as well as fed the big business of war.

Donor involvement in Uganda increased markedly between 1989 and 1994, during which time funds from Western donors nearly doubled (Hauser 1999). By 1996, foreign aid averaged more than US$800 million a year. Donors contribute to more than half the national budget and provide 80 percent of development expenditures. Much of the aid has gone toward state sector reforms like decentralization, privatization, civil service retrenchment, public expenditure reform, military demobilization, and, more recently, efforts to revive the northern part of the country (Tangri and Mwenda 2005). The aid transfers have occurred with little public accountability and transparency, so that ordinary Ugandans would not know where the funds were coming from and the purposes they were to serve.

One consequence has been that the donor-supported privatization initiatives have resulted primarily in the sale of privatized companies to people with connections in the government. Another has been that economic liberalization policies promoted by donors were carried out by individuals using their privileged positions to award their clients licenses, government contracts, credit, concessions, permission to evade taxes, and other "privileges" of office. Administrators have regularly been appointed not on merit but rather on political and personal connections. In other words, in their eagerness to privatize and liberalize the economy, many donors have not shown concern with the way in which these processes have been carried out and the ways in which they have perpetuated corruption. Meanwhile, dozens of semiautonomous agencies, secretariats, and commissions have been formed outside of the ministries to give them greater independence from the constitutional framework. They were often formed with the strong encouragement of donors; however, they only added to public sector expenditures and fostered a lack of accountability.

It was not until 2003 that donors began to issue statements regarding large-scale corruption and embezzlement at the top and started putting in place measures to monitor government procurement. For a long time, key donors had supported increases in military expenditure because Uganda was seen as one of the countries suffering from terrorism as a result of its battles with the Sudan-backed Allied Democratic Forces and Lord's Resistance Army. By 2004, Britain, which had provided much of the bilateral support, was scrutinizing military budget increases more carefully and insisting on guidelines for the procurement of military hardware (Tangri and Mwenda 2005).

Donors may have reasoned that Museveni's human rights record was an improvement upon the records of Uganda's neighbors and those of Amin and Obote. Uganda was consistently being compared favorably to Moi's Kenya, even though Uganda had more political prisoners and was involved in more internal and external warfare (Oloka-Onyango 2004). Yet with a few exceptions, donors rarely used threats of conditionality against Uganda as they had in the early 1990s against Kenya and Malawi. They usually overlooked many aspects of Uganda's political record because of the strength of the country's economic performance and the eagerness with which it adopted structural adjustment programs.

From time to time, donor countries made critical statements about the lack of political freedom in Uganda. They were uncharacteristically quick to pressure the Ugandan government when MP David Bahati proposed a draconian antigay bill in 2010 and several countries threatened to withdraw aid. But in general, the Movement and the opposition alike have interpreted continued increases in donor financial support as a vote of confidence in the Movement system. Several donors, including the British government, donated money to the 2000 referendum—a gift that, to prodemocracy advocates, could only be interpreted as an endorsement of the no-party system in spite of official statements to the contrary (see Chapter 4 for a discussion of the referendum).

Many opposition leaders and advocates of political pluralism are convinced that foreign donors have been misguided by Museveni, whom the Ugandan press frequently describes as more beholden to Britain and the United States than to his own people. Even though the United States had for years openly advocated multiparty democracy in Uganda and had been critical of restrictions on civil and political liberties, it undercut such pressure through other statements. Former Assistant Secretary of State for African Affairs Susan Rice, for example, endorsed the 2000 referendum as a "free and open decision" by the Ugandan people on the future of the country, as did other top US officials in the Clinton administration, including Reverend Jesse Jackson, who served as special envoy for the promotion of democracy in Africa, and Secretary of State Madeleine Albright (United States Information Agency 1998, 16). Most prodemocracy advocates regarded the referendum as a means of institutionalizing NRM dominance at the expense of multipartyism. And even though the United States temporarily suspended military aid to Uganda because of the latter's involvement in Democratic Republic of Congo, and relations between the countries became strained for awhile, President Bush was generally supportive of Museveni's government and praised Uganda for supporting the war in Iraq in 2003 and for its progress in HIV/AIDS prevention.

Donors and Problems of Citizenship

Donors have legitimated some of the more problematic elements of the Museveni government in other ways as well. One of the mistakes of donors has been to treat their role in programs like decentralization, privatization, and universal primary and secondary education as simply matters of technical assistance, rather than seeing the implicit political purposes of such programs. Donors frequently were eager to see their development objectives met and therefore were inattentive to or unconcerned with the political purposes for which their projects were being used, often with deleterious consequences for the intended beneficiaries. These concerns have implications for citizenship and the way in which donor aid may be disbursed in ways that make it difficult to develop productive relationships between citizens and the state built on mutual obligation, for example, paying taxes in exchange for the provision of public goods.

One of the clearest examples of the manipulation of donors for political purposes was the abolition of parent-teacher associations (PTAs) in 1996 in the process of implementing universal primary education (UPE). In a bid to gain votes in the 1996 presidential elections, Museveni announced the abolition of the PTAs and introduced UPE. As one teacher I interviewed in Mpigi in 2002 put it, "Parents think it is a gift from him." Later, running up to the 2001 election, Museveni promised a Grade IV health center in each subcounty of the country. And in 2005, he announced universal secondary education prior to the 2006 elections.

In response to the announcement of the 1996 UPE policy, the numbers of enrolled students shot up overnight from 2.6 million to 5.3 million in 1997 and up to 7.6 million by 2005. Before UPE, 60 percent of the school-aged children (those six to twelve) were in school compared with 90 percent in 2005. UPE was later modified to allow at least four children in each family to attend school.

Because Museveni introduced this measure as a campaign promise prior to the 1996 elections, it was hastily implemented without adequate preparation and therefore had disastrous consequences for many students. UPE was popular when it was announced because it promised to allow poorer households to send their children to school. However, the government did not have the resources to deliver quality education to the majority of schoolchildren, nor had the educational system prepared for the immediate and massive influx of students overnight. Teachers were not paid for months at a stretch, and large numbers of schools did not have adequate numbers of teachers, school supplies, or toilet facilities. Classrooms increased in size from 40 students to 110 on the average. More than 75 percent of students in the Jinja district, for example, did not have lunch, which affected their performance. Thousands of ghost teachers and students were constantly being uncovered, created to compensate for the low pay teachers were receiving. The poor construction of classrooms under the School Facilitation Grants was another of the many constraints facing UPE schools.

Apart from the enormous burdens the system put on teachers and the challenges students faced without adequate facilities, teachers and parents were concerned about the possibility of donors pulling out or reducing support given their own changing agendas. According to one teacher interviewed in 2005, "The aims of UPE are political: politicians stand up to talk about numbers of schoolgoers but not the quality of education." She added, "The responsibility for education should go to all: to parents, government, schools, and donors too. We should share the burden and make it a joint effort. The approach of UPE was wrong. Government should reconsider and let parents to help. Parents should be allowed to shoulder partly the maintenance of the schools and remuneration of teachers." One member of a Mpigi PTA explained, "Parents are dissatisfied with UPE because government is taking their role. [But] private schools are so costly and many parents cannot afford that."[1]

One consequence of the abolition of PTAs and the introduction of UPE was to strengthen vertical linkages between the central government and local communities by undermining local initiatives that gave communities too much perceived independence from the center. PTAs had once represented one of the largest areas of independent community mobilization. They were not formed into a national or even regional or districtwide network; rather, each PTA operated independently in its own respective school. In other words, their horizontal linkages were weak or nonexistent, making them easy targets for co-optation, manipulation, or elimination.

Formed after independence, the PTAs became especially important under Idi Amin's rule as the country fell into disarray in the 1970s and government sponsorship of the educational system unraveled. They represented in effect a local tax, but operated in a way that was meaningful to residents.

The case of Jinja reflects much of what happened in the rest of the country. Jinja parents responded, as did parents nationwide, to the collapse of the school system by creating PTAs and funding local schools themselves. Resources had dwindled after 1972, especially with the expulsion of the Asian population by Idi Amin. The Asian community had put considerable resources into Jinja's municipal schools, and Asian teachers had been numerous. Their exodus had a particularly serious impact on Jinja schools, since the Jinja Municipal Council was already struggling with the collapse of the national system. Enormous pressures on poorly compensated teachers and head teachers working under difficult conditions resulted in bribery and suspected illegal conduct on the part of both head teachers and PTAs. Inequalities arose between schools that had better PTA funding and those without adequate parental support. Nevertheless, most PTAs kept the schools open and running through these difficult years (Dauda 2004).

After the NRM took over in 1986, the Jinja Municipal Council, which had previously created obstacles for the PTAs, began to cooperate with them and encouraged the formation of new ones. Management committees were set up in schools involving the councillors, school heads, and parents. PTA funds, which were independent of other funds and controlled by the PTAs, were used to supplement teacher salaries and help construct new school buildings. Over time, the government contribution to education in Jinja District dwindled from USh 21.7 million (US$10.85 million) in 1991 to USh 1 million (US$500,000) in 1994. About USh 4 million (US$2 million) were generated by a local small education tax and the remainder and bulk of expenses came from the PTAs (Dauda 2004). By 1995, the schools were making a comeback. However, the government assistance was still negligible. In 1994 and 1995, for example, Jinja District was to have received USh 41.5 million (US$20.75 million) for primary education in Jinja Municipality; however, only a few million shillings ever made it to the town.

Nationwide, from the 1980s until 1996, 90 percent of the funding for the schools came from PTAs, which paid for school maintenance, salaries, educational materials, and furniture. Parents not only raised funds for tuition fees but also provided school transportation, midday meals, school supplies and textbooks, buildings, dormitories, teachers' houses, equipment, animals, and school farms that supplemented the teachers' salaries (Senteza-Kajubi 1991, 324). Undeniably, there were problems with the PTAs, including corruption and imbalances between parents who could afford schooling and those who could not, but overall they provided a perfect example of local participation in community development, whereby people had a vested interest and willingly invested in the quality of their educational system.

A more imaginative UPE policy might have used government or donor funds to supplement community input to address societal inequalities. But Museveni was not interested in tapping into one of the major areas where citizens of Uganda were contributing to their own welfare through civil society organizations. Instead he banked on massive donor assistance to implement UPE as a way of shoring up his popularity in time for the upcoming elections.

The donors supporting the UPE initiative included the World Bank, the United States, the Netherlands, Ireland, the UK, Canada, and the European Union, in addition to some international nongovernmental organizations. Eager to see an emphasis on education provisioning, none of the major donors funding the UPE, not even the World Bank or USAID, seemed to find the dissolution of PTAs in the rural areas problematic, nor did they put pressure to slow down the introduction of UPE to allow for more planning. The PTAs were eventually allowed to return to the more politically volatile urban areas, although with their powers considerably diminished. Their rural counterparts remained banned, and individuals were punished for making donations.

The results of banning the PTAs in rural areas have been disastrous. Inequality in education is widening as middle-class parents take their children out of public schools and put them into better-equipped private schools. Meanwhile, only 22 percent of the children who were in school nationwide when UPE was introduced reached standard (grade) seven. In Jinja, of the 87,000 children enrolled in the district's eighty-two primary schools upon the introduction of UPE in 1997, 26,000, or 30 percent, were no longer attending school by 2001 ("20,000 Primary Education Children Drop Out" 2001). Nationwide, only 19 percent, or 460,000, of the students who enrolled in 1997 sat for Primary Leaving Examinations in 2003 ("MPs Question UPE Statistics" 2003).

Conclusion

This chapter has shown how some of Uganda's economic successes have served to legitimate the Museveni government at key junctures and have helped garner political support for some undemocratic policies. Pleased with such progress on the economic front, foreign donors were often willing to overlook the less democratic aspects of Museveni's rule, further lending credence to the semiauthoritarian regime. Moreover, donors engaged central government in ways that sometimes diminished the obligations of government to become responsive to its citizenry. Donor resources funded government programs, like Universal Primary Education in Uganda, in ways that inadvertently weakened relations of accountability and reciprocity between central government and citizens. Instead of creating a quid pro quo between society and state through taxation of citizens and voluntary contributions to development in exchange for social services and security, donor funds were often used instead merely to create political networks of patronage.

Note

1. Interview with the author in Mpigi, July 5, 2005.

Epilogue

*N'akina obulungi yeena ava mu idhiiro. The greatest dancer of all must
leave the dance arena at the peak of his performance while the applause is
still ringing in his ears, lest by overstaying he undermines his earlier
achievements.*

—Lusoga proverb

The most important changes that have taken place in sub-Saharan Africa since
the early 1990s have been the shift away from authoritarianism. Less dramatic
have been the numbers of countries that have democratized. Economic growth
has taken an upward turn in this period, contributing to these changes. Moreover, there has been a gradual decline in conflict overall on the continent. This
book has shown that Africa, and more specifically Uganda, has seen a gradual
improvement of civil liberties and political rights since 1986.

But the changes are precarious in a semiauthoritarian regime such as
Uganda's, since they can easily be reversed and manipulated. Semiauthoritarian regimes embody both democratic and authoritarian tendencies to varying
degrees and both tendencies need to be accounted for. The democratic experiences and political openings form an important basis for potential shifts toward
greater democracy. Every country that has democratized has done so by building on such experiences. By contrast, the erosion of democratic measures has
serious consequences for state capacity and state building, which rely on legitimacy. Where and when democratic provisions have eroded in resource-poor
African states, the likelihood of conflict has increased while state capacity has
deteriorated; such was the case in Uganda under the regimes of Idi Amin and
Milton Obote II, as well as in northern Uganda under Museveni.

Why then do semiauthoritarian states exist in limbo between democracy
and authoritarianism? Why is it so difficult to dislodge them permanently from
their semiauthoritarian status toward democratization? Why do their leaders
hold so tenaciously to power? Which factors influence the capacity of states to
further democratize in Africa? Why do apparent steps in the direction of
democratization so often turn out to be corrupted by undemocratic practices?

Various explanations have been advanced to explain the persistence of
semiauthoritarianism. At one level, it is easy to point to structural arguments

of economic and class development and argue that the economic conditions in Africa are not generally conducive to democratization. However, some very poor countries have indeed democratized, so it is not enough to rely on determinism. Many have emphasized the weakness of state institutions and of the state itself; others have suggested a lack of elite pressures for change or an absence of democratic political culture, while still others have focused on the weakness of political or civil society in promoting democratization.

Uganda appears to be well suited to the examination of the constraints on semiauthoritarian states insofar as it seems to be in such limbo as it goes through the motions of democratization (for example, opening the country to multipartyism in 2005, allowing for the greater separation of powers, and creating a civilian government). It shares many of the key characteristics of such states: they democratize only as far as they are pushed by elites, civil society, parties, and foreign donors to do so; they combine elements of democratization with illiberal rule; they concentrate power in the executive branch, which attempts to encroach onto the judiciary and legislature; they invest power above all in the military and security forces, using elections to garner legitimacy; they generally ensure that a dominant party will win elections and that it will behave very much like a single party; they maintain power through clientelistic networks; and they are in perpetual contestation with civil society and the media over their independence, capacity to advocate policy changes, and ability to play a watchdog role. The state also vigorously contests the rights of political society to freedom of speech, assembly, and association.

In Uganda, these tensions have played out in what I call the "paradoxes of power": the more the ruling National Resistance Movement (NRM) has sought to eliminate sectarianism, one of the hallmarks of NRM ideology, the more it has been forced into relying on increasingly narrow bases of ethnic support. The more the country has sought to democratize in some areas, the less democratic it has become in others as it has sought to strengthen executive power. Decentralization has become yet another means of creating a patronage network to perpetuate NRM dominance through a local council system. The more the NRM sought at times to depend on the military and security forces, the less secure the country became. The stronger the economy has grown, the more it has helped legitimate undemocratic aspects of the system. Donors have reinforced this pattern by focusing on economic and social policy while ignoring the political and patronage dimensions of policy as well as human rights abuses.

This leads us to our final and central power paradox of why leaders who need to go seem unable to do so: rulers remain in power because the personal cost of leaving is too high. Because they have to feed patronage networks through the use of resources illicitly obtained through offices of the state and because they have used force or the threat of force against their opponents, they cannot leave office without dire personal consequences. Therefore, their imperative is to continue supplying the same patronage networks and using the same repressive tactics that have kept them in power. But unlike authoritarian regimes, which face many of the same constraints, semiauthoritarian regimes also need to relieve the pressures to democratize they themselves have invited, which come from civil society, political society, and members of the elite, the judiciary, and the legislature.

This study suggests that while many factors affect the ability to democratize further, it is particularly important to focus on those factors that break the catch-22 of semiauthoritarian regimes, whereby power is acquired and maintained through violence and patronage, which in turn make holding onto power imperative. Perhaps the most powerful forces influencing the Movement away from authoritarianism are splits within the elite and the military, which one finds in Uganda. But these splits alone are insufficient to ensure democratization; if they simply trigger a power struggle, then nothing will have changed from an institutional standpoint. A takeover by another set of rulers at the ballot box will be just that. Other elements need to come into play.

Establishing the rule of law is essential to moving beyond semiauthoritarianism. This is why the role of the judiciary has been so significant as a check on executive power in Uganda. The legislature is also important as a counterweight to the expansion of executive power, although in Uganda it has been compromised more than the judiciary has. The media has played an essential role in exposing undemocratic practices and areas where the executive and military have overreached. Political parties, civil society, and social movements like women's movements and labor have also played an important role in changing laws and norms, and the stronger they are, the more they can put pressure on the state to create productive synergies with society in order to strengthen both state and society. Donors and diplomats have the potential to help change incentive structures regarding patronage, but they have not always acted strategically or fully appreciated the way in which their aid has been used to prop up the very practices of semiauthoritarianism that they condemn. And finally, in the long run, the strengthening of the business sector and the economy can help create conditions for democratic change, although at this time, the business community in Uganda and in many parts of Africa still remains too vested in the status quo to be a significant force for political liberalization.

These are the main forces today that are pushing for greater democratization in Uganda, and in Africa more generally. Their very existence and impact on the political landscape suggest that in spite of all the daunting challenges a country like Uganda faces with respect to democratization—including its legacy of conflict and poverty—it has traveled far from the days of Idi Amin and the institutional decay that came with his rule. At the same time, the continuing limits on political freedom and civil liberties serve as reminders of how fragile those gains are and how easily the situation could reverse itself.

Acronyms

ACTV	African Centre for Treatment and Rehabilitation of Torture Victims
ADF	Allied Democratic Forces
CA	Constituent Assembly
CCM	Chama cha Mapinduzi
CMI	Chieftaincy of Military Intelligence
CP	Conservative Party
DES	District Executive Secretary
DP	Democratic Party
DRC	Democratic Republic of Congo
DSC	District Service Commission
ESO	External Security Organisation
FAR	Forces Armées Rwandaises
FDC	Forum for Democratic Change
FEDEMU	Federal Democratic Movement
FOBA	Force Obote Back Again
GoSS	Government of Southern Sudan
HIPC	heavily indebted poor country
HSM	Holy Spirit Movement
ICC	International Criminal Court
IDP	internally displaced person
ISO	Internal Security Organisation
JEEMA	Justice Forum of Uganda
KAP	Kalangala Action Plan
KY	Kabaka Yekka
LC	Local Council
LRA	Lord's Resistance Army

NALU	National Army for the Liberation of Uganda
NGO	nongovernmental organization
NOM	Ninth of October Movement
NRA	National Resistance Army
NRC	National Resistance Council
NRM	National Resistance Movement
PAFO	Parliamentary Advocacy Forum
PGB	Presidential Guard Brigade
PPU	Presidential Protection Unit
PRA	People's Redemption Army
PTA	Parent-Teacher Association
RC	Resistance Council
RCD-Goma	Rassemblement Congolais pour la Démocratie–Goma
RCD-K	Rassemblement Conglais pour la Démocratie–Kisangani
RCD-ML	Rassemblement Conglais pour la Démocratie Mouvement pour la Libération
RDC	resident district commissioner
RPA	Rwandan Patriotic Army
RPF	Rwandan Patriotic Front
SF	Special Force
SPLA	Sudanese People's Liberation Army
UCB	Uganda Commercial Bank
UFA	Uganda Freedom Army
UFM	Uganda Freedom Movement
UNA	Uganda National Army
UNLA	Uganda National Liberation Army
UNLF	Ugandan National Liberation Front
UNRF	Uganda National Rescue Front
UNRF II	Uganda National Rescue Front II
UPA	Uganda People's Army
UPC	Uganda People's Congress
UPDA	Uganda People's Democratic Army
UPDF	Uganda People's Defence Forces
UPE	universal primary education
UPM	Uganda People's Movement
VCCU	Violent Crime Crack Unit
WNBF	West Nile Bank Front
YPA	Young Parliamentarians Association

Basic Political
and Social Data, 2010

Capital	Kampala
Type of Government	Presidential republic
Independence	October 9, 1962 (from the UK)
Population	31,367,972 (2008 estimate)
Ethnicity	Baganda 16.9%, Banyankole 9.5%, Basoga 8.4%, Bakiga 6.9%, Iteso 6.4%, Langi 6.1%, Acholi 4.7%, Bagisu 4.6%, Lugbara 4.2%, Bunyoro 2.7%, other 29.6% (2002 census)
Religion	Roman Catholic 41.9%; Protestant 42% (Anglican 35.9%, Pentecostal 4.6%, Seventh Day Adventist 1.5%); Muslim 12.1%; other 3.1%; none 0.9% (2002 census)
Official Languages	English and Swahili
Head of Government	President Lieutenant General Yoweri Museveni (elected by popular vote February 23, 2006, for five-year term)
Cabinet	Appointed by the president from among elected members of the National Assembly
Prime Minister	Apolo Nsibambi
Legislative Branch	Unicameral National Assembly
	332 seats total

- 215 members elected to open seats by popular vote on February 23, 2006, for five-year terms
- 104 members elected to reserved seats, nominated by legally established special interest groups, including
  Women: 79 seats
  Army: 10 seats
  Disabled: 5 seats
  Youth: 5 seats
  Labor: 5 seats
- 13 ex officio members

	Seats held by party, 2010 National Resistance Movement (NRM): 205 Forum for Democratic Change (FDC): 37 Uganda People's Congress (UPC): 9 Democratic Party (DP): 8 Conservative Party (CP): 1 Justice Forum (JEEMA): 1 Independents: 37
Women in the National Assembly	31 percent (includes women in both reserved and open seats)
Speaker of the House	Edward Kiwanuka Ssekandi
Electoral System	Candidate with simple majority of votes wins
Districts	West: Bulisa, Bundibugyo, Bushenyi, Hoima, Ibanda, Isingiro, Kabale, Kabarole, Kamwenge, Kanungu, Kasese, Kibale, Kiruhura, Kisoro, Kyenjojo, Masindi, Mbarara, Ntungamo, Rukungiri North: Abim, Adjumani, Amolatar, Amuru, Apac, Arua, Dokolo, Gulu, Kaabong, Kitgum, Koboko, Kotido, Lira, Maracha-Terego, Moroto, Moyo, Nakapiripirit, Nebbi, Oyam, Pader, Yumbe East: Amuria, Budaka, Bududa, Bugiri, Bukedea, Bukwa, Busia, Butaleja, Iganga, Jinja, Kaberamaido, Kaliro, Kamuli, Kapchorwa, Katakwi, Kumi, Manafwa, Mayuge, Mbale, Namutumba, Pallisa, Sironko, Soroti, Tororo Central: Kalangala, Kampala, Kayunga, Kiboga, Luwero, Lyantonde, Masaka, Mityana, Mpigi, Mubende, Mukono, Nakaseke, Nakasongola, Rakai, Sembabule, Wakiso
Parties and Leaders	Conservative Party (Ken Lukyamuzi) Democratic Party (John Ssebaana Kizito) Forum for Democratic Change (Kizza Besigye) Justice Forum (JEEMA) (Suman Basalirwa) National Resistance Movement (Yoweri Museveni) People's Progressive Party (Jaberi Bidandi Ssali) Uganda People's Congress (Olara Otunnu)
Party Coalition	Inter Party Cooperation: includes Forum for Democratic Change, Uganda People's Congress, Conservative Party, and Justice Forum–JEEMA

Bibliography

"20,000 Primary Education Children Drop Out." 2001. *New Vision*, July 7.
Agaba, Grace. 2007. "Re-Centralisation: A Dilemma for Local Governments." *New Vision*, November 29.
Ahimbisibwe, Fortunate. 2007. "Who Are the PRA?" *New Vision*, March 3.
"Amama Glossed Over Issues Raised by Four NRM Party MPs." 2007. *Monitor*, January 17.
Amaza, Ondoga Ori. 1998. *Museveni's Long March from Guerrilla to Statesman*. Kampala, Uganda: Fountain Publishers.
Ariko, Charles. 2000. "Women Want UPDF Out of Congo." *New Vision*, May 25, 1–2.
Atkinson, Ronald R. Forthcoming. "'The Realists in Juba'?: An Analysis of the Juba Peace Talks." In *Understanding the Lord's Resistance Army: Perspectives on Uganda's War in the North*, ed. T. Allen and K. Vlassenroot. London: Zed Books.
Atuhaire, Alex. 2008a. "Did Officers Sell Arms to LRA Rebels?" *Monitor*, March 31.
———. 2008b. "I Am Not on Sale, Says Kyakabale." *Monitor*, March 31.
Barkan, Joel. 2005. "An African 'Success' Past Its Prime?" http://www.wilsoncenter .org/events/docs/Uganda.pdf. Accessed January 12, 2010.
———. 2008. "Legislatures on the Rise?" *Journal of Democracy* 19(2): 124–137.
Barya, John-Jean. 2000. "The Making of Uganda's 1995 Constitution: Achieving Consensus by Law." Unpublished paper. Kampala: Centre for Basic Research.
Bates, Robert. 2008. *When Things Fell Apart: State Failure in Late-Century Africa*. New York: Cambridge University Press.
Behrend, Heike. 1999. *Alice Lakwena and the Holy Spirits: War in Northern Uganda, 1985–97*. Oxford: James Currey.
Besigye, Kizza. 1999. "An Insider's View of How NRM Lost the 'Broad-Base.'" *Monitor*, November 7.
Bond, G. C., and J. Vincent. 2002. "The Moving Frontier of AIDS in Uganda: Contexts, Texts, and Concepts.'" In *Contested Terrains and Constructed Categories: Contemporary Africa in Focus*, ed. G. C. Bond and N. C. Gibson. Boulder, CO: Westview Press.
Branch, Adam. 2007. *The Political Dilemmas of Global Justice: Anti-Civilian Violence and the Violence of Humanitarianism—The Case of Northern Uganda*. New York: Columbia University Press.

Bratton, Michael. 1989. "The Politics of Government-NGO Relations in Africa." *World Development* 17(4): 569–587.

———. 1997. "Deciphering Africa's Divergent Transitions." *Political Science Quarterly* 112(1): 67–93.

Bratton, Michael, and Eric C. C. Chang. 2006. "State Building and Democratization in Sub-Saharan Africa: Forwards, Backwards, or Together?" *Comparative Political Studies* 39: 1,059–1,083.

Bratton, Michael, and Gina Lambright. 2001. "Uganda's Referendum 2000: The Silent Boycott." *African Affairs* 1000: 429–452.

Bratton, Michael, and Nicolas van de Walle. 1994. "Neopatrimonial Regimes and Political Transitions in Africa." *World Politics* 46(4): 453–489.

———. 1997. *Democratic Experiments in Africa: Regime Transitions in Comparative Research.* Cambridge, UK, and New York: Cambridge University Press.

Brett, E. A. 1994a. "Rebuilding Organisational Capacity in Uganda Under the National Resistance Movement." *Journal of Modern African Studies* 32(1): 53–80.

———. 1994b. "The Military and Democratic Transition in Uganda." In *From Chaos to Order: The Politics of Constitution-making in Uganda*, ed. H. B. Hansen and M. Twaddle. Kampala and Oxford: Fountain Publishers and James Currey.

Brownlee, Jason. 2009. "Portents of Pluralism: How Hybrid Regimes Affect Democratic Transitions." *American Journal of Political Science* 53(3): 515–532.

Bunce, Valerie J., and Sharon L. Wolchik. 2006. "Favorable Conditions and Electoral Revolutions." *Journal of Democracy* 17(4): 5–18.

Burkey, Ingvild. 1991. "People's Power in Theory and Practice: The Resistance Council System in Uganda." Unpublished paper.

"Busoga Gets Its 'Federo' First." 2002. *New Vision*, November 13.

"Busoga Rejects Mengo Federo Deal." 2005. *Monitor*, March 23.

Bussey, Erica. 2005. "Constitutional Dialogue in Uganda." *Journal of African Law* 49(1): 1–23.

Carbone, Giovanni M. 2003. "Under 'Movement Democracy' in Uganda Political Parties in a 'No-Party Democracy': Hegemony and Opposition." *Party Politics* 9(4): 485–501.

———. 2008. *No-Party Democracy? Ugandan Politics in Comparative Perspective.* Boulder, CO: Lynne Rienner Publishers.

Carothers, Thomas. 2002. "The End of the Transition Paradigm." *Journal of Democracy* 13 (January): 5–21.

Clark, John. 2001. "Explaining Ugandan Intervention in Congo: Evidence and Explanations." *Journal of Modern African Studies* 39(2): 261–287.

———. 2007. "The Decline of the African Military Coup." *Journal of Democracy* 18(2): 141–155.

"Colonel Kizza's Story." 2003. *Africa Confidential*, December 4.

Committee to Protect Journalists. 2008. "Tabloid's Printing Press Torched by Gunmen, Its Staff Followed by Unidentified Individuals." New York.

"Confession on Commercial Bank Was Government Cover-Up." 2001. *Monitor*, July 31.

"Constitution Has Become a Temporary Document!" 2005. *New Vision*, August 23.

"Contract Committees to Replace Tender Board." 2005. *Monitor*, April 25.

"Councillors Shouldn't Eat Where They Worketh." 2002. *Monitor*, April 26.

Dahl, Robert A. 1998. *On Democracy.* New Haven, CT, and London: Yale University Press.

Dauda, Carol L. 2004. "The Importance of De Facto Decentralization in Primary Education in Sub-Saharan Africa." *Journal of Planning Education and Research* 24(1): 28–40.

Ddungu, Expedit. 1989. "Popular Forms and the Question of Democracy: The Case of Resistance Councils in Uganda." Unpublished paper. Kampala: Center for Basic Research.

Decalo, Samuel. 1992. "The Process, Prospects, and Constraints of Democratization in Africa." *African Affairs* 91: 7–35.

Diamond, Larry. 1996. "Is the Third Wave Over?" *Journal of Democracy* 7(3): 20–37.

———. 2002. "Thinking About Hybrid Regimes." *Journal of Democracy* 13(2): 21–35.

"Did Saleh, Tinye, Jeje, Elly Deserve Promotion?" 2001. *Monitor,* October 23.

"Disagreements Rock Ankole MPs." 2007. *Monitor,* December 19.

Dolan, Christopher. 2005. "Understanding War and Its Continuation: The Case of Northern Uganda." PhD diss., Development Studies Institute, School of Economics and Political Science, University of London, London.

Doornbos, Martin R. 1978. *Not All the King's Men: Inequality as a Political Instrument in Ankole, Uganda.* The Hague (Noordeinde 41): Mouton.

Doornbos, Martin, and Frederick Mwesigye. 1995. "The New Politics of Kingmaking." In *From Chaos to Order: The Politics of Constitution-making in Uganda,* ed. H. B. Hansen and M. Twaddle, 61–77. Kampala and Oxford: Fountain Publishers and James Currey.

"DP Gives Museveni Memo." 2006. *New Vision,* August 1.

"Dusting Off the Jewel." 1988. *Africa Events,* November 14–15.

Edelman, Murray J. 1964. *The Symbolic Uses of Politics.* Urbana: University of Illinois Press.

Egeland, Jan. 2008. *A Billion Lives: An Eyewitness Report from the Frontlines of Humanity.* New York: Simon and Schuster.

Ekeh, Peter. 1975. "Colonialism and the Two Publics in Africa: A Theoretical Statement." *Comparative Studies in Society and History* 17: 91–112.

Electoral Commission of the Republic of Uganda. 2006. "Report on the 2005/2006 General Elections." Report submitted to parliament through the minister of justice and constitutional affairs in accordance with Section 12(1)(0) of the Electoral Commission Act No. 3.

Ellett, Rachel L. 2008. "Emerging Judicial Power in Transitional Democracies: Malawi, Tanzania, and Uganda." PhD diss., Department of Political Science, Northeastern University, Boston.

Englebert, Pierre. 2000. *State Legitimacy and Development in Africa.* Boulder, CO: Lynne Rienner Publishers.

Enloe, Cynthia H. 1980. *Ethnic Soldiers: State Security in Divided Societies.* Athens: University of Georgia Press.

"FDC Raps Kyankwanzi Movt MPs Retreat." 2007. *New Vision,* July 16.

Finnström, Sverker. 2008. *Living with Bad Surroundings: War, History, and Everyday Moments in Northern Uganda.* Durham: Duke University Press.

Flanary, Rachel, and David Watt. 1999. "The State of Corruption: A Case Study of Uganda." *Third World Quarterly* 20(3): 515–536.

Furley, Oliver. 2000. "Democratisation in Uganda." *Commonwealth and Comparative Politics* 38(3): 79–102.

Furley, Oliver, and James Katalikawe. 1997. "Constitutional Reform in Uganda: The New Approach." *African Affairs* 96(383): 243–261.

Geist, Judith. 1995. "Political Significance of the Constituent Assembly Elections." In *From Chaos to Order: The Politics of Constitution-making in Uganda,* ed. H. B. Hansen and M. Twaddle, 90–113. Kampala and Oxford: Fountain Publishers and James Currey.

Global Integrity. 2006. "Country Reports: Uganda." http://www.globalintegrity.org/reports/2006/UGANDA/facts.cfm. Accessed November 10, 2007.

Golooba-Mutebi, Frederick. 2004. "Reassessing Popular Participation in Uganda." *Public Administration and Development* 24(4): 289–304.

———. 2008. "Imagining 'Mchakamchaka for All.'" *Monitor,* July 28.

Graduate Institute of International Studies (GIIS). 2007. *Small Arms Survey.* Geneva.

Green, Elliott D. 2005. "The Politics of Ethnonationalism in Contemporary Uganda: The Case of Buganda." PhD diss., Development Studies Institute, London School of Economics and Political Science, London.

Gwyn, David. 1977. *Idi Amin: Death-light of Africa.* Boston: Little, Brown.

Gyimah-Boadi, Emmanuel. 1998. "The Rebirth of African Liberalism." *Journal of Democracy* 9(2): 18–31.

Hadenius, Axel, and Jan Teorell. 2007. "Pathways from Authoritarianism." *Journal of Democracy* 18(1): 143–157.

Haggard, Stephan, and Robert R. Kaufman. 1995. *The Political Economy of Democratic Transitions.* Princeton, NJ: Princeton University Press.

Hauser, Ellen. 1999. "Ugandan Relations with Western Donors in the 1990s: What Impact on Democratisation?" *Journal of Modern African Studies* 37(4): 621–641.

Herbst, Jeffrey. 2001. "Political Liberalization in Africa After Ten Years." *Comparative Politics* 33 (April): 357–375.

Hochschild, Adam. 1999. *King Leopold's Ghost: A Story of Greed, Terror, and Heroism in Colonial Africa.* Boston: Houghton Mifflin.

Howard, Marc M., and Philip G. Roessler. 2006. "Liberalizing Electoral Outcomes in Competitive Authoritarian Regimes." *American Journal of Political Science* 50(2): 365–381.

Human Rights Watch. 2004. "State of Pain: Torture in Uganda." March 28, http://www.hrw.org/en/reports/2004/03/28/state-pain. Accessed April 27, 2010.

———. 2007. "State Homophobia Threatens Health and Human Rights." August 22, http://www.hrw.org/en/news/2007/08/21/uganda-state-homophobia-threatens-health-and-human-rights. Accessed April 27, 2010.

———. 2008. "New Government Threatens Free Press, Expels Foreign Journalist, Prosecutes Local Media." March 14, http://www.hrw.org/en/news/2006/03/12/uganda-new-government-threatens-free-press. Accessed April 27, 2010.

Huntington, Samuel P. 1997. "After Twenty Years: The Future of the Third Wave." *Journal of Democracy* 8(4): 3–12.

Hyden, Goran. 1980. *Beyond Ujamaa in Tanzania: Underdevelopment and an Uncaptured Peasantry.* Berkeley: University of California Press.

Ikuya, James Magode. 2009. "NRM Pot Is Dangerously Tilting." *Weekly Observer,* February 25.

Inglehart, Ronald, Pippa Norris, and Chris Welzel. 2002. "Gender Equality and Democracy." *Comparative Sociology* 1(3–4): 321–345.

"In Search of Security: A Regional Analysis of Armed Conflict in Northern Uganda, Eastern Uganda and Southern Sudan." 2005. Feinstein International Famine Center, Tufts University. http://idl-bnc.idrc.ca/dspace/handle/123456789/30937.

"Is Museveni Using Kony War to Stay in Power?" 2004. *New Vision,* May 5.

Jabweli, Okello. 2003. "Judges Will Remain Professional." *New Vision,* January 29.

James, Robert, Paul Francis, and Godfrey Ahabwe Pereza. 2001. "The Institutional Context of Rural Poverty Reduction in Uganda: Decentralisation's Dual Nature." Ladder Working Paper No. 6. Kampala, Uganda.

Johnson, Douglas H. 2003. *The Root Causes of Sudan's Civil Wars*. Oxford, Blooming-ton, and Kampala: International Institute, in association with James Currey, Indi-ana University Press, Fountain Publishers.

Jones, Ben. 2009. *Beyond the State in Rural Uganda*. Edinburgh: Edinburgh University Press.

Joseph, Richard. 1987. *Democracy and Prebendal Politics in Nigeria*. New York: Cambridge University Press.

———. 1998. "Africa, 1990–1997: From Abertura to Closure." *Journal of Democracy* 9(2): 3–17.

Kabushenga, Robert. 1999. "Tinyefuze Owes Ugandans an Explanation." *New Vision*, November 7.

Kabwegyere, Tarsis B. 1995. *The Politics of State Formation and Destruction in Uganda*. Kampala: Fountain Publishers.

Kahigiriza, James. 2001. *Bridging the Gap: Struggling Against Sectarianism and Violence in Ankole and Uganda*. Kampala: Fountain Publishers.

Kakande, John. 2006. "NGOs Bill New Wine in Old Bottles." *New Vision*, May 14.

Kalyvas, Stathis. 2006. *The Logic of Violence in Civil War*. New York: Cambridge University Press.

"Kanyeihamba Criticises MPs." 2008. *Monitor*, October 9.

Karlström, Mikael. 1999. "Civil Society and Its Presuppositions: Lessons from Uganda." In *Civil Society and the Political Imagination in Africa: Critical Perspectives*, ed. J. L. Comaroff and J. Comaroff, 104–123. Chicago: University of Chicago Press.

Kasfir, Nelson. 1994. "Ugandan Politics and the Constituent Assembly Elections of March 1994." In *From Chaos to Order: The Politics of Constitution-making in Uganda*, ed. H. B. Hansen and M. Twaddle. Kampala and Oxford: Fountain Publishers and James Currey.

———. 1998. "'No-Party Democracy' in Uganda." *Journal of Democracy* 9(2): 49–63.

Kasfir, Nelson, and Steven Hippo Twebaze. 2005. "Limits of Institutionalization of Legislature Without Parties." Paper presented at the 2005 annual meeting of the American Political Science Association, Washington, DC, September 2.

Kasozi, A. B. K. 1994. *The Social Origins of Violence in Uganda: 1964–1985*. Montréal: McGill-Queen's University Press.

Katorobo, James. 1995. "Electoral Choices in the Constituent Assembly Elections." In *From Chaos to Order: The Politics of Constitution-making in Uganda*, ed. H. B. Hansen and M. Twaddle, 114–147. Kampala and Oxford: Fountain Publishers and James Currey.

Katunzi, Pius Muteekani. 1998. "Baganda to Submit Views on Land Bill." *Monitor*, May 9.

Kavuma, Richard M. 2009. "Great Expectations in Uganda over Oil Discovery." *Guardian*, December 2.

Kayanja, Ronald. 1999. "Counting Scribes' 'Dead Bodies' in NRM's Days." *Monitor*, November 30.

Kayunga, Sallie Simba. 1993. *Islamic Fundamentalism in Uganda*. Kampala: Centre for Basic Research.

———. 2000. "The Impact of Armed Opposition on the Movement System in Uganda." In *No-Party Democracy in Uganda: Myths and Realities*, ed. J. Mugaju and J. Oloka-Onyango, 109–126. Kampala: Fountain Publishers.

Kiggundu, Edris. 2008. "Why Saleh Disagreed with Amama, Tinye on Ghosts." *Weekly Observer*, April 3.

————. 2009. "Kazini Was Reckless, Says Museveni." *Weekly Observer,* November 12.
Kiggundu, Edris, and David Tash Lumu. 2006. "Omoro MP Jacob Oulanyah Has Crossed Over to the NRM from UPC." *Weekly Observer,* July 28.
Kwesiga, Jassy. 2001. "NGOs Call for Change." *Monitor,* March 6.
Kwesiga, J. B., and A. J. Ratter. 1993. "Realizing the Development Potential of NGOs and Community Groups in Uganda." Kampala: Ministry of Finance and Economic Planning.
Kyamutetera, Muhereza, and Emmanuel N. Mugarura. 2003. "Drop 3rd Term Bid, Churches Tell Movt." *Monitor,* June 3.
Kyazze, Simwogerere. 1999. "Time to Run Away from Journalism?" *Monitor,* November 12.
Langseth, Petter. 1996. "Civil Service Reform: A General View." In *Democratic Decentralisation in Uganda: A New Approach to Local Governance,* ed. S. Villadsen and F. Lubanga, 1–35. Kampala: Fountain Publishers.
Lemarchand, René, and Keith Legg. 1972. "Political Clientelism and Development: A Preliminary Analysis." *Comparative Politics* 4(2): 149–178.
Levitsky, Steven, and Lucan Way. 2001. *Competitive Authoritarianism: Hybrid Regime Change in Peru and Ukraine in Comparative Perspective.* Glasgow: Centre for the Study of Public Policy, University of Strathclyde.
————. 2002. "The Rise of Competitive Authoritarianism." *Journal of Democracy* 13(2): 51–65.
"Like or Hate Him, You Can't Ignore Tinyefuza." 2008. *Weekly Observer,* March 27.
Lindberg, Staffan I. 2006. *Democracy and Elections in Africa.* Baltimore, MD: Johns Hopkins University Press.
————. 2009. "The Power of Elections in Africa Revisited." In *Democratization by Elections,* ed. S. I. Lindberg. Baltimore, MD: Johns Hopkins University Press.
Linz, Juan J., and Alfred C. Stepan. 1996. *Problems of Democratic Transition and Consolidation: Southern Europe, South America, and Post-Communist Europe.* Baltimore, MD: Johns Hopkins University Press.
Lipset, Seymour Martin. 1959. *Some Social Requisites of Democracy: Economic Development and Political Legitimacy.* Indianapolis, IN: Bobbs-Merrill.
"Local Council Achievements and Failures in 2006." 2007. *New Vision,* January 3.
"Local Govts Revenues Fall After Tax Confusion." 2004. *Monitor,* August 11.
Low, D. A. 1988. "The Dislocated Polity." In *Uganda Now: Between Decay and Development,* ed. H. B. Hansen and M. Twaddle. London: James Currey.
Lumu, David Tash. 2009. "Gen. Tumwine Speaks on Army Imbalance." *Observer,* September 7.
Makara, Sabiti, Lise Rakner, and Lars Svåsand. 2009. "Turnaround: The National Resistance Movement and the Reintroduction of a Multiparty System in Uganda." *International Political Science Review* 30(2): 185–204.
"Makmot Joins NRM." 2006. *New Vision,* September 22.
Malloy, James M., and Mitchell A. Seligson. 1987. *Authoritarians and Democrats: Regime Transition in Latin America.* Pittsburgh, PA: University of Pittsburgh Press.
Mamdani, Mahmood. 1988. "NRA/NRM: Two Years in Power." Public lecture delivered at Makerere University, Kampala, Uganda. March 3.
————. 1993. "Pluralism and the Right of Association." Kampala: Centre for Basic Research.
————. 1994. "The Politics of Democratic Reform in Uganda." Paper presented at Conference Centre, Kampala. February 11.
Maseruka, Josephine. 2007. "Aggrey Awori Joins NRM Party." *New Vision,* March 27.

Mazrui, Ali A. 1977. "Religious Strangers in Uganda: From Emin Pasha to Amin Dada." *African Affairs* 76(302): 21–38.

Ministry of Finance, Planning, and Economic Development. 2009a. "Annual Report: Uganda's Economic and Financial Overview." Kampala.

————. 2009b. "National Budget Framework Paper (FY 2009/10–FY 2013/2014)." Kampala.

Mirzeler, Mustafa, and Crawford Young. 2000. "Pastoral Politics in the Northeast Periphery in Uganda: AK-47 as Change Agent." *Journal of Modern African Studies* 38: 407–429.

Mitchinson, Robin. 2003. "Devolution in Uganda: An Experiment in Local Service Delivery." *Public Administration and Development* 23: 241–248.

Mkutu, Kennedy Agade. 2007. "Small Arms and Light Weapons Among Pastoral Groups in the Kenya-Uganda Border Area." *African Affairs* (106): 47–70.

Moehler, Devra C. 2006. "Participation and Support for the Constitution in Uganda." *Journal of Modern African Studies* 44(2): 275–308.

Mpagi, Mwanguhya C. 2007a. "Uganda: Ruckus in the NRM Suits Museveni Just Fine." *Monitor,* September 30.

————. 2007b. "Muhwezi Trial: Beyond the Prosecution." *Monitor,* November 7.

"MPs Compile Torture Report." 2003. *Monitor,* February 20.

"MPs Question UPE Statistics." 2003. *Monitor,* July 29.

Mubangizi, Michael. 2007. "Arrested, Tortured, Dismissed for Fighting Ghost Soldiers." *Weekly Observer,* March 15.

Mudoola, Dan M. 1991. "Institution-building: The Case of the NRM and the Military in Uganda, 1986–9." In *Changing Uganda: The Dilemmas of Structural Adjustment and Revolutionary Change,* ed. H. B. Hansen and M. Twaddle. London: James Currey.

Mufumba, Isaac. 2010. "Election Violence: Is It Bursting Its Banks?" *The Independent,* March 23.

Mugerwa, Yasiin. 2009. "Movement, Opposition Talks Hang in Balance." *Monitor,* December 4.

Mugisha, Anne. 2003. "Museveni's Talk on Sectarianism Empty." http://www.mail-archive.com/ugandanet@kym.net/msg10211.html. Accessed November 11, 2007.

————. 2006. "Museveni: Words vs. Practices." *Weekly Observer,* March 30.

————. 2009. "Unmasking Country's 'Born Again' Fad." *Independent,* December 8.

————. 2010. "The Anti-homosexuality Bill: Snatching Victory from the Jaws of Defeat." *The Independent,* January 13. http://www.independent.co.ug/index.php/component/content/article/106-myblog/2374-the-anti-homosexuality-bill-snatching-victory-from-the-jaws-of-defeat. Accessed April 27, 2010.

Muhangi, Jossy. 2002. "Museveni Warns FM Radios on Besigye." *New Vision,* November 18.

Muhumuza, William. 2009. "From Fundamental Change to No Change: The NRM and Democratization in Uganda." *Les cahiers d'Afrique de l'est* 41(1): 21–42.

Mujaju, Akiiki. 1997. "Civil Society at Bay in Uganda." In *The State and Democracy in Africa,* ed. G. Nzongola-Ntalaja and M. C. Lee. Trenton, NJ: Africa World Press.

Mukholi, David. 1995. *A Complete Guide to Uganda's Fourth Constitution: History, Politics, and the Law.* Kampala: Fountain Publishers.

Mulondo, Emmanuel. 2005. "Judge Withdraws from Besigye Case." *Monitor,* November 19.

————. 2010. "Journalists to Debate Government over Media Bill." *Monitor,* April 27.

"Museveni Doesn't Survive on War." 2006. *New Vision,* October 25.

"Museveni—From Grand Reformer to Simply Surviving." 2009. *Africa Confidential* 50(8). http://www.africa-confidential.com.

"Museveni Mad with Judges over Nullifying 2000 Referendum Act." 2004. *New Vision*, June 30.

"Museveni Rigging Worse than Obote, Says Nekyon." 2001. *Monitor*, March 21.

"Museveni Warned Ankole in 2003." 2003. *Weekly Observer*, November 4.

Museveni, Yoweri, with Elizabeth Kanyogonya and Kevin Shillington. 1997. *Sowing the Mustard Seed: The Struggle for Freedom and Democracy in Uganda.* London: Macmillan.

Mutibwa, Phares. 1992. *Uganda Since Independence.* Trenton, NJ: Africa World Press.

Mutono, Allen. 1994. "Potholes on the Road to Press Freedom." *New Vision*, March 7.

Mwenda, Andrew. 2007a. *Mwenda's Prison Notes.* http://tortureinuganda.wordpress.com/2007/04/05/mwendas-prison-notes-testimonies-of-the-inmates. Accessed April 8, 2008.

———. 2007b. "Personalizing Power in Uganda." *Journal of Democracy* 18(3): 23–37.

———. 2008a. "Museveni Doesn't Favour Bahima, He Uses Them." *Independent*, April 4.

———. 2008b. "Kazini: The Untold Story." *Independent*, April 28.

———. 2008c. "Why the Uganda State Is Criminalized." *Independent*, April 29.

———. 2009. "Who Killed Gen. Kazini and Why?" *Independent*, November 24.

Mwenda, Andrew, and Roger Tangri. 2005. "Corruption and Cronyism in Uganda's Privatization in the 1990s." *African Affairs* 100: 117–133.

Mwesige, Peter G. 1999. "Movement Derailed—Col Kizza Besigye." *New Vision*, November 7.

Nakazibwe, Carolyne. 2002. "67 Percent Want Party Politics, Says Poll." *Monitor*, June 5.

Nakkazi, Esther. 2009. "Uganda: Alarm as Country Struggles to Save Economy." *East African*, December 21.

Namutebi, Joyce. 2009a. "Regional Tier to Increase Govt Expenditure." *New Vision*, December 12.

———. 2009b. "Regional Tier Bill Released." *New Vision*, December 7.

Naturinda, Shila. 2008. "Rugunda Report full of Lies—MPs." *Monitor*, June 20.

Ndegwa, S. N. 1996. *The Two Faces of Civil Society: NGOs and Politics in Africa.* West Hartford, CT: Kumarian Press.

Nganda, Ssemujju Ibrahim. 2003. "Museveni Names Team to Talk with Opposition." *Monitor*, May 7.

———. 2004. "Rukikaire Not for Museveni." *Weekly Observer*, September 2.

———. 2005a. "Gen. Museveni Rewards Loyalty." *Weekly Observer*, October 27.

———. 2005b. "Moment of Truth for Tumukunde." *Weekly Observer*, June 2.

———. 2006. "How Butime Fell Out with Museveni Favour." *Weekly Observer*, June 22.

———. 2009. "Banyankore Officers Most Qualified, Says Gen. Aronda." *Observer*, October 22.

Nganda, Ssemujju Ibrahim, and Benon Herbert Oluka. 2004. "Interview with Maj. Roland Kakooza Mutale." *Uganda Observer*, February 2.

"Ninety Days of War in Garamba Forest." 2009. *New Vision*, March 13.

"Northern Uganda 'World's Biggest Neglected Crisis.'" 2004. *Guardian*, October 22.

Novicki, Margaret A., and Martine Dennis. 1988. "Interview with President Yoweri Museveni." *Africa Report* (July–August): 18–21.

"NRM Boss Fears for His Life." 2006. *Monitor*, December 10.

"NRM Friction Spills to Spy Agencies." 2008. *Monitor*, February 13.

"NRM Historical Attacks Party." 2007. *New Vision*, January 1.

"NRM Policy a Must for Civil Servants—Party Official." 2007. *Monitor*, February 23.

"NRM Thrives on Rented Support—Col. Besigye." 2007. *Monitor*, January 10.

Nyakairu, Frank. 2007. "Military Spending Hits Shs 37 Trillion." *Monitor*, June 27.

———. 2008. "The Making of Joseph Kony: Failed Peace and the Sudan." *Monitor*, January 13.

Obore, Chris. 2006. "The Untold Story of the 1989 Mukura Massacre." *Monitor*, October 21.

———. 2007. "Tumukunde in U.S." *Monitor*, September 7.

O'Donnell, Guillermo A., and Philippe C. Schmitter. 1986. *Transitions from Authoritarian Rule: Tentative Conclusions About Uncertain Democracies.* Baltimore, MD: Johns Hopkins University Press.

O'Donnell, Guillermo A., Philippe C. Schmitter, and Laurence Whitehead. 1986. *Transitions from Authoritarian Rule: Prospects for Democracy.* Baltimore, MD: Johns Hopkins University Press.

Oguttu, Wafula. 2009. "Will the Opposition Alliance Kill Multiparty Democracy in Uganda?" *New Vision*, November 28.

Ojwee, Dennis. 2009. "190,000 People Still in North Camps." *New Vision*, December 13.

Oloka-Onyango, Joe. 1993. "Judicial Power and Constitutionalism in Uganda." Centre for Basic Research Working Paper No. 30. Kampala: Centre for Basic Research.

———. 1997. "Uganda's 'Benevolent' Dictatorship." *Current History* 9(6): 212–216.

———. 2000. "New Wine or New Bottles? Movement Politics and One-partyism in Uganda." In *No-party Democracy in Uganda: Myths and Realities*, ed. J. Mugaju and J. Oloka-Onyango, 40–59. Kampala: Fountain Publishers.

———. 2004. "'New-Breed' Leadership, Conflict, and Reconstruction in the Great Lakes Region of Africa: A Sociopolitical Biography of Uganda's Yoweri Kaguta Museveni." *Africa Today* 50(3): 29–52.

Omara-Otunnu, Amii. 1987. *Politics and the Military in Uganda, 1890–1985.* Basingstoke, UK: Macmillan.

Omoding, Obalell. 2007. "Behind Country's Police Story." *Monitor*, October 7.

Onyango-Obbo, Charles. 1999a. "Uganda Press: On the Short and Long Leash." *Monitor*, July 26.

———. 1999b. "To Cry or Not Cry for Independent Press." *Monitor*, July 24.

———. 2001. "Should We Run, Hide, or Stay Put Because Kazini Is Now Army Chief?" *Monitor*, November 7.

———. 2002. "Uganda Needs a Rich Mix of Educated and Illiterate Rulers." *Monitor*, August 14.

———. 2008a. "Strange: Govt Rapes Free Press as an Act of 'Love.'" *East African*, June 18.

———. 2008b. "It Is Not Always the Best Hunter Who Takes Home the Choice Cuts." *East African*, February 19.

"Onzima Tests FDC's Resolve: Party Will Bark But Not Bite." 2008. *Weekly Observer*, May 22.

Ottaway, Marina. 2003. *Democracy Challenged: The Rise of Semi-authoritarianism.* Washington, DC: Carnegie Endowment for International Peace.

Ouma Balikowa, David. 2002. "The Double Edge of Winnie Saga." *Monitor*, March 14.

"Parliamentarians Ignore Debates on Human Rights Abuses." 2007. *Monitor*, December 15.

"Part III: The Act Held No Substance." 2004. *New Vision*, January 30.

Plattner, Marc. 1998. "Liberalism and Democracy: Can't Have One Without the Other." *Foreign Affairs* 77(2): 180.

"Porter Commission a Joke, Says Byanyima." 2002. *New Vision,* November 13.
"President Museveni Donates Vehicle to Toro Clan." 2005. http://www.statehouse .go.ug/news.detail.php?category=News&newsId=430. Accessed June 18, 2008.
Przeworski, Adam, and Fernando Limongi. 1997. "Modernization: Theories and Facts." *World Politics* 49(2): 155–183.
Refugee Law Project. 2004. "Negotiating Peace: Resolution of Conflicts in Uganda's West Nile Region." Refugee Law Project Working Paper No. 12. Kampala: Refugee Law Project.
Remmer, Karen. 1991. "New Wine or Old Bottlenecks? The Study of Latin American Democracy." *Comparative Politics* 23(4): 479–495.
Rodríguez Soto, Carlos. 2009. *Tall Grass: Stories of Suffering and Peace in Northern Uganda.* Kampala: Fountain Publishers.
Rueschemeyer, Dietrich, Evelyne Huber Stephens, and John D. Stephens. 1992. *Capitalist Development and Democracy.* Chicago: Chicago University Press.
Schedler, Andreas. 2002. "The Menu of Manipulation." *Journal of Democracy* 13(2): 37–50.
———. 2006. *Electoral Authoritarianism: The Dynamics of Unfree Competition.* Boulder, CO: Lynne Rienner Publishers.
Sebunya, Crespo. 2003. "It's an Early Start for Optimistic Opposition." *African Church Information Service,* June 9.
Senteza-Kajubi, W. 1991. "Educational Reform During Socio-Economic Crisis." In *Changing Uganda: The Dilemmas of Structural Adjustment and Revolutionary Change,* ed. H. B. Hansen and M. Twaddle. Oxford: James Currey.
SIPRI. 2008. "SIPRI Military Expenditure Database." http://www.sipri.org/databases/ milex. Accessed April 27, 2010.
Ssenkumba, John. 1998. "The Dilemmas of Directed Democracy: Neutralising Ugandan Opposition Politics under the NRM." In *The Politics of Opposition in Contemporary Africa,* ed. A. O. Olukoshi. Uppsala: Nordiska Afrikainstitutet.
Sserwanga, Moses. 2009. "Kazini's Life: An Officer with Extraordinary Skills." *Monitor,* November 11.
Steiner, Susan. 2006. "Decentralisation in Uganda: Exploring the Constraints for Poverty Reduction." Research Programme: Transformation in the Process of Globalisation. GIGA Working Paper No. 31. German Institute for Global and Area Studies. Hamburg, Germany. http://www.giga-hamburg.de/dl/download.php?d=/ content/publikationen/pdf/wp31_steiner.pdf. Accessed April 27, 2010.
"Straining at the Edges." 1990. *Africa Confidential* 31(21): 14–16.
"Struggle for Equal Status—Women Enter 2007 with Hope." 2007. *New Vision,* January 1.
Szeftel, Morris. 1998. "Misunderstanding African Politics: Corruption and the Governance Agenda." *Review of African Political Economy* 25(76): 221–240.
Tamale, Sylvia. 2010. "Human Rights Impact Assessment of Uganda's Anti-homosexuality Bill." *Zeleza Post* (blog), January 17. http://www.zeleza.com/ blogging/african-affairs/human-rights-impact-assessment-ugandas-anti-homosexuality-bill-sylvia-tamal.
Theobald, Robin. 1999. "So What Really Is the Problem About Corruption?" *Third World Quarterly* 20(3): 491–502.
Tideman, Per. 1994. "New Local State Forms and 'Popular Participation' in Buganda, Uganda." In *The New Local Level Politics in East Africa, Research Report No. 95,* ed. P. Gibbon. Uppsala: Nordiska Afrikainstitutet.
"Torture Changes Face in Uganda." 2007. *Monitor,* April 15.
"Torture in a Safe House." 2008. *Independent,* May 14.

Tripp, Aili Mari. 2010. "The Politics of Constitution-Making in Uganda." In *Framing the State in Times of Transition: Case Studies in Constitution Making*, ed. Laurel E. Miller. Washington, DC: United States Institute for Peace.

Tull, Denis M. 2003. "A Reconfiguration of Political Order? The State of the State in North Kivu (DR Congo)." *African Affairs* 102: 429–446.

"Tumukunde, Muhwezi Attack Gen. Museveni." 2008. *Independent*, July 8.

"Tumukunde Case a Test of Court's Boldness." 2008. *Monitor*, October 27.

Tumusiime, James. 1999. "Uganda Sealed Omukago with Congolese-Museveni." *Monitor*, September 17.

Tutu, Desmond. 2010. "In Africa, a Step Backward on Human Rights." *Washington Post*, March 12. http://www.washingtonpost.com/wp-dyn/content/article/2010/03/11/AR2010031103341.html. Accessed April 27, 2010.

"Uganda: A Man in No Hurry." 1990. *Africa Confidential*, September 28, 2–4.

Uganda, Constituent Assembly. 1994. "Minutes of the Proceedings of the Constituent Assembly, July 8." Entebbe, Uganda.

Uganda, Government of. 1995. *Constitution of the Republic of Uganda, 1995*. http://www.ugandaemb.org/Constitution_of_Uganda.pdf. Accessed April 27, 2010.

"Uganda Ghost Soldiers Discovered on Army Payroll." 2007. *BBC Monitoring International Reports*, May 19.

Uganda Human Rights Commission. 2008. "11th Annual Report of the Uganda Human Rights Commission to the Parliament of the Republic of Uganda." http://www.uhrc.ug/index.php?option=com_docman&Itemid=111. Accessed April 27, 2010.

"Uganda in the Front Ranks." 2007. *Africa Confidential*, May 25, 9.

"Ugandan Leader Warns Army Officers Against Land Grabbing." 2008. *BBC World, Monitoring Africa*, August 18.

"Ugandan Radio Says Rebels Running Diamond Mines in Central Africa." 2008. *BBC World, Monitoring Africa*, September 21.

Uganda Participatory Poverty Assessment Project. 2001. "First National Report of the Uganda Participatory Poverty Assessment Project." Kampala: Government of Uganda.

"Uganda's Media Clampdown Part of Regressive Regional Trend." 2008. *Independent*, July 9.

"UJA Rejects Act." 1998. *New Vision*, October 30.

UNICEF. 2001. "Abductions in Northern and Southwestern Uganda 1986–2001: Result of the Update and Verification Exercises." Kampala: UNICEF.

UN Security Council Panel of Experts on the Democratic Republic of Congo. 2002. "Final Report of the Panel of Experts on the Illegal Exploitation of Natural Resources and Other Forms of Wealth of the Democratic Republic of the Congo."

United States Information Agency. 1998. "Africa News Report." Washington, DC. March 23.

US Department of State. 2002. "2001 Human Rights Report: Uganda, Bureau of Democracy, Human Rights, and Labor." http://www.state.gov/g/drl/rls/hrrpt/index.htm. Accessed April 27, 2010.

———. 2008. "2007 Human Rights Report: Uganda, Bureau of Democracy, Human Rights, and Labor." http://www.state.gov/g/drl/rls/hrrpt/index.htm. Accessed April 27, 2010.

——— 2009. "2008 Human Rights Report: Uganda, Bureau of Democracy, Human Rights, and Labor." http://www.state.gov/g/drl/rls/hrrpt/index.htm. Accessed April 27, 2010.

Van Acker, Frank. 2004. "Uganda and the Lord's Resistance Army: The New Order No One Ordered." *African Affairs* 103(412): 335–357.

van de Walle, Nicolas. 1999. "Economic Reform in a Democratizing Africa." *Comparative Politics* 32(1): 21–41.
———. 2002. "Africa's Range of Regimes." *Journal of Democracy* 13(2): 66–80.
———. 2003. "Presidentialism and Clientelism in Africa's Emerging Party Systems." *Journal of Modern African Studies* 41(2): 297–321.
Villadsen, Sørensen. 1996. "Decentralisation of Governance." In *Democratic Decentralisation in Uganda: A New Approach to Local Governance*, ed. S. Villadsen and F. Lubanga, 60–78. Kampala: Fountain Publishers.
Villalón, Leonardo Alfonso, and Peter VonDoepp. 2005. *The Fate of Africa's Democratic Experiments: Elites and Institutions.* Bloomington: Indiana University Press.
Waliggo, John M. 1995. "Constitution-making and the Politics of Democratisation in Uganda." In *From Chaos to Order: The Politics of Constitution-making in Uganda*, ed. H. B. Hansen and M. Twaddle, 18–40. Kampala and Oxford: Fountain Publishers and James Currey.
Wanambwa, Richard. 2010. "Ankole 'King' Caught Up in Bribery Storm." *Sunday Monitor,* January 3.
Ward, Kevin. 1995. "The Church of Uganda Amidst Conflict." In *Religion and Politics in East Africa*, ed. H. B. Hansen and M. Twaddle. Oxford, Nairobi, Kampala, and Athens: James Currey, EAEP, Fountain Publishers, and Ohio University Press.
Wasike, Alfred. 1995. "Journalists Reject Bill." *New Vision,* April 16.
Watson, Catharine. 1988. "Ending the Rule of the Gun." *Africa Report* (January–February): 14–17.
———. 1991. "Back to Normal." *Africa Report* (July–August): 13–16.
"What Does the Imprisonment of Former Army Chief Maj Gen James Kazini Mean?" 2008. *Monitor,* April 5.
"When the Loan Shark Comes Knocking, Even MPs Have a Price." 2005. *East African,* August 15.
"Who Maimed, Killed Civilians in Northern Uganda?" 2008. *Independent,* April 28.
Williams, Lionel. 1996. "Uganda-Ministers Museveni Says 'No' to Appointing Ministers from the North." Panafrican News Agency.
Woodward, Peter. 1978. "Ambiguous Amin." *African Affairs* 77(307): 153–164.
Young, Crawford. 1999. "The Third Wave of Democratization in Africa." In *State, Conflict, and Democracy in Africa*, ed. R. Joseph, 15–38. Boulder, CO: Lynne Rienner Publishers.
Zakaria, Fareed. 1997. "The Rise of Illiberal Democracy." *Foreign Affairs* 76(6): 22–43.
———. 2007 [2004]. *The Future of Freedom: Illiberal Democracy at Home and Abroad.* New York: W. W. Norton.

Index

About the Book

Aili Mari Tripp takes a close, clear-sighted look at Ugandan politics since 1986, when Yoweri Museveni became the country's president.

Museveni's exercise of power has been replete with contradictions: steps toward political liberalization have been controlled in ways that, in fact, further centralize authority; and despite claims of relative peace and stability, Uganda has been plagued by two decades of brutal civil conflict. Exploring these paradoxes, Tripp focuses on the complex connections among Museveni's economic and political reforms, his wars in the north and in Congo, the key roles of international donors and the military, and the institutional changes that have defined his presidency. She highlights, as well, efforts by the judiciary, the legislature, the media, and civil society to check executive power.

This is also a book about the semiauthoritarian regimes, like Uganda's, that characterize so many political systems in Africa. Tripp reflects analytically on the distinctiveness of this type of system—and on its implications for civil society, institutional growth, and real economic development.

Aili Mari Tripp is professor of political science and gender and women's studies at the University of Wisconsin–Madison. Her numerous publications include *Women and Politics in Uganda*, which is the recipient of several awards, and *Changing the Rules: The Politics of Liberalization and the Urban Informal Sector in Tanzania*.